John F. Kennedy

Vietnam

Mood Rings

Shag Carpeting

Al Kaline

Motown

grunge

bell bottom jeans

The Beatles

Make Love Not War

SIXTY TO LIFE

pet rocks

Psychedelic

	DATE DUE	

ISBN 0-9701342-5-8

First printing

Point Net Publishing
102 Division Street
Petoskey, MI 49770

This is a work of creative nonfiction. Some fictional names and scenerios have been created for the purpose of anonymity and clarity.

SIXTY TO LIFE
A journey through the decades

CHAPTER ONE

I was born on the ninth day of the decade under the presidency of Eisenhower, into an era that began with innocence and ended with upheaval. It was a decade of musical evolution and cultural revolution, slain Kennedys and men on the moon. I can trace my memory line to somewhere between late November 1963 and February 1964. I say that because I have no recollection of the John F. Kennedy assassination but I remember The Beatles making their first appearance on Sullivan. The latter I remember not because I was a fan of The Beatles at the time, but because of all the hoopla that surrounded the event. I do have other recollections before then, but they are distant and blurry like those experienced by one who is not quite awake. Yet, I do like to think back upon the early morning of my life. During my first two or three years my memories are faint, as though I were in a fog; still, they are some of my fondest. Everything I needed was provided and all I had to do was grow. I remember the sound of the very early sixties coming into our home via the Westinghouse transistor radio, playing songs like *Michael (Row The Boat Ashore)* by The Highwaymen and *Don't Let The Rain Come Down* by The Serendipity Singers, or *I Love How You Love Me* by The Paris Sisters. Looking back at that time the music was simply part of the memory, just as when you look at an old photo and see a sofa that's been long removed or a pet that has passed away, and the recollection of the part paints the whole. For me in the early sixties the sound was a mere accouterment to the whole and not yet a catalyst for thought. Yet at times I can picture myself so clearly sitting by the heat register in our living room, wearing my little pajamas, observing my parents immerse themselves in the world with all its must-be-dones, while I sat back comfortably without the hindrance of foresight of what would await me. But as one grows, so does their awareness, and a less obscure early memory is that of my third birthday. An aunt asked me how old I was and I remember saying three-and-a-half, knowing full well that I was three. My mom and aunt laughed at how cute the answer was, thinking that I didn't know any better, but I had pulled one over on them. I let them laugh at my innocence and never let them know that I just wanted to see their reaction. Looking at that now makes me realize why I want to write this book. I have always been an observer of people, culture, and the world around me. I can't remember when the revelation was made clear to me, but the only qualities one needs to be a philosopher are cognizance and introspection. There have been many books written about those who have survived war or who have been in the presence of greatness, but there is wonder in every life and universal profoundness when experiences are shared. We see a bit of ourselves in lives lived by others; life paths that perhaps we considered before heading down the one that became our reality.

Although autobiographical for structural and developmental purposes, this isn't a book about *my* life—this is a book about *our* lives and the era that took us from birth and helped mold us into what we've become. My goal is to go through the years of the life of a baby-boomer and recall some of the happenings and look at the effects they had on us, to again hear the music and follow its progression, to analyze societal trends and movements and throw in some how-and-why opinions, and for those younger than us, to show what everyday life was like from 1960 through the mid 2000s. As you read this, those who have read my fiction novels will recognize that I got fodder for my stories from real life.

My biological mother had died less than an hour after giving birth to me, and as the youngest of eleven children, and at the request of my dying mother, I was raised by my aunt and uncle in Manistique, Michigan, a town roughly fifty miles away from my siblings. Having taken me directly from the hospital, this aunt and uncle were nothing less than a mom and dad to me; that's how I addressed them in life, and that's how I'll refer to them in this book. Conversely, I will make the distinction by using the terms biological or natural for my birth parents. I was never close to my natural father and my brothers and sisters were, and in some ways still are, more like cousins. They would come to Manistique, or we would go to their hometown of Garden, Michigan about once a month, where we would visit for a few hours. I never felt comfortable there. We would spend the first half-hour in the living room with my natural father, him asking obligatory questions, and me answering politely but feeling no kinship with the man. The birth order of the family was four boys, six girls, then me. The boys never seemed to be around when we'd visit but I remember my sisters staying in the other room and shooting glances at me, some with curiosity and some with shyness, while they whispered and giggled. When the chat with my natural father had concluded I was allowed to go outside where I'd romp through the fields in search of something interesting, or climb atop the old cars in the junkyard that my brother Jimmy ran—anything to kill the time. Sometimes my two youngest sisters, Jackie and Mary, would come out, too. We'd climb trees and pick apples, or look for berries, or pick vegetables from the garden. Then with much gratefulness I would return to my own world and my own life. I never felt the blood connection with my siblings as we led different lives and we ourselves were very different. As I got older, relatives would say how much I looked like my brother Tony. I particularly hated that—nothing against him, nothing against me—but I wanted to be the one and only me and not the offshoot of a forerunner. My four brothers and six sisters felt the bond of family that I have never felt, though some blame me on a subconscious level for their mother's death.

I always thought of myself as an only child. I hated the fact that I wasn't my mom and dad's biological child (and I still do to this day.) In school, I never admitted to having any brothers and sisters, and if word got out to any of my classmates that I did I would deny it. I'd even balk when my dad or mom would tell me of my heritage. I enjoyed my individualism and my life the way I knew it best. It was my dad who was my biological mother's brother, and in later years I would look at him for bloodline information, as he would have had the same as my biological mother. I am of French descent, for example, and I could legitimately say, "Just like my dad." This, I'm sure, is one of the reasons that I now feel closer to him than my mom. Yet, I loved both my parents. They were my mom and dad and I didn't want their authenticity to be compromised by anyone. Occasionally an adult would refer to them as my aunt or uncle or make a reference to me being adopted, but whenever that happened I would play dumb or simply wouldn't respond. I never addressed my natural father as Dad or Father. He was either John, or I said whatever I had to say without the formality of any title. In legal realms I had my biological father's last name, but when I entered school, which became the first time I needed to be referred to by a last name; I wanted to go by LaMarche, the family name of my dad. In 1975, when I reached the age of consent, I was legally adopted by him and the name LaMarche became official.

My dad's name was Roy. He was a simple man, a millwright by trade, and he was usually gone from Monday till Friday. He would build the machinery for paper mills or power plants and had to travel to wherever there was work. My mother, Geraldine, was a professional musician. She would play solo for church services, weddings or funerals in the day, then play organ or accordion in the clubs at night, either as a solo performer or with the full band and her family, The Gorsche Orchestra. Their music was of the Big Band variety, swing and ragtime mostly, and I didn't relate to it at the time. Still, I knew my mom was talented. We had an old piano at our house that had been played by her family for a generation. The black keys toward the center had deep grooves of wear, which fascinated my young mind as I contemplated how many times each note must have been played for it to get to such a condition. Yet I wasn't inspired to learn to play, something I now regret. For as gifted as my mother was, hearing her play every day had me believing that everyone had a piano in their home and that everyone's mother could play, at least to some degree.

We lived in an old two-story house that belonged to my mother's family's estate. It was located on Arbutus Avenue in a quaint little neighborhood that was wrapped on the backside of the block that housed the business district on its front. Next door to us were my Uncle Pete Gorsche and his wife Maxine, and their four children. Suzie was the youngest and was two years older than me, but the proximity in age and location made us pretty close cousins. I want to make a note here; I had mentioned earlier that it was my dad whom I was related to through my natural mother, so his brothers and sisters were blood relatives—authentic aunts and uncles. I say this because I want to make clear that the relatives on my mom's side, to whom I was not related by blood, were nothing less than actual to me. Additionally, the third branch of relatives, those related to my biological father, were obscure to me and they remain so to this day. So back to Suzie. There weren't many other kids in our neighborhood, which drew the two of us even closer. She was lot of fun to hang around with, especially in the nineteen-sixties, before she was old enough to leave the neighborhood and meet up with her friends from school. We would play hide-and-seek or tell ghost stories on summer evenings, in the fall we'd bury ourselves in the huge pile of leaves in the center of the yard between our two houses, and in the winter we would have snowball fights. We'd walk to school together, and when Aunt Maxine died in 1965, Suzie would come to our house for lunch on school days. The Ford Garage was past Uncle Pete's and beyond that was the marina, which would be a port of departure for a cruise on Lake Michigan whenever one of mom and dad's friends had a boat docked there.

My parents were considerably older than me. My dad was forty-five when I was born and my mom was forty. Their friends were their age and my aunts and uncles were in that range as well. Consequently, I had the same values instilled in me as someone who was raised in the mid to late forties. But that notwithstanding, the kids of my time were raised differently then those born a mere ten years later. Despite the tumultuous reputation that the sixties had, the beginning of the decade was quite innocent. Kids were brought up to respect their elders. *Little children should be seen but not heard,* was a saying often thrown at me. We ate at the dinner table and not in front of the television. When I balked at food that was short of being my favorite dish, i.e. carrots, I was told *you'll eat it and you'll like it!* If I did something grievously wrong I was spanked or my dad's belt came off. Today this may even be considered child abuse by some, but I think we came out of our childhood better because of the discipline we received. We behaved in public, and when we didn't we only had to be told once, and we were never sarcastic to adults.

Suzie and I both attended St. Francis de Sales Catholic School, which was three blocks from our homes. It was a small school that ran from first through eighth grade and had about thirty kids to every class. In my early years of attendance most of the teachers were Franciscan nuns, a fact that would change with a shortage of nuns by the early seventies. St. Francis church was adjacent to the school and we would begin each day by attending mass. I had attended kindergarten at Central School. Kindergarten was an adjustment for me. My first day was probably typical to that of many other children throughout the country and around the world. My mom walked me to the school on a bright and beautiful late-summer morning. We even stopped at the grocery store for a bottle of pop, a treat that had never before been allowed in the morning, and I was fine until I realized that Mom wasn't going to be staying with me. I was left alone in a room full of strange looking kids with faces that seemed to be concocted by a cartoonist and not by

God, but as the day progressed I forgot that I had been abandoned and became intrigued with my new situation. Yet, having lived the life of an only child I was used to being the center of the universe, and I was soon smacked in the face with the fact that the world didn't revolve around me. Despite the chastisements that led to that revelation, I believe I still was one of Mrs. LaFave's favorites. I was interested and inspired, and although I was a little hyper, I was a good little student.

I always looked forward to weekends when Dad would come home. I'd run and cling on him and ask if he got me anything. Sometimes his answer was, "Une petite nouveau rien," and on those Fridays I'd look for the une petite nouveau rien but I'd never be able to find it. Now my dad's first language was French so he had one up on me, and finally I had to ask what a une petite nouveau rien was, to which he replied, "A brand new little nothing." Still, he would always leave his pennies in his suitcase for me. His clothes smelled of a man who worked, but I'd scurry through his them like a little rodent until I found every last cent. Occasionally I'd get lucky and find a dime that had been inadvertently put in with the pennies. My mom didn't drive, so when Dad was home we spent a lot of time in the car. The first car I remember was a 1960 Oldsmobile, complete with a gauge that measured speed with a thermometer-like green line that would change to yellow and then to red when we reached higher speeds. Often we would go to Dad's hometown, Escanaba, which was fifty-seven miles to the west—fifty-two after the new highway was built. (He was actually born in Riverland in the Danforth area, which is considered rural Escanaba.) Sometimes we'd go for the day, but often we'd stay for the weekend. When we did we'd sleep at my Uncle Phil's. My cousin Ricky was just a year younger than me and we always found plenty to do. There were seven other kids in the family, but only three that I knew well, as the older kids would be out and about most of the time. One time we took an evening ride from Escanaba to Gladstone, I can't remember what the purpose was, but Dad got our car hung up on the railroad tracks while going up an access road that led to The Gladstone Bluff. I remember seeing a distant train approaching slowly, Dad yelling at us to get out of the car—we did—Mom yelling back at him to leave the car and get out himself as he frantically rocked the vehicle back and forth until it finally released and Dad screeched the car to the other side of the tracks. In retrospect, the train was slow moving and didn't get that close to our car, but that train held horrifying possibilities to me at the time.

Mom and Dad also had friends, Leo and Ester, who had a cottage on Thunder Lake, which was about a half-hour ride from Manistique. I would love going there for three reasons: the gravel road leading to the cottage had several steep hills and Dad would take them fast enough where I'd get a tickle, Thunder Lake was warm and had a soft, sandy bottom, unlike the gravely bottom of the Lake Michigan beach on the highway, and Leo and Ester had a pontoon boat that they'd take us out in. On other occasions we'd visit my Uncle Lawrence and Aunt Luella at Indian Lake, but it was never as much fun as Thunder Lake.

There were plenty of times when my inquisitive nature got me into trouble. I remember going on an errand with Dad. I was probably six, maybe younger but no older. I had always watched him drive and knew the concept of the pedals; brakes on the left and gas on the right. He pulled over to the side of the road for some reason, and when he went to take off again I decided it was time to help him push that gas pedal all the way to the floor. Dad managed to dodge everything until he regained full control of the vehicle, and needless to say he immediately pulled back over to the side of the road. That's when I realized that I didn't think things through, and the end result was a whipping by a father whose adrenaline level was spiking from the shock of my shenanigan. Our house was heated with fuel oil and every cold-weather month a tanker would pull into our driveway and the driver would extend the hose from his truck and dispense fuel into the tank in our basement from the fill pipe at the side of the house. One summer day as I was filling my inflatable pool with water I thought it would be helpful if I topped off the fuel tank with the garden hose. I would soon learned that not everything that comes out of a hose goes into the fuel tank, and like in the previous anecdote, there was a thickening of the skin that came with a learned lesson.

I was healthy as a child, but had a tendency for breaking bones; always the ones in my left arm, which I broke three times in five places. We had perfect attendance awards at school, which I took home most every year; not that I didn't get sick, but back then more than now you went to school unless you had something serious, and the only time that that happened was in '65 when I had the three-day measles. It was in the last days of doctors making house calls and Dr. Waters came over and diagnosed me. He told me that I had to stay in bed for three days and that I had to avoid light, which meant staying in my parents' room as it was darker, and I couldn't watch TV. I recall that I didn't feel all that sick, but my senses were somewhat distorted. In fact, some fifteen years later when Pink Floyd came out with the song *Comfortably Numb* and I first heard the line "My hands felt like two balloons," I immediately related it to how I had felt during that childhood illness. What I remember most, though, was being incredibly bored. As Sunday evening came I got out of bed and went into the living room to watch *The Ed Sullivan Show* with Mom and Dad, a show that I had limited interest in but one that they liked to have me watch. I fully expected their approval and that Mom would snuggle up to me and ask how I liked the jugglers or dancing chimps or Topo Gigo, but the avoidance of light still trumped all and I was sent back into my exile of physical and quasi-punitive darkness. I also remember the final time I broke my arm. I was trying to dive from a ladder into my inflatable pool and landed with my left arm by my ear. I told my dad that I knew it was broken because I heard it crack, but he didn't believe me because I wasn't crying and I went through the night with an untreated break. By the next morning, when my parents saw that I was still in writhing pain, I was taken to the doctor's office and then to the hospital. They told me they were going to reset my arm and they put the sleeping-gas mask over my nose and mouth and told me to count backwards from ten. I probably made it to eight and I was out. Unfortunately they weren't able to reset my arm properly because the radius and ulna had already begun to fuse together. To this day my left arm is slightly crooked and I can't rotate it to where my opened palm is facing upward.

Aunt Irene and Uncle Pete's house was always a place of sunshine. They had five children: Robert, Louise, Paul, Carl, and Mabel Ann, whom were twelve to nineteen years older than me. I believe they enjoyed having a youngster like me around most of the time, but I'm also certain there were times when my rambunctious nature wore on them. Aunt Irene was a saint. She was kind, gentle, and patient. I remember how soft it felt when she washed my hands before she fed me, and she knew that raspberry jam sandwiches should be cut diagonally. My mom insisted that they tasted the same regardless of how they were cut, but I guess this was an accrued knowledge that Aunt Irene had over my mom, being her older sister and having raised more kids. She only lived a block from my school and I'd go there at noon for lunch at least a couple times a week. On Friday nights Uncle Pete refereed high school football games and for the rest of the week he was the chief shipping clerk at Port Inland, where they shipped limestone to other Great Lakes ports for processing. Uncle Pete always had projects and on occasion he'd have me help him, or in hindsight, humor me into thinking I was useful. They had a cabin on Lake Michigan and he would often level out the dirt road by dragging a large iron grating behind his truck, which was about twelve feet long and the width of the road itself. We would sing *John Jacob Jingleheimer Smith* or something of the like until the grater got hung up on a large stone or a root, at which point we'd get out to take a look, and I'd help him jostle the device around until the obstruction was cleared. When the job was finished, either that one or some other project, we'd go down to the lake for a swim, or take the row boat out onto Lake Michigan, or build a fire, or go fishing at the mouth of the creek that ran past his cabin. Many of the images from the cottage scenes in my sixth book, *Falling From Delaware,* came from those times at Aunt Irene and Uncle Pete's cottage.

Their house was on Walnut Street, about a block up from the courthouse and in a quaint little area of town. Even from the street it was a warm, comfortable looking place, especially in the summertime. There were always tulips planted in front, and as you climbed the cement steps you saw a porch swing that faced the cement birdbath where robins and blue jays could been seen splashing their wings in the water, and if you were fortunate you'd be there on one of the several days a year that you could hear the soothing whistle of a visiting cardinal. To the right of the house was a driveway that ascended up and behind their home to the garage, and the building next to it housed a full-court gymnasium. Behind the garage and gym was a football field with the old H-bar goal posts at each end. Lining the backside of the garage were perhaps eighty to a hundred fifty-five gallon drums that Uncle Pete had gotten at Port Inland. Although I occasionally dribbled a ball around the boxes that were now being stored in the gym and shot a few baskets, and went around back and aimed field goals at the by-then rusted goal posts with the ball landing into the tall grass that at one time was the end zone, both of these facilities were of another day. As a young boy growing up alone, I tended to look at inanimate objects as if they had feelings, and I always felt sorry for the gym and the goal posts to have been abandoned and left feeling so alone.

My Uncle Seb and his daughter Mary Eloise lived in an upstairs apartment that was above one of the local businesses. Mary El, as we all called her, was about twenty-five years older than me and was more like an aunt than a cousin. There was a long stairway that led up to their place, longer than any I had seen anywhere else, and I would love to run up the steps ahead of my parents in an I'm-faster-than-you manner. Inside was a grayish-stained skylight that in its earlier days probably gave a nice view of the moon and stars from inside the living room. Mary El would often take me for car rides on Sunday afternoons, and as I got a little older, she'd take me golfing.

Our town was small enough where the sight of an airplane was relatively rare, and whenever one went over many of the residents would shade their eyes to the sun and try to spot the plane, myself included. By the summers of '65 and '66, Dad, Mom and I would go for airplane rides about every other Sunday. My dad had a friend named Verne Bernard who chartered flights, and he'd take us up for a half-hour or so. As we'd fly over town, my parents would point out where things were: our house, the school, Aunt Irene's, and I remember thinking how narrow the river looked from our aerial vantage point. On a couple of occasions Verne put me in the copilot seat and let me take over for perhaps some thirty seconds. I remember holding the bar tightly and making sure I did exactly what I was told. I can't remember why we stopped flying, but eventually we did, and I wouldn't fly again until my mom and I went to Detroit in 1970. After that came the hijackings to Cuba that were so common in the early seventies. That and the fact that I began to listen to the news and hear of plane crashes engendered a fear of flying that would keep me out of the air until '82 when I was flown to Milwaukee for an Army physical. That was followed by another twelve year hiatus, which has had a subsequent eleven year interim. I give you this litany as a contrast between how I look upon air travel now as opposed to when I was a little boy who eagerly sat in the copilots seat and, if only for a few brief seconds, flew the plane alone.

My entrance into St. Francis had brought more structure and discipline into my educational process. The nuns were strict, and like the societal acceptance of harsher disciplining from parents, the nuns weren't opposed to giving you a good whooping when you needed it. We had uniforms: the boys wore navy slacks, black oxfords, a light blue dress shirt with a navy tie monogrammed with an SFS. The girls wore a white blouse with a knee-length blue and white plaid skirt and blue socks. I hated the uniform and as soon as the school day was over it was back to jeans, a tee-shirt, and my Red Ball Jets. The educational process was more formal as well and I wasn't allowed to be as hyperactive as I'd been in kindergarten. But with the added legitimacy, I found myself even more inspired to learn and soon was thought of as one of the smart kids by my classmates. My curiosity continued when I got home. I was always asking questions, and in doing so testing my parents' patience. When I was old enough to read well, I became a junkie for statistics. Thanks to an almanac that my mom had bought me, I knew all the states' ranks in land mass and population, and within a few thousand, I could tell you the population of the fifty largest cities. And thus planted the seeds for the wanderlust of my later years. I would circle any cities on the list that I had visited, with the intent of eventually seeing all fifty of them. I traced a map of the United States, complete with individual state borders, and would color in each state in which I had set foot. Again, the goal was to see all fifty states. This goal was being achieved slowly at first, though, as by 1968 the only states colored in were Michigan, Wisconsin, and Minnesota. Whereas I started off with three, today I can say that I've been fortunate enough to have visited all but three states.

With my interest in statistics came the need to know all the superlatives. It started off with a desire for common and practical stats—Alaska, for instance, was the largest state land wise, but California was the most populous. But as I became more and more of a junkie, it became objective and obsessive, or as Dylan said, "Useless and pointless knowledge." I'm sure my parents' nerves were often frayed with all the questions like, "Which one's better, Anacin, Bufferin, or plain and simple Bayer aspirin?" or "Do Firestone tires last longer than Goodyear?" and "Does Wonder Bread really taste better than Mrs. Karls." Based upon the nature and presentation of their commercials I developed my favorite products, without giving regard to the fact that I was too young to use many of them. Firestone would usually have cool ads, such as tires carving their way through pristine snow. Uniroyal, however, had race car drivers standing next to each other and wearing their names on their uniforms: Uni, Roy, and Al. So based strictly on how such commercials held my interest, Firestone had to be a better tire than

Uniroyal. Another deciding factor in my evaluation of these "bests" was what my dad used. If I was over at a friend's house and I saw that his father had a Dodge, I made sure to let that him know that it was inferior to our Oldsmobile, which by this standard of testing was without a doubt the best car ever made.

Except for music, the culture of the early to mid sixties existed but didn't surround me. Nor did it draw any interest from me. I was living the life of a child and spent most of my free time trying to entertain myself. Life was an adventure, and when my dad turned on Cronkite, I shot off in another direction. After all, there were trees to climb and apples to plug at passing cars from the cover of shrubs. And as for the music, I guess it was somewhere around 1965 that the sound caught up with me. I think back to the invasion of The Beatles in '64, and walking down the street with my mom holding my hand, singing, *I Want To Hold Your Hand*, and me crumpling my face and trying to pull away from her. To me it wasn't a teenybopper love song, but a song about impeding my independence with my mother's hand keeping me from running down the block ahead of her. Through the years, and for as popular as it was, that song never did grow on me and perhaps it was for that reason. By '65, however, the sound of garage bands and the second British wave had begun to at least tweak my attention. The first song I called my favorite was *I'm Henry VIII, I Am*, by Herman's Hermits. It remained my favorite song until *Snoopy Vs. The Red Baron* came out in late 1966, with its catchy refrain, "10, 20, 30, 40, 50 or more," which in turn was replaced in '68 by the bubble-gum sound of *1,2,3 Red Light.* But pop music at that point of my life was still something that I only appreciated when I caught it by happenstance. I wasn't listening to the radio in hopes of hearing my favorite songs.

If I ever owned the world it was in the early sixties. After all, I was the fastest, best looking, and smartest child in all of Manistique. I was loved by all and it was a pleasure for people just to see me. At least that was the perception I had at the time. Age, however, brings reality and truth. Sometimes the truths are cold and harsh; other times they are simple adjustments to correct the course you're on. Aging can be pejorative, and just as you are born with a certain number of days to live, it also holds true that the innocence of youth is not inexhaustible. There were firsts that were to come which would bring a new reality: my first lost fight, the first time I'd find my dad to be wrong, the first time I'd be ignored or laughed at by other kids. But those things were all in the future and life in Manistique was good. The sun shone brightly and the grass was green, and the blue sky was interrupted only by the purest white clouds.

CHAPTER TWO

As with any era, there are things that occur that the next generation will find hard to fathom, and the period of time in which I grew up was no different. Many things were better the way they were back in the sixties, but some things needed to be changed. Littering was one example. It was a common practice that when traveling down the highway, trash went to the side of the road. Now were not talking household garbage, but beverage cans, wrappers, and the like. And at least where I lived, no one looked in their rearview mirrors to see if there was a cop behind you, because even if there was, it was an accepted practice. The insult, "woman driver," was frequently used and seldom found to be offensive to women other than the one being referred to, for the fact was that not many women drove and it was generally accepted that they were overly cautious. Also, the struggle of the Black American was even more incomplete than it is today. Though we were almost entirely white in Manistique, racism was still manifested in jokes, jokes that would be told today by only a classless few. Outside of those examples, overall we were a better society in my opinion. For one thing, we benefited from the discipline I had mentioned earlier. Children of today would be in the custody and so called protection of the state if they were disciplined the way we were. Now I'm not talking about people who punch their kids or lock them in closets; parents who do those things are not acting for the betterment of their children. I'm referring to common sense discipline, and back to differences in the times, you seldom saw kids talking back to their parents the way you do today. I understand that many people think these beliefs are antiquated, but dubbing something as an antiquation is arbitrary and therefore inherently leaves the matter undetermined. Another notable difference between the sixties and today is long distance calling. To begin with, we had to call the operator on our black rotary phone and say, "I like to make a long distance call to," and then give the number and she would connect you. The calls were more expensive and the connection would be bad if it was cross-country; consequently the person on the other end would place their hand over the receiver and shout out something like, "Pipe down, it's long distance!"

But we didn't think of such things as being unusual in those days. We were simply kids looking for the next exciting thing to do, vis-à-vis, finding ways to kill time, and in doing so we grew in mind and body with each year that passed. There was an elderly woman in the neighborhood that didn't get out much in the winter. One spring as she was watching us frolic about she said to me, "You know you children are like little trees, you grow so fast." At the time it didn't mean any more than the oft heard cliché *you're growing like a weed,* but now I can imagine how we must have seemed like different children to her each spring, with our growing bodies and maturing faces. Now, life has gone full circle and I see this happening with the kids in the town where I now live. It doesn't seem long ago that neighborhood mothers were pregnant, and now there are little individuals listening to their own music and bouncing basketballs, on their own journey to coming of age and eventually making similar observations, thereby make their circle round.

The movie theater was three blocks from us and occasionally Mom would take me to the matinee on Saturday afternoons for movies like *That Darn Cat, The Love Bug,* or other kid's movies. The first family movie I saw was *The Sound Of Music*, but as I got old enough to see those types of films, Mom also took me to see some which I found to be extremely boring, like *My Fair Lady*. When I got yet a little older she'd give me the 35¢ and let me meet my friends at the theater. We'd watch the Westerns like *True Grit* with John Wayne, with the actors riding up to the camera for a quick introductory pose at the beginning of the movie. As we got still a little older we'd meet girls at the theater. We'd usually sit in the row behind them, throwing candy at the backs of their heads during cartoons like *The Road Runner* or *The Pink Panther* that preceded the film. If the movie was good we'd squat down in our seats and stay to watch it again. On the way home we'd evaluate our performance with the girls, trying to figure out who had a chance with whom. Then I'd go home, but I never told my mom about the girls. In school we got *The Weekly Reader*, and within it there was a site from which we could order books. Outside of children's books, they were the first that I read voluntarily. From there I got into westerns that were written for kids; books like *Kit Carson* and *Buffalo Bill*. Yet, as a child I wasn't that much of a reader; instead, I sought activity.

Christmas without a doubt was the most exciting time of the year when I was young, perhaps because signs of the season began to appear two weeks before the holiday, not in mid November (or in some cases late October) as it does now. Across from the post office was Triangle Park, which was simply a small open block in the shape of a triangle. Every holiday season they put up a musical shed called Santa's Workshop, where flat wooden elves whose arms and legs would move back and forth played musical instruments in tempo with tinny sounding songs of the season. In our living room we had a set of bay windows and at Christmas time we'd put the tree into the inlet of the bay windows where the couch usually rested. Upon entering the house I'd get the feel of the special time of year by seeing the furniture arranged to accommodate the tree. We'd have a lot of company during the holiday season, some of whom I wouldn't see any other time of year, and Mom would get on the piano and play Christmas songs while our guests would sing and drink holiday cheer. By the mid sixties I had become old enough to remember the songs that I would only hear during the holiday season and I listened for my favorites: *Walking In A Winter Wonderland, O Come All Ye Faithful,* and *Silver Bells.* Also, I eagerly awaited the seasonal television specials. In my younger years they would be shows like *The Andy Williams Christmas Special,* but later, shows like *A Charlie Brown Christmas, How The Grinch Stole Christmas,* and *Rudolph The Red Nose Reindeer* became the standards. On Christmas Eve we would go to Aunt Irene's and Mary Eloise's and I would collect presents. As a young boy it was cool to see different ornaments on their trees. Aunt Irene had little glass-enclosed propellers that would twirl when the lights below them warmed. Mary Eloise had bubble lights, which were tubes of colored liquid that bubbled, just like the light in our Frosty The Snowman that went on our kitchen windowsill. All the gifts would go under our tree until Christmas morning. It'd be hard to get to sleep on Christmas Eve night and when I did I would dream fantastically colorful dreams, then I would get up before daybreak, anxious for the phenomenon of Christmas toys. In the sixties I would always wake Mom and Dad before opening my presents; on a couple of occasions I got sent back to bed because it was too early. Opening presents was nothing less than a frenzy. Wrapping paper would fly as I'd tear into boxes that certainly held wondrous things. Every once in a while I'd stop and coax Mom and Dad to open one of theirs, and then go back to shredding those carefully wrapped gifts. Once all the presents were opened we'd get ready for church, where I'd sit impatiently, waiting to get back home to play with all my new toys.

It was in the summer of '67 when a new member entered our little family. I was told that there was a surprise for me in the living room. I went in eagerly and saw a box with the top open, sitting at the end of the couch by the bay windows. I went up and peered inside and saw two little black eyes peering helplessly back at me. "What's his name?" I asked my mom with a broad smile. "He doesn't have one yet," she told me. And without putting a lot of thought into it, I named him Kelly. I don't know what inspired the name, and he stayed Kelly for two or three days until my dad convinced me that this peekapoo, which was a cross between a Pekinese and a poodle, needed a French name. So, in spite of the knowledge I now have that this mixed breed is more Chinese than French, Kelly became Pierre. He quickly became my buddy and companion, but when weekends rolled around there was no doubt that he was Daddy's dog, as I was young and probably a little too rough with him at times and my dad was very even keeled.

If any time came close to capturing the magic of Christmas it was The 4th of July and the days leading up to it. The festivities would begin with the arrival of the month and would conclude with the fireworks display at the football stadium. Mom would take me to the store to buy sparklers, smoke bombs and snakes. (For those who don't remember, they were these little tablets that you would ignite and ashes would rise in the shape of a snake.) She didn't let me buy firecrackers, but I knew that Dad had several packs of ladyfingers in the vanity underneath his underwear. At night we'd run up and down the street waving our sparklers and right before they were about to extinguish we'd throw them up in the air; something Dad always yelled about on the first lawn-mowing after the 4th. The older kids would have M-80s, Roman candles and cherry bombs, and a couple years later bottle rockets came onto the scene. *The Kiddie Parade* was on the 3rd and I won the award for best costume one year as I rolled down the street with my bike patriotically decked out with red, white, and blue crepe paper around the frame and amidst the spokes of my tires and my little dog Pierre trotting along by my side. On the day of the 4th was the parade down main street, with the marching band playing *Stars And Stripes Forever* and other patriotic songs and proud veterans from World War One and Two and Korea passing by to applause from the crowd. Guests would come to the house after the parade and Mom would get on the piano and play songs like *You're A Grand Old Flag* and everybody would sing. The coup de grâce, though, was the fireworks. It seemed that everyone in town went down to the football field. The grandstands would be filled and so would the track that rimmed the field. Also filled would be the parking lot atop the cliffs. The fireworks were lit at the far end of the quarry and were distanced so they'd explode above the stadium. I don't have to explain the thrill of watching fireworks when one is young—we've all experienced it—but I will say, like with many things in life, it is best when we're young.

It seemed like once every summer there would be a tornado warning. In the narrow and seldom used passage between the living room and the dining room was the door that led to the basement. I never went into the basement except when there was a tornado warning, for it was a dank and foreboding place to anyone under ten years old. The cobwebs matched the dark gray skies that came with such a weather phenomenon, as Mom and I would descend the narrow staircase and go back to the far corner of the basement where piles of wood and coal were left orphaned by the addition of an oil furnace. Support beams ran overhead and into an area where the foundation stopped shoulder high to an adult, leaving an earthen crawl space where lumber was stored. The fact that my mother took these warnings seriously filled me with fear as I waited for the upper portion of the house to get sucked up into the sky at any moment, while visions of *The Wizard of Oz* played in my head, augmented by the eerie sounds of *Telstar.* But every time, the Westinghouse portable transistor radio would eventually give the all clear and our house never did get blown away.

As I had said Uncle Pete Gorsche lived next to us. In the front half of our yard, centered between the two houses, was a huge elm tree. In the spring of 1968 Dad and one of his friends cut the elm down, leaving the stump projecting just an inch or two above the grass and thus creating a natural home plate. Some thirty feet ahead of that and in decent alignment with the stump was a small cherry tree, i.e., second base. Uncle Pete's clothesline pole acted as first, leaving only third that had to be improvised, usually by a stone that would again prompt Dad to yell at me whenever he cut the grass. The game was Wiffle ball, played solitaire style—me throwing the ball up and then hitting it. Toward right field, the alley was a home run and the grape terraces and raspberry bushes marked the fences in center and left. In the yard on the other side of our house, the side we seldom used for anything, was an early fifties car that had been parked there for as long as I could remember. I do recall my dad working on it from time to time, and I even saw it run on a couple of occasions. The Robinsons lived just beyond the old car and behind their house was an old shack where a homeless man found shelter. One cold winter morning I was awakened by Pierre jumping and hitting the edge of my bed, his way of telling me that he wanted to go outside, and when I opened the door to let him out I saw the homeless man dead and frozen on our steps. Past the Robinson house were the MacGregors. Angus Macgregor and his wife were old when I was young. He would veer from side to side as he walked down the sidewalk. I had once asked his wife if he was drunk all the time, but she said that it was just the way he walked. Now with the wisdom of age behind me I understand that he usually *was* drunk. Don McLean lived where Arbutus Avenue jettisoned itself into a dead end, past the curve that directed most traffic onto Elm Street. In my small world I had once asked him if he was related to Denny McLean, the thirty-one game winner for the Detroit Tigers. We had neighbors across the street, the Babladelises, who were Greek. I was too young to have any understanding of the origin of names; I only knew they were Greek because my parents said they were Greek. I also remember the oddity of the women's names: Evanthea, Leftarea, Ogalaouia. The patriarch we simply addressed as Mr. Pete. Also on the other side of the block were the Millers, the Schubrings, and the Rushfords. At the far end was a woman who ran a chiropractic office out of her house. The only thing I remember about her was that she ended up committing suicide.

I knew every nuance of the neighborhood. There was a slab of sidewalk between the MacGregors and Robinsons that had been uplifted by a tree root and made a natural jump for my bike. In the alley businesses discarded their unwanted boxes behind their shops for garbage-day pickup and if one cared to sift through them he could find truth to the adage *One man's junk is another man's treasure*. I would often find little toys and such; either they didn't sell or were at the bottom of a box that was thought to be empty.

Either way, I had my gold. The grapes and raspberries and asparagus that grew wild in our backyard were indigenous and exclusively ours, and the little cave of shelter created by the grape vines growing over a trellis was my place of solitude. In my backyard on sunny days I would sometimes wonder, in a rudimentary youthful way, of course, if everyone in the world lived the same life that I was living. Did they look for shapes of known things in the clouds? Did they get bored on days that were too glorious for one to be bored? Or was there always something to do where they lived?

The fascination with places different than my hometown grew when my parents bought me a set of World Book encyclopedias. My focus was on states and as I read the entries I learned to spell each of them. (I still find myself spelling the states with the rhythm I used when I was young: *MissIssIppI, ConnEctIcut, TennEssEE*. Each long-named state was accompanied by its own cadence—De da da da De da da De De. I looked up all the states one by one. Within the articles were pictures of both historical sites and interesting places, along with a list of average monthly temperatures. The combination of climates and terrain being different than that of the Midwest prompted my interest in faraway states and California became the place I would one day have to visit. The encyclopedia listed addresses for each state's bureau of tourism and I mailed out requests for brochures for the ones that intrigued me the most. When they arrived at the house I'd go off by myself and look at the pictures of what the world had waiting for me. But the trips of my youth were mostly to Escanaba. We had gone to Wisconsin several times to visit friends of my dad. Most of his jobs were in small northeast Wisconsin towns and he had a smattering of friends in these communities. Then in 1968 we made our first lengthy trip—up into Canada and around Lake Superior, then down through Duluth and back across Wisconsin. Suzie came with us. I remember stopping in Sault Ste. Marie, which is right on the Canadian border, and visiting our Aunt Gen and Uncle Lou. I always loved it there, with the red, brick sidewalk, something I hadn't seen anyplace else, and a quaint little backyard, complete with an apple tree. There was a trail across the street that led to Lake Superior, and I would summon Duchess, my aunt and uncle's dog, and we would go down to the lake shore where I'd see how far I could throw rocks or how big of splash I could get them to make. We stayed overnight, and when we were getting ready to leave the next morning, Uncle Lou gave Suzie a twenty-dollar bill, which was a considerable gift for a child in those days. I remember feeling slighted when he handed me a five, as I was too young to take into consideration that she was traveling without parents from whom she could coax money.

We made the Lake Superior loop, through Wawa and Thunder Bay, spending another night along the way. We refueled as soon as we crossed back into the United States. I rolled down the window and asked the attendant if I could pump the gas, and he said that I could. Having watched the process before, I was prepared for this next step toward adulthood. I went behind the car and pulled down the license plate and took off the gas cap, then went to the pump, got the hose and pulled the reset lever. My dad told me to put five dollars in, and when I told that to the attendant, he said, "Don't you mean five gallons?" I told him that I was sure it was five dollars 'cause that's what my dad always got. He didn't believe that someone would want to spend so much on gasoline, so he asked my dad to make sure.

We stopped in Rhinelander, Wisconsin on the last night of the vacation and stayed with Len Cournaya, who was a friend of my dad. I can't recall how many kids Len and his wife had, but there were a couple that were our age. There was a carnival in town and Suzie and I went with their kids to catch the rides. I lived life minute by minute back then and took everything for what it was at the time. I went to the carnival without reservations about the trip coming to an end. I was content going around and around on the Tilt-a-Whirl and Ferris wheel. Perhaps these are the steps you have to take to learn about letdowns and anticlimax, for by the following evening I was back in my hometown, restless and bored. Yet, I had my first substantial vacation under my belt, along with the memories I would take from it. I enjoyed spending the week with Suzie, although I can no longer recall many of the particulars that comprised the brunt of the journey. She was an influence with the two years she had on me, especially when it came to popular music. I paid closer attention to the songs that caught her attention. Whereas I knew which songs were sung by The Beatles, The Monkees, or Herman's Hermits, she knew the names of other less famous groups, groups where I knew the song but not the singers.

Back in the sixties, businesses closed at 5:00 p.m. from Monday through Thursday, stayed open till 9:00 p.m. on Friday, and all businesses would be closed on Sunday. Once a year in the middle of July, however, there was an event called *Midnight Madness*. It took place on a Friday night. There was excitement in the air, especially for me as youngster, as it would be the only night that I could stay up until midnight. One year in particular comes to the forefront whenever I remember Midnight Madness. It was a warm evening and Mom and I went downtown at about nine. It seemed strange to see crowds of people milling about as we turned the corner onto Main Street. We went into Ben Franklin, or The Franklin Store as we had called it up there. They had nothing new on the shelves, no toys or games that I hadn't looked at many times before as I'd kill time while my mom looked for new dresses at Peoples, the adjacent clothing store, but on that night back in 1968 all the toys and games seemed extraordinarily enticing. The night, after all, hosted an event where such toys and games weren't to be looked at casually but with an added air of reverence, for it was their special night. I followed Mom around from store to store, having a soda at the Liberty Cafe somewhere in-between. The setting was so cool that I didn't even get bored in the stores where I'd usually become antsy and annoying within the first couple minutes, for as uninteresting as they were, I was out late on a magical night. We continued to go from store to store, hitting nearly all of what downtown Manistique had to offer. I felt shortchanged when we got home at eleven-thirty, so Mom said I could stay outside until midnight as long as I didn't leave the yard. I went to edge of the alley and listened to the last sounds of Midnight Madness;

sounds of shutting car doors and starting engines and people calling out greetings and farewells. I looked up at all the stars in the sky and let my young body soak in the warm night air while my young mind contemplated one more small step I had made in my journey toward adulthood. It was midnight.

While I was still busy being a boy, those ten years older than me were beginning to make their mark on the world. One of the hallmarks of the late sixties was the songs of peace and love, and perhaps for the first time since classical music was modern, we listened to our music with solemn seriousness. Hearing *Get Together* by the Youngbloods made the open-minded evaluate how their lives were being conducted. *For What It's Worth* had us look at national policies with a critical eye and the direct implication that things should be better. Perhaps the epitome of such songs was by Scott McKenzie, singing about San Francisco, the ground-zero home of the anti-war sentiment, and reminding us to put flowers in our hair if we should visit. The unavoidable negativism that came from this movement (I say this without inference of blame and rather to illustrate that we were moving farther from the nation I had known to be pure and wholesome) was that we began to first look for the bad in people, especially our politicians. This trend would later become full blown and lasting with the Watergate scandal and would leave us a distrusting and cynical citizenry. 1968 was a tumultuous year in America. On April 4th Martin Luther King was assassinated in Memphis by escaped convict James Earl Ray. A month later Bobby Kennedy was shot and killed by a Palestinian named Sirhan Sirhan. The Tet Offensive by the Viet Cong caught American and South Vietnamese troops off guard as they celebrated the Vietnamese New Year. The Americans regrouped and won a technical victory, but the event advanced sentiment back home that the war was unwinnable.

The songs of the late sixties were beginning to catch my attention on a level higher than that of a young boy with a tune in his head. I became more pursuant of these songs and learning the names of the groups that sang them. One source was the jukebox at The

Liberty Cafe, the restaurant around the block. My mother had many talents, but cooking was not one of them. On summer weekdays when I was out of school and my dad was out of town, we would have lunch at The Liberty almost daily. I remember loading up the jukebox, I'm sure to the annoyance of the other patrons. I would pass through the Sinatra, Tony Bennett, and Nat King Cole selections to find my repertoire: *Green Tambourine, Lady Madonna, The Letter, Crimson and Clover,* and *Sugar, Sugar* to name a few. Due to the energy change in music and the dislike many of the older people had for the new sound, there was one selection that was frequently played—by them—titled *Three Minutes of Silence.* To my chagrin, they sometimes would put in enough dimes to have it quiet for the duration of our stay.

My intrigue with pop music and the culture that surrounded it continued to mount. There was an alley behind our house that expanded into an open space. So looking out from our backyard we faced the backside of the business district. There was a dance hall on the second floor of one of the buildings and on Friday nights they would have live bands. In the summer they would have the windows open and the sound would resonate throughout the neighborhood. That's where I had begun to dig the sound of garage bands, and by 1967 I was introduced to a new sound, one that grabbed me immediately and would stay with me until this day—psychedelia. The psychedelic sound was new, it was exciting, and when I saw the groups that performed it on various television programs, I was fascinated by all the color. In the phraseology of the time—it was groovy. Now Manistique was by no means the cultural center of the Midwest, and soon I was tuning in WLS out of Chicago at night to hear more of this new sound. I would take the transistor radio into my room at night and listen until I fell asleep, playing it as loud as I could without getting scolded.

Despite this interest in the sounds of the sixties, I was still boy. When I saw my mom and dad watching all the Detroit Tiger players running toward the mound the moment they won the '68 World Series, baseball quickly became my obsession. Dad would tell me stories of the Tigers of the nineteen-forties, with players like Rudy York, Hank Greenberg, Dizzy Trout, and Hal Newhouser. He had already finished his stint with the army and was working for Packard Motor Company in Detroit. When The U.S. joined the fight in W.W.II, Packard Motors was turned into a tank assembly plant. Overtime was mandatory and leaving was not an option. My dad would tell me that the only way he could get time off was to say that he was going to the dentist, but he'd instead head to Tiger Stadium and take in a game. He did this until his boss said, "According to my records, Roy, you've had all thirty-two teeth pulled." Baseball evolved into the sport of my youth and I loved tuning the game in on the radio and listening to the calls of Ernie Harwell and Ray Lane, and later Paul Carey. Similar to the difficulty I had finding the music I liked on our local station, I would have to tune into WJR out of Detroit, *The Great Voice of the Great Lakes*, to get Tiger broadcasts. I can still picture my mom sitting in a lawn chair on our front porch as I rode my bicycle up and down the block, with the game on the radio that sat next to her. The signal would often fade for minutes at a time, seemingly always at crucial points of the game, and I'd sit frozen on my bike while I waited to see if Willie Horton would deliver Kaline home from third. I had mentioned how I was a junkie for statistics regarding cities and states. Well, that was nothing compared to my interest in baseball stats. I knew the home run leaders, by season totals and all-time, and who the career strikeout leaders were, and I rooted vigorously for my home-state heroes to reach such heights of individual acclaim. Sometimes it was more important to see Mickey Lolich strike out twelve batters or for Al Kaline to hit three home runs than it was for the Tigers to win. When there wasn't a game I would throw a rubber ball at the side of the house and I would make the great fielding plays of my idols. Sometimes I would throw the ball high and hard off the house so I'd have to make an over-the-shoulder diving catch, to the displeasure of my mother. "Look what you've done to your clothes!" was something I often heard. If there was a phrase I had heard more than that, it was "Eat your vegetables!"

Like my dad I was a meat and potatoes guy, but I guess my dad ate his vegetables because I can't recall him getting yelled at. There were some vegetables that I genuinely disliked, but for the most part I passed on them whenever I could get away with it due to the time constraints I was under. After all, there were pickup games waiting for me, and they by far outweighed any benefits derived from eating vegetables.

When Dad was home the meal was steak, mashed or baked potatoes with lots of butter, and a vegetable, usually carrots. The steaks were tenderloin, sirloin, and occasionally cube. When we did veer from red meat the choice was either a casserole or smoked chubs. I liked smoked chubs and it didn't bother me that the heads were still attached, unlike sardines, which I liked but was repulsed by the little fish looking at me. Occasionally Dad would like a shot of blackberry brandy after a meal. Back then he'd have to buy his brandy at the Michigan Liquor Control Commission, as it was not yet legal for grocery or party stores to sell hard booze. When Dad was on the road and we weren't eating at The Liberty Cafe or The Eat Shop, the other option was *Pasty Day,* where pasties were made by volunteers from a local church and sold in a hot box outside Gambles. Barney's Grocery was a half-block from school and we'd stock up on candy before going to our first class. My favorite was the wax harmonica; you could play them then eat them. Of course we had to conceal all our goodies from the nuns to avoid either a beating or some form of humiliation. These snacks were best eaten at one of the several reel-to-reel movies that'd be shown during the course of an average week.

In those days I also became a gatherer. Aluminum cans were becoming a popular choice of manufacturers and I could redeem them at the junkyard for 25¢ a pound. Granted, it took a lot of aluminum cans to make a pound, but a pound of cans equaled one-half of my weekly allowance. I would also get extra money from the DNR in exchange for the bodies of lamprey. They had gotten into the Great Lakes through the St. Lawrence Seaway and eventually made it to the Manistique River. If you don't know what a lamprey is, it's an eel-like creature about eight to twelve inches in length that attaches itself to its food with a suction-cup mouth. They were doing serious damage to the fish population, hence the bounty on them. The Manistique River has a limestone bottom and the lampreys would latch themselves to it as they waited for prey. We would wade upstream with ice choppers and cut off the heads of any we came upon and collect their bodies in burlap sacks. The DNR paid 25¢ apiece for these parasites, so a good day at the river bought you a fountain soda, a banana split, and several 45s. Another item that fit into the things-gathered category would be cigarette butts. A couple of my school friends and I began smoking by finding half-burned cigarettes on the street. Admittedly, it's disgusting to think about now with all the newly diagnosed diseases of our day, but back then such things weren't a consideration. At the end of the street where I lived was a trail that led to an odd-looking, lone-standing tree which we named *The Jungle Tree*. We would take the cigarettes we collected, climb and take perch on one of the limbs and smoke the day's take. Although I must admit that I did like the taste of tobacco, the real craving was the thrill of doing something forbidden.

Due to the fact that I had W.W.II generation parents, I became interested in the years that preceded my birth, not as a historian but as someone who was captivated by the stories I heard. Later in life I'd look at those years with an even keener eye as I tried to retrace the path that took society to where it is today. With that in mind, I had earlier touched upon the simplicity of the early sixties and I want to elaborate on that. There was almost a seamless merge that took us from 1958 to 1962. You can see it in the movies and the music, and in fact, many people mistake groups like The Shirelles for fifties acts. The simplicity of the early sixties perhaps can best be evidenced by movies like *A Summer Place*. They were pure and modest, non sexual by today's standards, and there was that well-groomed wholesomeness about them. Now don't get too far ahead of me here. I would go through several longhaired beatnik phases of my own, but that's not where we were at this time. But if the merge was seamless that took us from '58 to '62, the merge that brought us from there to 1969 was anything but that—on the national stage, at least. I believe that everyone is familiar enough with the era's radical social changes that they needn't be enumerated here, but what I find intriguing is the dynamic of each movement. Take the anti-war crowd, for example. It would make for an interesting social study to dissect this group. I look at the Vietnam war protesters and split them into four groups: those who genuinely didn't believe in the war or who were pacifists at heart, those who were afraid they'd be killed if sent to war, those who looked at such gatherings as a huge party and had no strong convictions, and those who wanted to gain persona or create an identity for themselves, that is, be the next Ira Einhorn. Unfortunately, from the television images, it seemed like most of the protest crowd fit into the latter two categories, which contributed to the lack of respect they got from older Americans. (They already despised our long hair, they detested the sexual revolution, and they deplored the fact that we were unraveling the culture they had woven.) Another interesting aspect of the societal change was how some people went forward and some stayed behind. To me it can be exemplified by the song *Caroline, No* off *Pet Sounds* by the Beach Boys, as the boy asks the girl, "Where did your long hair go?" for in that time while the boys hair was getting longer, the girls started to cut theirs short. In my interpretation, he was used to sitting on the beach with his quintessential domesticated girlfriend. As the changes began to occur, he stayed in the world of the Four Seasons and The Drifters, while she explained to him that exciting things were happening in San Francisco's Haight-Ashbury district. He didn't understand and had no desire to, when trying to comprehend would have been the only thing he could have done to keep her. I believe that most of us deal with dichotomy at some point in our lives, and in the preceding scenario I can sympathize with both parties. I would guess that to many lovers and friends the example I gave was reality. Another more dramatic paradigm of cultural change as seen through music is found in the song *Triad* by Jefferson Airplane

33

with Grace Slick singing the provocative lyric, "Why can't we go on as three?" The innocence was gone and the sexual revolution was in full swing.

I believe that in some ways I took in the flavor of the sixties more than those who were older than me. Children are more observant to detail, and when something intrigues them they can be enthralled in it. The way it was with me was that I absorbed it as it happened. Then, some ten to fifteen years later, and as I will elaborate upon in due course, I went back to it with an insatiable hunger. It was the sound and it was the color, but it was also was nostalgia. It was where I was and who I was, and it was a remnant of what no longer prevailed. It was a pulled back curtain letting in a glimpse of sunlight into a darkened room. It took me back to a time when all doors were opened and the road would go wherever I wanted it to lead me. The innocence of the era merged with the sound and the color and played on my no-longer innocent self and fused in symbiotic fashion and brought me to completeness. I now knew not only where I had come from, but who I was.

For many people the innocence of the early sixties ended with the escalation of the war in Vietnam and the subsequent protests. Another Kennedy had been shot, and so had civil rights hero Martin Luther King. Riots infested summers in Detroit and Los Angeles, and the aftereffects of *The Summer of Love* were sending young people in directions that were new and exciting to them, but not all that popular with most of the citizenry. However, life in our small Northern Michigan town didn't change as quickly as the rest of the country. There was only one colored family in town, and although it was noticed that they were different, they were always considered to be no different than us. In fact, the locals were friendly to anyone and everyone, regardless of who they were or where they were from. Other social issues that were on the front burner nationally seemed unimportant in our town. For instance, a woman's place was still in the kitchen, and the women felt as strongly about this as the men did. So with most of the country submerged in social upheaval, I innocently watched on that warm summer evening as Neil Armstrong planted a human footprint on the moon, not reminiscent of where we had been, but curious as ever about where the next decade would take us. Yet, I was also still a kid who loved to hear Dick Van Dyke singing *Chim Chimney* and Jiminy Cricket singing *When You Wish Upon A Star*.

CHAPTER THREE

It was the first business day after the new year and the new decade when my mother took me to the State Savings Bank to open my first savings account. I remember the teller writing the entry into my book, *Deposit - $10.00, January 03, 1970*, and the date stood out as if it was all she wrote. 1970! It seemed impossible; the sixties were all I had known. But there I was, heading into the first vast unknown since I had reached an age where I could make such a delineation. My inaugural decade was in the books and so was the most innocent part of my childhood. I was still young, but now I had aspirations. The savings account was but a start. I was building and so was the society in which I was immersed. I was at I point where the world would soon be mine and anything would be possible. Rejection had yet to be encountered and I had no reason for pessimism. Furthermore, the age of freedom was at least within sight. My parents had no desire to go to California, for instance, and I wouldn't be able to talk them into taking me no matter how much I pleaded, but in just a few years I'd be able to do it alone if I so would choose. I'd be able to make my own decisions: what kind of job I would hold, what my hair length would be, and whether to purchase a motorcycle.

In some ways the entrance of the decade was very profound and distinct. There was optimism that the war in Vietnam would soon end and there was intrigue over where industrial innovation would take us. But to look back at the sixties through the prism of time, we see from a cultural standpoint—and this was a decade remembered for its culture—that the sixties, when thought of as an idealism, didn't end on the first of January, 1970, but rather on May 1st, with the shooting of four students by National Guardsmen during an anti-war protest at Kent State University. It was the epitome of the type of events that mobilized the counterculture revolution. Yet it would be the last major stand by the anti-war movement. After a little time passed there was a change in our nation. It was subtle at first, but on a national level the zeitgeist was shifting, with an ebbing of war protests and more energy and emphasis put on protecting the environment. Changes in music followed. Just as The Supremes and The Four Seasons had stepped aside to make way for The Doors, Hendrix and the like, the prevailing cultural sentiment prompted a restart of the succession process and groups like America, Seals and Crofts, Chicago, The Carpenters, and Bread took their places as musical heirs. The sound was lighter and more melodic. The hair continued to grow, but the colors softened. The bright tie-dyed shirts and union jack pants were replaced by earthy attire. To get a feel for the look of the day one only need watch *Jesus Christ Superstar.* On a local level, though, the tumultuous nature of the late sixties and the influence the various movements had on teenagers was just beginning to hit our community. Some of our stop signs had **THE WAR** stenciled in underneath, hair on the boys who were five or so years older than me began show some length, and in our class, the girls were talking about the Women's Lib movement. In May of 1970 the inaugural Earth Day took place, and shortly after, I formed an environmental club at school. I laugh now—my intentions were good and I didn't do it as a farce, but talk about appearing malfeasant. The kids who joined had to pay me ten cents a month for membership, and in return they got to go around and pick up trash. I chuckle now at the absurdity of the dues, but that aside, we had become part of the movement. Songs with progressive lyrics were moving forces in having us take our posts as good human beings. Those our age began thinking in global terms for the first time and realized the responsibility we had in doing our share. I'd like to note here that regardless of where we evolve politically, it's gratifying to take liberal stands when you're young, and so it was with us. Like everything in life, though, there are those who take things too far, and so it was with the environmental movement. I remember one specific occasion. It was common back then to hear the sonic boom of jets breaking the sound barrier. I was walking down a trail and a hippie was approaching me. A startling blast came out of the sky just as we converged. I made some small-talk comment in a jovial way, but he said dead seriously, "I wonder if it was really necessary." In terms of logic he was right, but in the confines of our small town he sounded foolish, and from that I realized the wisdom in fighting the larger battles and conceding some of the impractical ones.

Unlike in the sixties when all the unrest seemed to either avoid our small town or postpone its arrival for a later date, the changes in the early seventies were more immediate. Perhaps it was because the changes themselves were less drastic. With the environment being the hot-button issue of the day, public service commercials came into play. We had the Indian shedding a tear on a littered riverbank, Johnny Horizon was taking us to where the air was clean and the water was clear, but reminding us that it was more than a song, we had a lot of work to do. The general theme of the times was progress through unity. It was even in a Coca-Cola commercial as Melanie's raspy little-girlish voice sang about teaching the world to sing in perfect harmony—but of course this required buying them a Coke.

In the end, though, it was still small-town America. Moms stayed at home and drove large station wagons while dads earned the family wages. There was still a butcher shop down the block, and people went out to eat on Sundays after church. Everybody knew everyone, which was an additional deterrent for anyone doing anything too far from the mainstream. Yes the hair was getting longer and there were incidents of anonymously committed protest vandalism, but, for instance, if one wanted to organize an anti-war march down Main Street word would get out that so-and-so's kid was a troublemaker, at which point so-and-so himself would be sure to castigate the kid, telling him he was an embarrassment to the family and the community. So anything that was done in the name of counterculture had to be done on the sly. We were still pretty wholesome. We liked playing baseball during the day and listening to the Tigers in the evening, watching *The Brady Bunch, Lost In Space, Marcus Welby M.D.,* and *Gilligan's Island* on TV, and all family members were still expected to be present at the dinner table.

We grew up in a world of different names, too. The Vietnam War Theater (Cambodia, Laos, and North and South Vietnam) was referred to as Indochina. Taiwan was still called Formosa, The United Arab Emirates was the Trucial States, and Sri Lanka was Ceylon. We freely called Native Americans Indians without insult being implied or received. Those of us who were offspring of older parents celebrated Memorial Day and Veteran's Day as Decoration Day and Armistice Day.

I distinctly remember the breakup of The Beatles. Having said that, most of what I write is from what I learned ten to fifteen years after the fact. There had been friction forming between the members of the band, primarily between Lennon and McCartney. They needed a new business manager and John, George, and Ringo wanted Allan Klein, but Paul didn't trust Klein and tried to strong-arm his father-in-law, Lee Eastman, into the position, but he was outvoted. Also, John had been bringing Yoko into the recording studio, violating a long-standing rule that the band had imposed upon itself and making the rest of the members uncomfortable. From there they all began to entertain thoughts of going their own way, and when Paul released the album *McCartney* in April of 1970 it solidified the fact that they would never work together again. When the other members came out with their solo albums, shots were taken at Paul, such as in Lennon's song *How Do You Sleep* and in Ringo's single *Back Off Boogaloo.* In *Abbey Road,* the last album they recorded, (even though *Let It Be* was released after, it was recorded before *Abbey Road)* the album essentially ended with perhaps their most profound line, "And in the end the love you take is equal to the love you make." Despite the devastation the fans felt at the time, The Beatles had gone out on top. They didn't suffer the compromised end to their careers that Sinatra or Elvis had. They didn't stick around for the post-glory attempts of an aging boxer; they were James Dean—forever preserved at their best, leaving us to marvel at what it must have been like to go on one of the greatest rides in all of history. My initial memory of them had been of screaming girls drowning out the music they were playing; my final memory was pulling for *Let It Be* to win the Grammy for song of the year. (It would lose out to *Bridge Over Troubled Water*, a bridge that would metaphorically catch aflame from the covetousness Simon felt over the accolades given to Garfunkel for a song that he had written.) I knew all The Beatles' singles and I liked them. News of their breakup was surprising and was one of the few events in my young life that I found newsworthy. But time can be the only true measuring stick, and in ten years society would look through that prism and see that The Beatles hadn't been forgotten. In actuality their fan base would explode, adding fans who hadn't been born when the group disbanded, and as time would continue to pass The Beatles' mystique would only intensify.

Like with many boys my first job was a paper route, delivering papers for *The Escanaba Daily Press*. (We had a local paper, *The Pioneer Tribune,* but it only came out on Thursdays, so most residents relied upon the Escanaba paper for printed news.) We would pick up the papers outside the office, but there wasn't anyone working inside the office except on Saturdays. Because there was no supervision it was important to be one of the first to get your papers, as we would raid the stacks that weren't picked up, taking two or three from each bundle. Before beginning the route we'd take our papers, fold them into squares and put them in our bags, then fling them to their destinations like Frisbees. When we finished, those of us with "extra" papers would sell them in bars. My route was thirteen blocks long and I had thirty-some customers. Some of them were friendly, some of them weren't, and a couple were just weird, like the lady who would hand me my money while standing behind the cracked-open door and all I would ever see was her left arm.

One winter in the early seventies my mom signed me up for a Saturday intramural basketball league and we played at the old public school gym, which even then was a portal to the past. The square brick building stood alone, on the same block as Central High School but separate, and upon entering it looked both small and monstrous; small because of the mere several rows of spectator seating which in turn made it seem large because the court dominated the rest of the building. Small windows cast profuse lighting at strange angles onto the floor that was rickety, yet solid. There was a cast iron spiral staircase that led to a hardwood track that circled the court below. After changing into our shorts and tee-shirts we'd go up to the track and run warm-up laps while the game scheduled prior to ours finished. On occasion there'd be high school boys running laps. It wasn't common for me to be around kids that age, as the Catholic school I attended only went up to eighth grade, and they looked odd to me, being as big as our dads but having the faces of kids. I noticed how the floor would creek when they ran and I'd run toward the upper side of the sloped track to make sure that they didn't bump into me, sending me through the scant railing and onto the court below.

I saw my first professional sporting event on August 2nd, 1970 at Tiger Stadium in Detroit. I remember the date because it was Al Kaline Day. Dad drove Mom and me to Pellston and wished us a good time, then the two of us boarded a plane for Detroit. Mom's friends Alice and Hector, who lived in St. Claire Shores, picked us up at the airport. It was also the first time I'd been in a big city; previously, the largest city that I'd been to was Duluth. I had some distant cousins in Detroit whom I'd never met and I stayed with them for the day and night while Mom had some time with her friends. We went to Greenfield Village, whose science exhibits were a world away from anything I would see in Manistique. We spent the night in a tent in their backyard; they lived inside the city of

Detroit and we were just three years removed from the riots. I experienced that thrill you get as a kid when you're in a frightening situation but no one will admit they're scared. On Sunday Mom and I went to the game. Al Kaline was my boyhood hero and this was his day. They gave him a white convertible before the game and the organist played *Thanks For The Memories* as he sat in the passenger seat while the car circled the inside of the stadium. An announcement was made that Cherry Street was being renamed Al Kaline Drive, and then it was time to play ball. I had hit rocks with a stick the night before we'd left Manistique and in doing so I learned that Kaline would hit a record five home runs that day, while Norm Cash and Willie Horton would hit two apiece. Unfortunately it turned out that that method of predicting lacked scientific merit and the only home runs came off Minnesota Twin bats, a monster upper deck shot by Harmon Killebrew and a solo homer by Tony Oliva. The Tigers lost that day, but I had been to a pro baseball game and for the first time in my life I saw in person the players that I'd seen so many times on TV.

I was a baseball junkie in those days, or more accurately, an American League junkie. I rarely watched National League games, and when I did it was to see a specific player, like Ernie Banks or Willie Mays or other players who were climbing their way up the ladder of history. The Kansas City Royals of 1970 had players with catchy names like Paul Shall, Cookie Rojas, and Amos Otis. I was a naive small-town boy and didn't realize the latter two were Latinos, nor did I realize that about Tony Oliva or Luis Aparicio. They were simply baseball players to me, as they should have been.

In late summer of 1970 I watched the Detroit Lions beat the Green Bay Packers 40-0. They would beat them again that year 20-0, much to the chagrin of the many Packer fans in Manistique. Soon, football became a passion. Like love for a wholesome girl but lust for a sultry one, I loved the Tigers but found football to be dynamic. Just as with the baseball team I learned all the players by name, number, and career stats, and I rooted for them passionately, partially because I wanted them to win and partially for school yard bragging rights. Like with Kaline, Northrup, and Horton with the Tigers, I had my Lion favorites, too: Dick LaBeau, Charlie Sanders, Mike Lucci, Wayne Walker, the last being a linebacker who in times of injury did the place kicking. The Lions of my youth seemed to be a perennial 7-7 team and only made the play-offs once when I was young, a 1970 game which they lost 5-0 to the Dallas Cowboys.

Whereas I had grown up as a fan of the Detroit Tigers and Lions, it was a different story with basketball. Pete Maravich had caught my attention with his long hair, floppy socks and old tennis shoes, slick passing and fancy dribbling. After he shattered NCAA records while playing at LSU, he was drafted by The Atlanta Hawks in 1970, joining the likes of Lou Hudson, Walt Belamay, and Walt Hazzard, making the Hawks not only a competitive team, but one that was fun to watch. I hadn't gotten into the NBA previously so I hadn't formed an allegiance with The Pistons, so from 1970 through '74 I was an Atlanta Hawks fan. It was a good time for basketball, with stars like Jerry West and John Havlicek, Wilt Chamberlain and Oscar Robertson, Lew Alcindor and Dave Bing.

I played on the St. Francis basketball team for four years, and though I was a good outside shooter and had a knack for getting a lot of rebounds for being the second shortest kid on the team, I seldom got into a game. I remember one occasion when I did, it was at Engadine, the score was lopsided, and I entered with one minute to play. Within ten seconds I tied up their center and was in a jump ball situation with a kid ten inches taller than me. I lost the tip, but my teammates managed to get me the ball before the end of the game and I hit an outside jumper. It may have only been two points in a decided game, but it was my first bucket and I've seldom since been so proud. At one of our practices there was an incident in the locker room, one where my friend Tom punched me in the face. It didn't hurt much, but I did something spontaneously; something that backfired on me. As the punch landed, without any thought, I pretended I was stunned. I took a step backwards and let my head wobble around as if I were disoriented. Everyone began to hoot and holler and I tried to explain that I had faked it, but it was futile. To this day I don't know exactly why I did it, only that I did it without the foresight of consequence. Perhaps on a subconscious level I did it with the same reasoning as when I told my aunt I was three-and-a-half; to observe the reaction. On another occasion at practice I was quitting the team because I was mad at the coach. I was getting to an age where I was a little hot tempered and when I decided I'd had enough I kicked the ball from half court. The ball went in the basket. Everyone started laughing and soon I relinquished my anger and slowly began to smile. The most unlikely basket I've seen in any game, pro or otherwise, kept me from quitting the team and I remained a St. Francis Raider until I finished the eighth-grade season.

Our music teacher in fifth grade was Sister Marcus. She was one of the few nuns we had that didn't follow the Franciscan tradition of having Sister Mary in front of a male saint's name, such as our principal, Sister Mary Peter. What I remember most about her, though, was that she, like some adults I had encountered during my childhood, didn't have a concept of where a child's knowledge and interests were at any certain age, and she would talk to us as though we were younger than we were. She'd have us sing songs meant for first graders, songs with lyrics like:

> *Little Tom Tinker got burned by a clinker*
> *and he began to cry*
> *Ma, Ma, what a poor fellow am I!*

She'd teach us such songs while we'd roll our eyes and moan, trying to give her hints that she was underestimating us, but she never got our message. The older kids had a nickname for her, nothing nasty but by no means complimentary. Still, even though my mother was a musician, it was Sister Marcus who taught me about syncopation and the effect of changing musical cadence. She had been mocked and ridiculed behind her back, but yet I learned that everyone, regardless of how uncool they may be, holds the potential to offer something.

There are certain rights of passage that we all experience. Some are routine, such as learning to ride a bike—it's simply a matter of time before they are achieved—while others put you in a more exclusive category, like throwing your first curve ball that actually breaks, skating backwards, or later in your teens, dunking a basketball. They are milestones in our development and they're seldom forgotten. I was always interested in sports; hence my examples. But just as significant to someone else may be reading music for the first time, preparing a meal without your mother's assistance, or being entrusted to baby-sit. Sometimes these achievements happen later in life, like learning a foreign language in your adult years, but when they do I wouldn't qualify them as a passage. I look at passages as experiences take us from childhood to adulthood. And I believe that there is a synergistic value to them; more importantly than throwing a curve, you learn that if you're persistent goals can be achievable.

In the early seventies I would go to Escanaba and spend three days every August with my Aunt Laura during fair week. For a young boy, The U.P. State Fair was an event topped only by Christmas and The Fourth of July and I'd look forward to it for weeks in advance. Aunt Laura lived in a mobile home court that was owned by my Uncle Phil, who also had a mobile home dealership, and Aunt Laura's trailer was a mere two blocks from the fairgrounds. I remember how anxious I'd be on the first day. My aunt would be at the kitchen table with a can of Tab, a lit cigarette that seemed to eternally burn in its ashtray, and a deck of cards spread out in a game of solitaire. Through her overbite she'd tell me to be careful and I'd run the two blocks to the admissions gate and toward all the games and rides that I'd been waiting for since the previous fair had ended. I'd be in constant motion between venues: from the double-decker Ferris wheel to the Tilt-A-Whirl, then over to the games where I'd try to dunk Bozo, through the House of Horrors, past the side shows with the man yelling, "Gorilla-gorilla-gorilla-gorilla-gorilla-gorilla-gorilla...come see the gorilla," back to the clown yelling, "High and dry looking for a ballplayer," regardless of how wet he was. I became highly skilled at popping balloons by

45

squirting water into a clown's mouth and was a prodigy at looping rings over Coke bottles. In short, I was a fair rat.

One of the most humbling experiences of my life occurred when I was eleven. It was Memorial Day and I was waiting with some friends from school for the parade that would go from the high school and down Main Street as far as the post office. We were goofing around as eleven year-olds do when I decided I had to jump over the fire hydrant. I alerted my friends to watch my soon-to-be heroic achievement, then backed up to get a good running start. I remember thinking as I was about to launch that perhaps it wasn't a well thought out idea, but I knew that bailing out would bring ridicule. So I jumped. As you well know there's a bolt-like object that projects from the top of a hydrant; without getting too graphic, I didn't make it. I had never felt such a sensation in my young life. My groin was shooting pains that went up my back-bone making me feel cold and sweaty and instantly nauseous. I hobbled over and leaned against the side of the Ford dealership, eventually sliding down to the sidewalk, while my friends laughed and adults asked if I was okay. One old woman pulled a wrinkled and used looking tissue out of her purse and handed it to me, I don't know why. So there I was, in excruciating pain and holding old-lady snot. Yet the most humbling part was still to follow. I checked myself out when I got home, of course to find that area black and blue. It didn't really hurt anymore but I didn't know the repercus-sions of having black and blue testicles and I did the only thing I could—I showed my dad. Now my dad was not much for sympa-thy, regardless of the situation, and true to form he asked, "Why on *earth* did you do something *stupid* like that?" But he told me that it would be okay in time, and the discoloration eventually did go away. With the price I paid for my fiasco I became more aware of the possible consequences to every action.

The price of gas in 1971 was 31¢ a gallon. One day I was riding with my dad when we noticed a long line of cars at the local Clark station. We didn't pay it any mind until we came to the next gas station and saw the same type of lines. I looked at the price sign,

46

tugged at Dad's sleeve and said, "Look, only 17¢ a gallon." And so began Manistique gas war of 1971. It would last only several weeks and when it ended gas shot up all the way to 34¢. The gas war had come from nowhere. There had been no outrage at the price and the event seemed rather strange, yet everyone filled their tanks and some even bought and filled hundred-gallon holding tanks. Word spread throughout the central part of the peninsula of the cheap fuel and soon people were driving from Marquette, Escanaba, Munising, and other communities to take advantage of the price break.

I find it intriguing to look back in time and realize we were more than we gave ourselves credit for. Personally I find it in some of my writings from thirty years ago, when I see correct hyphen-ation or exquisite verbiage, and I think *I had no idea I knew that back then.* Similarly, I remember the first time I had a desire to go to Europe—England in particular. It was a sunny summer after-noon in 1971. I was in the backyard doing nothing in particular, just hanging out while my mom hung laundry on the clothesline that was strung in an little extension of our backyard that ran be-hind the storage shed and in front of the raspberry bushes and grape vines that buffered our yard from the alley. The radio was playing *Here Comes The Sun* by the Beatles and I pictured myself walking down a tree-lined British thoroughfare amongst mini-skirted girls that looked like Petula Clark. I thought how groovy it would be to see those red double-decker buses pass by on tight, curving streets with buildings that looked nothing like the ones we had in or any-where near Manistique, and how refreshing it would be to see a place so different than the small town in which I lived. In later years I had thought my desire for Europe had come in the mid-eighties, but writing this has excavated memories that were long forgotten and in doing so I exposed the budding of my transoce-anic dreams.

But while I was dreaming such things, new ground was being broken for America as a whole. In 1972, Nixon made a historic trip to communist China. I can remember my dad saying, "What the hell does he want to go over there for?" which was the sentiment of many Americans. I felt some intrigue with our president going to such a strange land, but like my dad, I wasn't able to see the benefits of the visit. The fact that wasn't comprehended by the commoner was that new doors were being opened in terms of trade and normalization. When the same efforts were made with the Soviet Union, however, I understood the importance. Even in our small town the black and yellow symbols of fallout shelters were visible and just a few years had passed since school children participated in drills where in event of a nuclear attack they would hide under their desks (which today, of course, we know would be a futile evasive measure). Furthermore, despite the fact that the world community generally accepted that there were two superpowers, I believed the prevailing sentiment in the early seventies, which no one cared to talk about, was that we were number two. Russia was a larger country territorially, the impression was that they were more ruthless and thus trigger-happy, and the word was that their arsenals were considerably larger than ours. Nixon's '72 visit brought signing of arms limitation treaties and made plans for a joint U.S.-Soviet space mission. This visit to The Kremlin caught American's attention more than the China visit, but I believe our citizens didn't want anything less than a compromised Russia and American supremacy.

My interest in sports was rounded with the '72 Olympics in Munich, which promised to be a microcosmic showdown between the United States and the Soviet Union. I was growing up with baseball, basketball and football, Sunday boxing matches and occasionally some tennis, but with this event I was introduced to many new sports. I particularly enjoyed the track and field events: the shot put, pole vault, discus, and javelin throw, because they were so different from any sport I was used to watching. I was also a patriot and when Mark Spitz won a record seven gold medals in the pool. I was as proud of him as any American sports figure, Al Kaline included. However, the '72 Olympics would be remembered for political events more than anything else. My first

48

experience with Islamic terrorism was burned into my memory as Jim McKay broke the news of eleven Israeli wrestlers held hostage while we watched the unforgettable image of the black hooded terrorist on the balcony with a submachine gun. Sadly, all eleven athletes were murdered. The event left a dark cloud over the first Olympiad that I was old enough to appreciate and set the stage for a modern day resurgence of Islamists pursuing philosophical imperialism and revenge through the harm of innocents.

For one weekend during the summers of 1972 and '73 I attended a retreat at St. Lawrence Seminary at Mount Calvary, Wisconsin. The object of the weekend was to try to get young kids interested in joining the priesthood, which was not a consideration for me, but the experience was actually quite fun. The seminary was located atop a hill. It was complete with dorms, (something I had never stayed in before) a mess hall, church, bell tower, and a gymnasium. There were catacombs that ran from the dorms to the gym, which made going there even more cool to a twelve year-old. Brothers would guide us and provide the schedule, and they kept us from being bored for just about all of the weekend. I was the only one to go from my Catholic school so I was a little apprehensive at first, but I fit right in as soon as I arrived. Perhaps when I said apprehensive it was misleading. What I really felt was that I'd be with a bunch of kids who wanted to be priests—stuck with a bunch of no-fun kids who were holier-than-thou. It was not the case. The first thing we did after settling into our dorms was meet in the gym for a game of bombardment (dodge ball). I had only played a few times before, but I was good at it, both in firing the ball at other kids and at catching what they threw at me. Staying in dorms was a blast; no one wanted to go to sleep and the first two hours were spent trying making comments that would prompt the other kids to laugh, whereupon one of the brothers would come in and tell us that we had a full day ahead of us tomorrow and we better get our sleep. The church was modern, not stiff and formal like the one I was attending in Manistique, and the service was less rigid as well. To this day I think of it as refreshing. The alter was made of wood, not marble, and the walls and ceiling were also wood and not stone, which fit the back-to-nature theme of the early seventies. Even though it was by no means of Spanish design, for some reason I associate it to the little church in Spain that Jake entered in Hemingway's *The Sun Also Rises*. The food in the cafeteria was good and the drink of choice was *bug juice*, a combination of Kool Aid and something else that I never found out. The rest of my memories of those retreat weekends are less clear; yet the high points of those six days split between two years are something I'll always look back at with fondness.

The boys in our class knew each other well, as there were only seventeen of us, most of whom had been together since kindergarten. Often we would organize games after school: baseball or kickball in the spring and football in the fall. We would imitate our favorite players as we played our positions. While playing football and on defense I played backfield (we were too young to designate whether you played safety or corner) and I was always Dick LaBeau, number 44 from the Detroit Lions. Early on, I got the knack of playing off the receiver to make the quarterback think he was open, then closing in at the last moment for the interception. After school on weekdays many of us would watch *Bill Kennedy At The Movies*. On Friday nights we'd stay up late to see *The Ghoul*. Saturday evenings had what I consider to be the best lineup in the history of television: *All In The Family, Bridgette Loves Bernie, The Mary Tyler Moore Show,* and *The Bob Newhart Show*. Most of us would watch the full block at our own homes and then repeat the catchy lines to each other during Monday morning recess. Late Saturday night it was *All Star Wrestling*, with stars like Bobo Brazil, The Mighty Igor, Andre The Giant, Baron Von Raschke, and Chief Wahoo McDaniel. Sunday evening programming included *Mutual of Omaha's Wild Kingdom* and *The Wonderful World Of Disney*. Another notable when we were that age was the occasional Raquel Welch film. There'd be a buzz in the classroom amongst the boys whenever she'd be on the CBS late movie, and when we got home we tried to talk our parents into letting us stay up late on a school night to catch a show, not saying what we planned on viewing. Television commercials were catchy too, and I still hum some of them to this day. There was the Ken-L Ration commercial, "My dog's bigger than your dog," the Armour ad, "Tough kids, sissy kids, even kids with chicken pox love hot dogs," and the recently revitalized ad from Oscar Meyer, "My bologna has a first name."

There were three girls in our class that I thought were cute, but Sally was the one who was cute and sweet. In fifth grade I was trying to show off for her and I yanked Pat Waters' chair out from behind him as he was going to sit. End result—he was okay but he did hit his head on the way down and consequently I spent the rest of the school year, three months, with my desk in the corner facing the wall. I had been vilified for my actions, but more importantly, I didn't get to gaze at Sally. Many after-school fights were scheduled because of the aforementioned girls, but the fights were an event of their own and word of them would quickly spread through the classroom and subsequently throughout the school. Throngs of students would migrate to the designated site at the sound of the bell that ended our day, and they would form a circle around the two gladiators. Most of the fights would be quite lame; either a name-calling contest followed by a mutual chickening out, or a bigger kid tackling the smaller one in about three seconds, perhaps punching him in the head a few times or rubbing his face in the snow until he cried out that he quit. Occasionally, though, we did have some classic matchups, like in seventh grade when Bob Rozich took on an eighth grader and won. Bob was one of my best friends, but I felt bad for the eight grader, knowing the humiliation he'd face for losing to a younger kid.

For a period during the early seventies my all-time favorite song seemed to change every year. As I had dubbed some of the garage band songs my favorites in the sixties, the new progression opened with *Hitchin' A Ride* in 1970, then went to *Want Ads* in '71, *Brandy (You're A Fine Girl)* in '72, and *Brother Louie* in late summer of '73. From there I would go through a period, lasting about a year, where neither music nor anything else was much a part of my life.

By late '72 music was once again shifting directions. The light sounds that had replaced the psychedelic music of the sixties were being replaced by a harder and more driving sound. The color bands, as my friends and I referred to them back then, Black Sabbath, Deep Purple, and Pink Floyd, along with Grand Funk Railroad, became standard-bearers of the new sound. It was like Father Chronology was saying, "It's time to move on and here's what I have for you now." But like a kid whose puppy had run away, I just wanted my old dog back. Along with the changes in music came a change in the drug culture. Mind-opening experimentation had turned into a search for wasted incoherence and there was an air of darkness as users became troubled and distant black-hole zombies. The shift was from acid to heroin, which was less mind altering than mood altering and the fun-loving aspect of usage took on a more dangerous image. It was viewed so by society, too. Perpetrators of many of the violent crimes being committed were users, something that wasn't happening with the pure hallucinogens of the sixties.

On occasion I'd watch the nightly news with Walter Cronkite. By the early seventies we were all familiar with the names from the war: Saigon, Phnom Penh, Hanoi, My Lai massacre, Tet Offensive, The Demilitarized Zone, Mekong Delta, Ho Chi Minh Trail. They would give nightly casualty reports, separating the dead and wounded into three categories: Vietcong, South Vietnamese, and Americans. Most of the time the numbers would show heavy casualties for the North, moderate for the South and only several for U.S. forces. Not long after I began paying attention to these numbers, Suzie's older brother, Jimmy, came home from Vietnam. One night he came to our house for supper and I blurted out the question that prompted stern looks to be shot at me from both my parents. "Did you kill anybody?" He didn't answer, he just got really quiet, and from that I assumed that he had. He had bought a fast car—a bright yellow Oldsmobile Roulette, complete with a spoiler on the back. One afternoon, Jimmy went to the cemetery with my mom and aunt to visit some passed relatives, and while he was there he mentioned where he wanted to be buried. The following Sunday while I was in church with my mom, the priest included in his dedications, "And for James Gorsche for whom this mass is being offered." I tugged on my mom's sleeve and asked if Jimmy had died, but she assured me that he hadn't. Still, I had never heard a dedication presented that way for anyone who hadn't died. For a living person it would always be something like, "And for the special intention of John so-and-so." So despite the reassurances of my mother, I sensed my analysis was right. When we got back from mass the word was out. Jimmy had crashed his car into a tree while rounding a sharp curve near the Three Mile Supper Club. I didn't see the police report, but I heard it said he was traveling in excess of 100 mph.

They towed the car to a body shop across from our school. A couple boys from the class and I went to look at it one noon hour. The front end was horribly crushed and there was shattered glass everywhere. There was blood on the windshield and throughout the interior, but what I will never forget is the chunk of flesh on the dash. I would guess that ten to fifteen years passed before I recalled Jimmy's statement concerning where he wanted to be buried, and correlated it to the proximity in time of the accident. Could it have been sheer coincidence? Sure. However, considering the fact that he was infantry in the front lines of a vicious war, that he had probably seen some horrible things, that he had made the statement at the cemetery, and that he was rounding a curve that was known to be dangerous at such a high rate of speed leads me to believe otherwise. I have since asked another cousin who is sixteen years older than me and had experienced that period of time as an adult if she would make the same conclusion that I did. She said that she wouldn't. Jimmy's death wasn't the first our family had experienced in my lifetime, but it was the first time I experienced the death of someone who was still in his prime. It brought me to realize a little about the finality of death, at least from an earthly standpoint. Except for his time in the service I had seen Jimmy nearly every day of my life and it was hard to accept that I would never see him again. Yet, I didn't contemplate the fragility of life as it applied to me. At that point I was still invincible, but that perception would change the following year.

As we entered 1973 the war in Vietnam was still not over. Although I was still young, whether or not I'd be drafted was something that was on my mind as I grew closer to eligibility. I had observed those who were five to ten years older than me, how some went to war without complaint, how others protested in the streets, and how some went to Canada. I had come to the decision that if I were drafted I would go, but would do so reluctantly. One of the factors in this resolution was that if the person drafted in my slot was to be killed, his death shouldn't be a result of my decision. Now I know that this assessment is arbitrary—perhaps I would be more alert or agile or vice-versa—but I felt going-if-called was the only way I could keep respect; self-respect and respect from the older generation. I waited for either the war in Vietnam or the draft to come to an end. The end of the war would come in late January with the fruition of the Paris Peace Talks that I'd been hearing about on the nightly news. The cease-fire agreement was signed in January and the last U.S. troops would leave Vietnam in March. With the United States finally out of the war, political news had not only to be broadly covered, but of interest to a thirteen year-old for me to take note. So in January of 1973 when the Supreme Court ruled that a woman had a constitutional right to make private decisions, ergo legalizing abortion, I was unaware of this landmark ruling. The fact is that the ruling gets more attention today than it did when Roe v. Wade was ruled upon. At that time it was quite unpopular to those old enough to understand, (issues like abortion weren't discussed with children at that time) but support for the ruling grew through the years as the older Americans with values of the era in which they grew up began to die. To this day that ruling highlights one of the most divisive issues in American politics.

On some Sunday mornings Dad would take us to The Al-O-Ray restaurant after church. There was a motel adjacent to the restaurant with a heated pool and non-guests could use the facility for fifty cents. One Sunday I wore my trunks under my pants and went to the pool while my parents were eating, promising them to stay in the shallow section as I hadn't yet learned to swim. There was a girl tanning in a lawn chair beside the pool. She was a couple years older than me and she was cute, so the showoff in me came out and I began to brag about how well I could swim. I stood on the deck near the center of the pool but a couple of steps toward the deep side, then dove into the deep side and coasted into the shallow. I did this a couple of times until I finally misjudged. My hands felt the incline but I didn't have enough momentum to make it all the way up. Using my feet, I tried to climb back, but the slippery blue-painted cement sent me sliding further into the deep section. I began to panic. I managed to get my head above water and call a muffled "Help!" but went back down again. I made another surge and tried to yell again, but took in a mouthful of water instead. It was then that the girl dove in and pulled me out. I was too scared to be embarrassed and didn't care what I looked like as I coughed out a couple mouthfuls of pool water. I can't remember if I thanked her—in fact I can't recall any specific image of her other than that of her tanning before the incident happened. The rest is just blurred images: an arm as she was helping me out of the water, and a foot as I lay prone. Looking back I realize how lucky I was that a girl of fifteen or so knew how to swim and was strong enough to pull me out. But with that, the seeds were planted that would grow into the realization that I was not invincible.

The main realization of mortality in my young life came on September sixth, 1973. I had come home from school for lunch and found my mother lying on the bedroom floor. I rushed to her and grabbed her wrist to check for a pulse, but she was cold and her lips were blue. I dialed zero and had the operator send an ambulance, then called my Aunt Irene. I knew my mom was dead and I sensed that she had been for a few hours, but my aunt thought I was overreacting. She told me that she had probably just passed out and that she would come right over. I went next door to Uncle

Pete Gorsche's and told him. In the previous year or so, Uncle Pete had begun to see me as a young man and not so much a kid anymore, and he found more credence in my words. He came back to the house with me. We got there as the ambulance was arriving.

I was beginning to feel the finality of never seeing my mom again, but over the course of the next several hours there were a lot of people showing up at the house. To this day I can only make assumptions as to why I did what I did next, which was run my paper route. I have since heard that when President Kennedy was shot, some of his staff who flew back from Hawaii laughed and played cards on the flight to the mainland, but once they landed they all broke down. I suppose I went on some type of emotional automatic pilot as well, perhaps trying to have one last hour of normalcy before dealing with a tragedy that I knew was bound to change my life profoundly and infinitely.

My dad had been working in Marquette. Aunt Irene got hold of him and he met me at her place. I remember that he sat on the couch crying, something I didn't see much of from him, with his left hand shaking uncontrollably. After that I remember John (my natural father) and two of my sisters, Jackie and Mary, stopping in. It was strange for them to be at Aunt Irene's, and it seemed like two worlds were colliding. But John was particularly nice that day. From time to time over the previous couple of years he would take me aside and make sure I knew that he was my quote, unquote real father, but he didn't do it that day. Still, a panic came over me. With my mom gone and my dad working out of town I feared that my biological father would insist that I go live with him, and having that on my mind wasn't what I needed, with everything else I was dealing with. Looking back, I give him credit for having the intuition to understand the power of the bonds that had been formed and never suggesting that I be uprooted. If there is one thing that I'll forever thank him for, it is that.

People were still arriving to pay their respects, some I knew well, some I had only met a few times. Aunt Gen came in from Sault Ste. Marie. I handled myself well; in fact, I wonder if my relatives worried about me, as I hadn't cried openly since the tragedy occurred. And that was something I was well aware of; I was determined to be the good little soldier and not break down and look like a kid. In the meantime all the plans were being made. I went to Aunt Gen and told her that my mom had once told me that when she died she wanted *Ave Maria* played at her funeral. But for a reason that I can't remember, Aunt Gen didn't think that song would be appropriate. I felt the fear of letting my mother down on something that was important enough for her to tell me in advance. I restated my case, emphasizing that it was what my mom had wanted, but it was to no avail. I remember shortly thereafter Mary El getting mad at Aunt Gen on my behalf because she felt Gen had been nit-picking at me. Adults in conflict on the Gorsche side of the family was something I hadn't seen before, but when Mary El stuck up for me I felt that I was relevant in the decision making process. My mom's wake was one of the largest ever in Manistique. Through her music, she was very popular. I continued to hold it together until an unlikely event happened. Our neighbor across the street from us never seemed to like me, perhaps because I used to roughhouse his kids. However, when he came up to me at the funeral home the best of human nature came out in both of us; after all, he was an adult and I was a boy who had just lost his mom, and when he hugged me I broke down and cried. I couldn't stop it; his act of compassion had gotten to me more than those of my closest relatives. Despite trying hard to be strong and succeeding for so long, everyone was watching me break down, and I once again became the young boy they expected me to be.

After all the services were complete, Aunt Irene and Uncle Pete told my dad that I could stay with them on weekdays for the rest of the school year, which had just begun, and Pierre could stay in the utility room towards the back of the house. My dad agreed, and this was a huge relief to me, as my worries about being taken away from my dad would not be substantiated. Still, with the death of my mother, I would find that the days of certainty were over for good. I would go back and stay at our house when my dad came into town. Aunt Irene's house was warm and full of life, but our house wasn't the same. It was now dark to me and had the feel of death. When I was little I would sit by the register on cold winter days and let the flow of air warm me, but sitting there on those late autumn days of '73 just made me notice that the closet that harbored my mom's clothes was empty, and that's how I felt about the whole house.

I spent the night of New Years Eve of 1973 at my brother Harold's. Harold was nineteen years older than me and had kids just a few years younger than I was. I can't remember how I came to stay there on that particular night, but I didn't want to be there. I was still messed up from the loss of my mother and I felt crushed not to have my dad around, especially with a brother who refused to acknowledge him for what he was to me and referred to him as "Your Uncle Roy." On top of all that, Jean Dixon or someone had predicted that the world would come to an end at midnight, and I hadn't yet had the experience of bypassing unfulfilled predictions. So with my nieces and nephews tugging and pulling on me as if I were a happy person, I watched the clock and wondered how it was going to feel to experience *The End*.

Right after Christmas of '73 I had my first taste of normalcy, watching *The Sting* at the theater. It's a movie I consider to be one of my three all-time favorites, perhaps because of the hope it brought when I found that I could at least temporarily be distracted from my thoughts. It wasn't until the Watergate hearings, though, and the interest that I found in them that I felt the oncoming of sustained normalcy. Years earlier, I had become aware of the political process, especially with our selection of presidents. In '68 I told the other kids in our class that Hubert H. Humphrey should be the next president. I didn't have a clue as to why the man should hold that office, I was strictly a myrmidon of my father's position. By '72, however, I had become more aware, and for reasons that I had put thought into I didn't want to see Nixon get reelected. He did, but by '72 the Watergate scandal was starting to break and in early '73 everything was beginning to unravel for the president. Vice

President Spiro Agnew was forced to resign amid charges of corruption and income tax evasion. When the impeachment hearings began in the spring of 1974, I was glued to the TV, and I believe it was the first time my attention was diverted from my mother's death for any considerable length of time. The pressure was on the president and the missing eighteen minutes of tape were something he couldn't explain. John Ehrlichman, H.R. Haldeman, John Dean, and G. Gordon Liddy became household names. I kept up with the situation until Nixon finally resigned under pressure of an upcoming house vote that would have certainly impeached him. Watergate changed the way we looked at our elected officials, both as citizens and members of the media. The unconditionally respectful tone was gone and so was the trust.

I was staying at Aunt Irene's watching the Braves' game the night that Hank Aaron passed Babe Ruth on the all time home run list. I didn't want to see Aaron get the record. I had hoped that the opportunity would've gone to Willie Mays. Willie was dynamic while Hank was consistent. Willie hit longer homers and compiled higher seasonal stats. I appreciated Aaron for what he did, though; he earned the record, and on the night he achieved it I applauded him. In a way the same comparison can be drawn between Al Kaline and Willie Horton. I loved Al Kaline, he was my favorite player, but there was an excitement I felt when Willie came to the plate that I never felt when Kaline batted. There was another notable sporting event that I had also watched while staying with Aunt Irene, and that was *The Battle of the Sexes*, the tennis match between Bobby Riggs and Billie Jean King. Being a boy I rooted for Riggs, as I didn't want to face the inevitable ridiculing by the girls in our class if King would win. She did, I took my lumps, and with the perspective of time I'm glad that she did. Riggs was brash and boastful while King had a cause resting on her shoulders, and her victory lent more fuel to the Women's Lib movement.

I felt comfortable staying at my aunt and uncle's. I had the bedroom that Paul and Carl had when they were young. It was upstairs and toward the back of the house, overlooking the garage and gymnasium. At night I would tune in WLS from Chicago on the transistor radio and listen to John "Records" Landecker and Steve King play songs like *The Joker, Little Willie,* and one of my aforementioned favorites *Brother Louie* by The Stories, a song about a racially-mixed relationship—something we hadn't had in Manistique—and I again realized how diverse the world was and how much more there was for me to see.

There was an old limestone quarry behind the band shell where I spent many a summer day. I had learned to swim shortly after the incident where I nearly drowned and my friends and I would swim in the warm, clear water and jump off the lower shelf of rock that protruded out below the top of the cliff. Some of the older kids would dive off the upper shelf, having to clear the lower formation that jettisoned out about ten feet when looking straight down. Occasionally someone would miss and catch part of their body on the rock and bounce from it into the water. Seeing that, along with the word that years earlier two kids had drowned when they got tangled in some old car bodies that had been pushed into the quarry kept me from ever diving off the high cliff. We'd drop-line for rock bass at the quarry, too, which usually meant a ten second wait between the time the hook hit the water and we had a bite. If we ran out of worms we'd hook the eyes out of the fish we caught and use them for bait. When we had poles we'd hook the smaller rock bass on for bait and cast out for one of the several pike that were said to be in the middle, but neither I nor any of my friends ever caught a pike there. On other occasions we'd go to Intake Park and fish near the dam. There we get bullhead, sunfish, and bluegills, and there we did occasionally catch a pike. My main fishing venue, though, was three blocks from my house, wading in the Manistique River in my blue jeans and tennis shoes. By the time I was fourteen I knew all the holes and would often exceed the legal limit, which meant following the river and then cutting through the woods, as the DNR office was along the path I would take to my site.

There was a lay teacher at our school whom I will call Mr. Jones. I haven't changed any names up to this point, but for reasons that will become apparent I'll change this one. Anyway, Mr. Jones was a pretty hip guy. He was liked by the students because he made class interesting and because he was cool. The school was somewhat rigid when it came to social events like dances, so when his suggestion to have them was nixed, Mr. Jones decided to have them at his house instead. He had everyone bring some 45s and we danced in his living room. We were all a little apprehensive at first, but he took his wife out onto the dance floor, and those of us willing to dance slowly followed. Janice Creeden asked me, but I still had an eye for Sally Turan, who was now with my friend Bob Rozich. The first song I slow danced to wasn't a slow song, but *I Can See Clearly Now* by Johnny Nash. I liked the song, but Janice was dancing much too fast, and I believe that when I told her to slow down it was the first time that I had ever asserted myself with a girl.

And now the reason that Mr. Jones became "Mr. Jones." He had gotten a different job and had moved to a small town seven miles outside of Marquette. My dad was working in Marquette on the construction of their new power plant. Mr. Jones had heard of my mother's passing and invited me to stay with them for two weeks. Dad agreed and dropped me off on a Monday morning. Mr. Jones and his wife had become vegetarians and had a huge garden and they introduced me to many new and exotic vegetables, but it was another herb that he introduced me to, marijuana, that is the reason for preserving his true identity. His wife was a glass blower and she had blown some pipes that we used to smoke hash oil. He was part of *The In Crowd* and had some of his friends staying with him as well, most notably, a playboy centerfold from the previous year. So they all got high and watched as I caught my first buzz. There was an old piano in the garage and somehow we all got out there; one of those sensations you get when you're stoned where you were *there* and then suddenly you're *here*. I told them I could play, but I started banging out a bunch of trash. Jones said. "Just relax and let the groove find you, man," and when I did I extemporaneously brought forth a rhythmic sound that was as new to me as it was to them.

61

By the end of the night it was discovered that there weren't enough beds, and so came the situation that perhaps has brought me more ridicule from my friends than anything before or since. It was decided that the playboy bunny would sleep in the same bed as me. I remember her wearing only an oversized nightshirt and panties as she crawled over me to the other side. And what did I do? Nothing! For the duration of the night I did nothing. I didn't even cop a feel under the guise of rolling over in my sleep, although I contemplated it. But as I did, I pictured her storming out of the bed and screaming, "You disgusting little pervert!" and then telling Mr. Jones, who in turn would say, "Sorry bud, but I'm going to have to ask you to leave, man." And I thought how there I would be—seven miles away from my dad's hotel and seventy miles from my hometown, too young to drive and walking down the highway, stoned, in the middle of the night. So the decision was made and that was that. In the end I was a fourteen year-old Catholic boy who didn't want to risk offending the girl in bed with him, regardless of who she was.

After my two-week stint with Mr. Jones had concluded, I ended up staying with Dad in Marquette for much of that summer, residing at The Heritage House, a vintage hotel atop a hill that overlooked the city. I was fourteen and was getting my first real taste of freedom and I found plenty to do without getting into trouble. He'd get back to the hotel around five and we'd get something to eat, and then watch television or perhaps go for a ride. I enjoyed both aspects of my tenure there: being free during the day and being with him in the evenings. While he was working I loved walking around town, traversing the steep hills that made up the downtown district. I'd go into various stores and look around, occasionally buying something with the extra money I now received from Dad, or I'd walk down to Lake Superior, which was a mere two blocks behind us, and watch the ore boats unload. During the course of the summer I met a retired college professor from Virginia Commonwealth University named Earl McIntyre, who was summering at the hotel. He was a kindly older man and offered to take me to different places of interest around the area. Dad did some inquiring about the fellow and had enough people tell him that he was an okay guy that he let me go with him. He took me to local places that were too far to walk to, like Presque Isle Park where there were steep cliffs and other cool rock formations and where the deer were plentiful and approachable. Mr. Mac, as I came to call him, would become a pen pal and a respected friend until he died, some twenty-five years later.

The independence I had that summer made me feel like less of a child and more like a young man who, despite the tragedy of the previous year, still had a lot waiting for him. My time in Marquette served as another step of the bridge between losing my mother and gaining self-reliance. Things were new and intriguing and I really don't remember thinking about my mother that much during that period of time. Also, it's interesting how certain songs become permanently linked with certain events, and to this day whenever I hear *Midnight At The Oasis* I think of walking down the hill from The Heritage House and those transitional days of 1974. The experience had also helped me bond with my dad. I had always held him in the highest esteem, but during our time in Marquette I realized two things: my dad was perfectly able to take care of me, and he allowed me a certain amount of freedom that I hadn't had with my mother.

CHAPTER FOUR

For nearly a year I had stayed with my aunt on school days, then went back to our house when Dad came home. It was nearing the end of the summer of '74 when my cousin Louise had me sit with her on the steps and told me my dad was probably going to have us move to Escanaba. I tried to reassure her that I could convince him to stay in Manistique, but she didn't believe me and it turned out she was right. In August we made the move. My Aunt Celia had a house and the upstairs wasn't being used. Next door to her were my Uncle Elmer and Aunt Betty, and their kids, Kenny, who was two years younger than me, and Pat, who was a year younger than Kenny. So once again I'd be living next door to cousins who were close to me in age.

So we cleared out the house in Manistique. When moving day came, I decided that I wanted to ride the ten-speed my dad had bought me for graduating from St. Francis. Dad and Pierre were going to be about an hour behind, so I told him to watch for me and that I'd flag him down if I wanted to abort the journey. I had never rode my bike for a stretch longer than the seven-mile ride to Indian Lake and this run would be over fifty. I hadn't gotten five miles out of town when I hit a stiff head wind. I remember telling people at the time that I had to buck a 30 MPH wind, but in practical retrospect I would put it at about ten, which was still substantial when you add your travel speed. By the time I reached Thompson Creek

I was already tired and my face was wind-burned. I was thirsty, too, but the water in the bottle that was handily designed to fit on the frame of the bike was hot and tasted like plastic. There was a bar up ahead and I went in for water. The next stop I made was at a boat launching area about fifteen miles away from Manistique. The access road sloped down to the lake at probably an eight-point grade, leaving me out of sight from highway traffic. And there went my dad. I can't remember feeling as deflated or intimidated as I did then and there. I had made up my mind that I was going to bail on my effort and catch the ride. I was tired and sore, hungry and insatiably thirsty, and I wanted no more of this undertaking. But there I was at the boat launch, now with two-thirds of the ride left to go and with no choice but to do it myself. It was another five hours before I pulled into Escanaba. I rode to Aunt Celia's, only to find that Dad had gone to Uncle Phil's, which was two miles back in the direction in which I had come into town. The last thing I wanted to do was ride any more, but Aunt Celia didn't drive and I needed to find my dad. Finally I caught up with him. He had been worried when he didn't see me on the road and was contemplating what to do. Now my dad was never a hugger or one to readily show affection, but I could tell by the way he was scolding me that he was very glad to see me. We put the bike in the back of his truck and headed to our new domicile.

Aunt Celia had come to visit us several times when we lived in Manistique. She would go on walks with me and tell stories and was a lot of fun to be around. However, the situation was different now. She became the person in charge of me while my dad was working out of town and I was at an age where being controlled by someone who had never had that role in my life was hard to accept. We genuinely annoyed each other, and looking back at the situation now I take half the blame, blame I didn't accept at the time. I saw her as trying to interfere in my life, but the fact was that it was her house and at times I acted like I owned it. She was retired and spent a lot of time chatting on the phone with her friends, and I found it particularly annoying when she would switch from

English to French whenever I'd walk by, sometimes glaring contemptuously at me as she did. The French I knew was limited and I had forgotten most of what my dad had taught me when I was young, but I knew she was talking about me. Eventually, though, we came to an unspoken understanding; I would spend most of my time upstairs—I had my stereo and my own TV—and she would only minimally interfere. Likewise, I kept from getting on her nerves as much as a fourteen-year-old possibly could.

The autumn of '74 was incomparable to any period of my life. The first day of school in Escanaba was also my first day as a high school student and it was as traumatic for me as my first day in kindergarten. My world had changed drastically. Mom was gone, I had left all my friends behind, and now I was in an environment that was totally foreign. The faces seemed just as strange as they had on that first day of kindergarten—like they weren't real but images haphazardly created without thought of the outcome. In the hallways outside of classes there was laughing and joking and telling of summer conquests, but I was no longer included in such talk. I cowered at being in an environment where I didn't know anyone, or more correctly, where they didn't know me or what I'd been through. I felt out of place and uncomfortable. The situation collected its toll—it took my childhood. I changed from being a fun-loving kid to a sad and introspective teenager; a young guy trying to figure out the *hows* and *whys* of the world. The school itself was much larger than St. Francis and in our freshman class alone there were more students than there had been in all eight grades back in Manistique. The walk to school was about a mile and a quarter and it took around twenty minutes, but the walk there and home became the best part of my day. In fact I believe it was on those walks that I became a writer. It was there that I'd wonder about life and death—my own, my dad's, and everyone's with whom I was close. I thought about the imponderables, such as God having no beginning or how the universe could come to exist without his hand, how photoelectrons could turn light into perceivable vision, how the immune system could work against viruses it had never seen before, or why my right arm swung back and forth perfectly as I walked like that of a soldier but my left arm would veer off to the front. I counted the days till Christmas vacation, and once that passed I counted the days till the end of the school year. There was a time and temperature sign that towered a hundred or so feet in the air, so even though it was blocks away I could see it on my walk, and I began to keep track of the warmest and coldest days of each month. When I saw other kids in front of me I'd either slow down so not to catch up to them or speed up to get around them quickly. The school might have been theirs but the walk was mine. My search for solitude and contemplation continued when I got home. Things with me were no longer this-is-this, but why is this like this. I was aware of the world and its ways more than most kids my age. In those days I also became very aware of my dad's age. He was sixty, and having lost my mother I didn't know what I would do if I were to lose him, too. The fact was that my dad and I were closer than ever.

His cousin had a hunting camp about twenty miles out of town and we would go there often, sometimes alone, sometimes with the owner, Bill LaVallie, and other times with another cousin of his, Clarence. Dad and Bill bought a tractor together and Dad cultivated three old and unused fields that surrounded the camp. In them we planted rye for the deer, and on the perimeter of each field we planted buckwheat for the partridge. Helping them with this kept me occupied in a time where I didn't have any friends. During deer season I'd go into the woods with my 30-30, find a stump to sit on, but mostly I would think. Clarence had breathing problems and couldn't hunt, so he'd keep post by the window and watch the fields while we were out. I was usually the first one back to camp and he seemed to always catch me by abruptly saying, "Oh!" and when I'd ask what he'd say, "I almost saw a deer." My job at camp was to split the wood for the stove; the old kitchen stoves where you'd take a prong and lift the griddle and put the wood in from the top. Most of the wood was elm and it had to be split with a wedge and a sledgehammer. It was hard work but I felt good about having a role. There was no running water at camp. The water came from the pump house and if you held a filled glass up to the sunlight you could see animal hair and an assortment of other interesting things that you really didn't want to drink. Obviously, no plumbing also meant an outhouse, and needless to say it wasn't pleasant to get yourself out of bed and walk fifty yards in the middle of a frigid night. A chilly wind came into the upstairs loft where we slept through the cracks between the logs and I caught some dandy colds from sleeping there; I use the word sleep liberally because between the cold and the fact that everyone snored—Bill was the worst—I never got much. The sheets always seemed a little damp and the blankets smelled of must, but I looked forward to going for weeks ahead of time. In November there were an abundance of flies and when Dad made corn fritters in the morning and you felt a crunch when you chewed you only hoped it was a kernel of corn. Bill and his sons Billy and Terry, along with Dad's cousin Emery from Chicago, were musicians and would have bluegrass sessions in the evenings. Emery was the best musician and played mandolin. They'd play songs like songs like *The Robert E. Lee, Arkansas Traveler, Springtime In The Rockies,* and *The Dark Town Strutter's Ball.* Dad would buy me a bottle of Boonesfarm so I could get a little drunk with the rest of the guys. A smile comes to me whenever I think of those times at camp.

Like the Watergate hearings had occupied my time and thus helped me get over my mother's death, the beginning of the '74 NFL season brought familiarity to the new world in which I lived. I loved football and collected cards and kept stats on all the era's great players. It had also been more than a year since Mom passed away, so things were slowly returning to normal. All the anniversaries had passed: the first Christmas without her, the first time we passed her birthday, and the first anniversary of her death. I would still think of her often, but not as often as before, and although I could still picture her vividly, I was beginning to forget the sound of her voice. But life was continuing and I was beginning to take root in Escanaba. I had slowly acquired a handful of friends, most of whom I made through a mutual interest in football and betting a quarter per game on the weekend schedule. I was getting familiar with the town and was finding my places of solace. Like in Manistique, we were situated one block from Lake Michigan, and between our house and the coal docks was a huge mountain of sand which the kids called horseshoe hill. Named because of its shape, it became a natural backstop. I would stand at the railroad tracks with a baseball and bat and hit toward the hill. It took a good poke to make it over the hill, and if I did it was a home run. If I didn't make it over, the contour of the hill would send the ball rolling right back toward me, regardless if it went left, right, or down the middle. The other kids in the neighborhood weren't really sports fans so I had the hill to myself, and consequently, it replaced The Jungle Tree of Manistique as a place where I could get away from everybody.

The train yards were also behind our house. Trains would come in to switch tracks several times a day, but most notably around ten at night. This was notable because the process shook the house enough to make nearly everything in it rattle. This was hard to get used to at first, but eventually I found it to be relaxing; it was the sound of being home. Again with symmetry, we had train tracks about a block from the house in Manistique, but the trains only came through a couple times a year and never shook our house. I didn't realize it at the time, but these similarities made the transition easier for me: living one block away from the lake, being two blocks away from downtown, having cousins that lived next door, and having train tracks to walk. Familiarity is a friend and it can manifest itself in simple ways. I believe I could have moved to Romania or Algeria and still would've found something to link me to my roots; something to latch onto and bring that feel of being closer to home than I really was.

Also, there was a link between the two towns concerning the big boats of the Great Lakes. This comes to my mind because as I'm writing this today, in fact at this very hour, it's the thirtieth anniversary of the sinking of the Edmund Fitzgerald. I've had a special association with Great Lakes ships throughout the years and the wreck of the Fitzgerald hit me in a way it may not have with others. As I had mentioned, Uncle Pete Berger was the chief shipping clerk at Port Inland near Manistique, where the big ships took limestone south to Inland Steel for the making of iron, as well as to paper mills, power houses, and other ports for aggregate use. Occasionally Uncle Pete would take me on the boats to eat in the galley with the crew. I believe that one of the ships was the Arthur M. Anderson, and if not, I had definitely heard my uncle speak of it many times. It was the boat that trailed the Fitzgerald on the evening that it went down. The two captains kept in radio contact as thirty-foot waves pummeled them, and it was the captain of the Anderson who radioed the Coast Guard when he suspected that the Fitzgerald had been lost. Then, twenty years later when the families visited the site where the Fitzgerald sank and officially designated it as a burial place, they would see the Anderson pass by them upon their return, as if it were an eerie specter forever linked with the fate of their loved ones. When we moved from Manistique to Escanaba I lived two blocks away from the coal docks and perhaps a mile and a half from the ore docks, so I could always see Great Lakes freighters from our backyard. In '75 and '76 when shipping was at its peak it wouldn't be uncommon to see both docks of the ore docks full and ten boats in the bay waiting to load. In the summer we'd sneak onto the coal docks (as they would only have an occasional boat) and dive into the deep water below.

I counted the days till summer vacation as the end to that first school year in Escanaba came into view. I had always loved the summer sabbatical when I was a child, but the year had been hard and for the first time in my young life I needed the time off more than I desired it. I remember taking the usual shortcut through the cemetery one mid-May morning and counting seventeen days till the end of the school year. I think I had the countdown started earlier, but the number seventeen hit me in a way that told me I was getting close. (Since that day I still use seventeen when anticipating a vacation or other noteworthy event.) From the first hour of classes the year had been a chore; I didn't know where anything was and I knew no one. I missed the camaraderie I'd shared with my old friends, and because I was a quiet, lamenting kid who didn't showcase what he had to offer, I had unconsciously impeded kids from befriending me.

With summer in our sights Dad began talking about taking a trip, and he said I could bring my friend from Manistique, Tom Guertin. I was still into statistics and had maintained my dream visiting all the largest cities in the United States and I wanted to go to New Orleans, but Dad wanted to go to Quebec. I petitioned him steadily, and for a while I believe he was considering it, but we ended up going to Quebec. I missed my friends in Manistique and the few new friends I'd made in no way compared to my old ones. After all, we had went through eight years of Catholic school together in small, intimate classes where we got to know each other well. Now Tom and I would be connecting in two weeks, and even if we weren't going to New Orleans, it was going to be a blast. The final days passed, and on Saturday, June 14th, 1975 at 6:10 in the morning, Dad and I began the trip. Tom's mom dropped him off at Jack's Restaurant in Manistique and we had breakfast before taking off. Even though I was fifteen I could still be a handful to my dad at times, but when Tom and I got together we were over the top, and looking back I credit my dad for letting me take a friend. One of the early highlights was going over The International Bridge at Sault Ste. Marie and entering Canada. I have since been over many bridges in my lifetime, including The Golden Gate, but I have to say there was something about The International Bridge that made it as cool as any I've seen. We traveled through Blind River, Sudbury, and North Bay, then settled in for the night in the small town of Mattawa. We found a hotel on a river with the foothills of eastern Ontario behind it. It was a picturesque setting. Tom and I camped in the back of our truck while Dad took a room inside. I had our Kodak Brownie Hawkeye, the kind of camera you held at waist level and looked down through the view window to aim, and Tom and I took snapshots of each other by the river. I recall that as we were doing this a drunken vagrant walked past us and asked if we had any money. When we told him no, he said with a slur, "I thought you were dead anyway." Tom and I laughed about it on and off throughout the night, and that was the sort of stupid stuff that I had missed.

We stopped in Ottawa and Montreal as we made our way to Quebec City. It was cool to hear my dad speaking French with the people we encountered. I had never thought of my dad as an intellectual. In fact, his English had poor structure, and I wouldn't understand until I got older that with French being his first language he went by that syntax. He would say things like, "Toss the horse over the fence some hay," or, "Toss me down the stairs my coat." I couldn't get him to say the TH sound; he would pronounce think "tink" and fourth was "fort." But listening to him speak a foreign language fluently with people whom he didn't know kind of blew my mind.

My disappointment with not seeing New Orleans dissipated as I saw the larger and rather cosmopolitan Canadian cities. Montreal's population was over a million and Ottawa's was around three-hundred thousand. There was life and activity that I'd been deprived of experiencing, growing up in Northern Michigan. The buildings were tall, people were of different races—I even found the air pollution to be notable from a sightseeing perspective, one of those things I'd heard about on the news but had never seen. It was interesting as well to be dealing with the metric system, as it sounded like the United States would be converting to it by 1976. The distances measured in kilometers on highway signs made it seem as if we were farther from home than we actually were, and the same was true for the weather reports with temperatures gauged in Celsius. I still had plenty of catching up to do with Tom, which we did in the smaller towns and on the vast stretches of Canadian highway that separated them. I wanted to know what was happening with all of my friends. I wanted to know if Tom dug the same new music that I did and shared the experiences the culture had prompted over the past nine months. There was a record store in the next town. We stopped in and Tom and I browsed through the top forty section while Dad looked at French albums. Bachman-Turner Overdrive had just come out with a new single, *Hey You.* I dug the song but had only heard it a couple times. I distinctly remember the conversation with Tom as I tried to explain how it went; it could've been something out of Joseph Heller's *Catch-22.*

"Did you hear this new song by B.T.O. yet?"

"No. How's it go?"

"It's like, Hey you, pa pa pa pa pa."

"That's what it says? Hey you, pa pa pa pa pa?"

"No, but it's really cool."

"Sounds cool."

I spotted the 45 and snatched it off the rack to show him. "This is it," I declared.

"Oh yeah, Hey you, pa pa pa pa pa. I love that song."

I rolled my eyes and took the record to the cashier. Tom bought a couple Elton John 45s and Dad bought an album that contained a favorite song of his, *Bon Madeline.*

Tom and I were having a great time and enjoying the trip, but it was something different for my dad. For him, it was a religious pilgrimage and a retracing of steps from a trip he had made more than twenty years earlier. While we were in Montreal we visited St. Joseph's Cathedral, and in Cap-de-la-Madeleine was saw a statue of the Virgin Mary that was said to have opened its eyes. Our ultimate destination was Ste. Anne-de-Beaupré, which was seventeen miles north of Quebec City. There was a magnificent Cathedral there, along with Stations of the Cross that were on a hill across from the church. Tom and I tried to be as reverent as fifteen year-olds could. Yet, there were times when I goofed around, though even as I was doing it part of me wished that I wasn't—that I could be the appreciative son. Although kids don't put a lot of thought into outcomes, somewhere inside I knew that my dad was being more than patient with us and that he deserved a few hours of this trip to be primarily his. Also, I was a Catholic schoolboy and I understood the meaning behind the edifice to my right and the stations we escalated. In the end, however, I couldn't resist trying to make Tom laugh so he would get in trouble. As we began to head home, Tom and I began to get a little bored and perhaps had had enough of each other's company. There was no major blowout or confrontation, but just the annoying pecking that goes back and forth between kids. By the time we dropped him off it was good to be alone again.

When I got back home it became the summer of Elton John, and more specifically, the summer of Captain Fantastic. For as much as I'd like to look back and say I came of age under The Beatles' reign, the truth was that when we were mid-teenagers Elton ruled the charts. From the melodically acoustic intro to the harmonic lamentation in the outro, *Captain Fantastic And The Brown Dirt Cowboy* was unconventional and brilliant. Like *Sgt. Pepper* in The Summer of Love, its sum was greater than the total of its parts. It debuted at number one and left no doubt as to who was the most popular artist of the era. 1975 brought me into my own musically, as well, and *Captain Fantastic* became the *Sgt. Pepper* of our age group. The symmetry continued as it was now my turn to begin growing my hair long. I was beginning to feel more independent, slightly rebellious, not toward my dad but toward other adults who weren't relatives or friends of his, and the doors of possibility seemed to be opening faster than ever before. Despite digging the sound of the late sixties and having an assortment of favorite songs throughout the preceding years, I was at an age where current songs were now meant for me. In direct correlation with the music, adolescence was upon me and so was my desire for girls, but the changes from the previous few years still impeded me. When my mother died I was at an age where it was frowned upon to have girls at the house. In a way her death left me trapped in time, as that was the last edict I had gotten from her. This was all subconscious, of course, and I didn't think about it deeply enough to realize that she would have given me more leeway as I got older, which I now had. If this sounds familiar to you it's a sentiment I laid upon Sara McClair, one of the characters in my first novel, *Hiding From*

Hemingway, but it was something so profound that I found it therapeutic to make such a transference.

If any group came close to The Beatles in the aspect of being a phenomenon it was Kiss. They hit the scene by storm in the mid-seventies and took glitter rock to the edge, with forceful vocals, painted faces, and a hard driving sound. For those of us who were teenagers the names Ace, Gene, Peter, and Paul rolled off our lips as freely as John, Paul, George, and Ringo. I remember buying their first hit single *Rock And Roll All Night* on 45 and that the edge of the vinyl was beveled like that of an album; I had never seen a 45 like that before nor have I since. I liked many of their songs, but I only really dug a couple. Once people got over the novelty of their elaborate attire, platform shoes, and the length of Gene Simmons' tongue, they became just another rock band. Ironically, their biggest hit was *Beth*, a mellow ballad that was the antithesis of what their music was about.

I would love to open the window of my upstairs bedroom and play my records loud enough that the sound would resonate through the neighborhood. In doing so I was making a statement of what I liked, ergo, who I was. On summer Saturday nights I would listen to the sound of stock cars racing at the speedway some two miles away. Even though I was never a fan of auto racing, I found the loud sound somehow to be soothing. In the fall I'd listen to *Radio Mystery Theater* in the evenings after school, or read books like *The Red Badge Of Courage, Love Story,* and *Around The World In Eighty Days.* I also remember watching *The Summer Of '42* that year and drawing the parallels between my life and the boy whose adult self narrated the movie. I also remember assuming that the soldier killed in battle had been killed in Vietnam, a sign of the impact of the times I grew up in. Dad had to remind me that I was watching *The Summer Of '42* and that the soldier had been serving in W.W.II.

That summer Dad and I and Bill LaVallie took a ride to Chicago, and Illinois became the fourth state on my states-visited list. We had made the trip to pick up a wood stove for the hunting camp, but while we were there we went to the observation deck of The Sears Tower, and we visited my brother Tony in Berwyn and my other brother, Joe, who lived in Cicero. Chicago became the largest city I had been in and I found it fascinating to see all the skyscrapers from my vantage point atop the Sears building. I also dug Bill's company and he kept the ride interesting for the six-hundred round-trip miles we traveled.

Tom came over a couple more times for weekends during the summer of '75 and I stayed a couple weekends with him in Manistique, but the distance, the large spans of time in between visits, and the different directions we were heading eroded our friendship rather quickly. I would see him one last time, as we went to a Manistique Emerald basketball game. We sat and talked about what was going on with us—but he was strange to me, like I never had known him. The physical changes of adolescence left him looking different enough that I couldn't picture us ever having hung around. If I had realized it would be our last encounter I would have reminisced more about the past, instead of making small talk about the new album by Kiss and the other matters of current culture we discussed that evening. I would like to have shaken his hand knowing it would be adios, and wished him well with a sincerity that suited the friendship we'd had. But it was simpler than that. I told him goodbye, then walked back to Aunt Irene's to meet my dad, whereupon we drove back to Escanaba. And I believe from that time on I began to think of Escanaba as my home.

An impediment I had in social development was that I still didn't know a lot of my classmates. I had made a few friends that were moderately close to me, but our class had nearly four hundred stu-dents, and hardly any that I had met in my freshman year were in the classes I took as a sophomore. With the death, the move, and the lack of friends, my social confidence was shot. I would occa-sionally catch eyes with one of the girls I thought was cute, and sometimes I would see the look of interest in her eyes, but I couldn't bring myself to do anything about it. So it was with Ann Marie.

She was as pretty and pure as any girl I had ever seen. I first laid eyes on her in my U.S. History class. She walked in and sat to my left. She had fairly long blonde hair with soft curls, a beautiful complexion, and an unpretentious personality that matched everything she appeared to be. I was instantly fascinated with her, but she transferred from the class after only a few weeks. I learned that she was a cheerleader, though, and I went to the football and basketball games to see her as much as I did to see the team. She knew I had a thing for her and I believe she was waiting for me to approach her, if just to get acquainted. But I couldn't. Yet, she'd smile at me as we passed in the hall, and sometimes we'd say hello.

In that fifth-hour U.S. History class of my sophomore year we had a teacher who was easily sidetracked. I liked history, and especially U.S. history at that time, but it was cool to waste an hour of what I considered to be forced attendance. Some days this teacher would get off on tangents on his own, while other days we'd have to work him. On those days he might have been talking about The Battle of Gettysburg and someone would raise their hand and ask something like, "Don't you think Gerald Ford's pardoning of Nixon had a bad smell to it?" The topic we diverted him to didn't have to be interesting to us; it just had to be something we wouldn't get tested on, and once diverted he could be manipulated from subject to subject until the bell rang. We'd manage to pull this off for either the full hour or most of it about two to three days a week. Looking back it wouldn't be hyperbole to say he was a poor teacher and I probably didn't learn anything that I hadn't learned in Catholic school, which happened to be the case with most of my high school curriculum anyway.

In 1976 our country celebrated its bicentennial on the 4th of July. The event was extraordinary, culminating in massive fireworks shows in all the major cities, the likes of which I hadn't seen and would not see again until the arrival of the new millennium. The observance actually began on the arrival of the new year with a series of events and activities leading up to the climactic celebration. I remember one television network running nightly spots called

A Bicentennial Minute, highlighting significant moments in American history. I was writing for the school newspaper and at the end of the school year we published our bicentennial issue. There was an article about Nixon commissioning two committees in 1971 to plan for the commemoration of our 200th birthday, one about The Netherlands presenting us with one million Dutch flowers to be planted in one hundred U.S. cities, an article looking ahead to the next 200 years, and I was assigned to write about The Washington Monument. On the night of July 4th the most spectacular fireworks displays were in Washington D.C. and New York City, but it was a special night throughout the nation and we were all filled with a sense of pride and patriotism. As I watched the bursting bombs that night I silently sensed that I was amidst what would eventually be the most memorable Independence Day of my life.

I had mentioned that Dad and I pretty much had the upstairs of the house to ourselves, which was nice because I still needed a space where it was just him and me. I awoke before him on August 20th, 1976. It was a red-letter day for him, but one for me as well. I went into his room and shook him till he woke, which I now realize isn't how one should be wakened on one's birthday. "Congratulations, Dad!" I said. "You're officially retired!" I thought he'd smile or pat me on the back or something, but instead he told me to let him sleep a while longer. I was disappointed at his lack of enthusiasm, but in retrospect retirement and enthusiasm need not go hand in hand. Yet even though he continued to sleep, the milestone meant something to me. My dad, the millwright, the guy who could fix anything, had retired, and the thought of him being retired made him seem instantly older. After having lost my mom and already worrying about losing him from time to time, it seemed like that fear now had more substantiation. But I looked forward to having him home and being able to go to camp more often. Also I had been concerned about him doing the work he was doing at his age. It was physical and sometimes dangerous and for that I was glad he was retired.

During the presidential election of 1976, there was a sentiment to distance ourselves from the Watergate scandal and move ahead. Gerald Ford was and honorable man and had done a decent job and I remember many of us proudly wearing his WIN (Whip Inflation Now) buttons, but many people remained angry over his pardon granted to Richard Nixon. Jimmy Carter had come out of nowhere and won a close election, largely because of his campaign promise, "Jimmy Carter will never tell a lie."

For me, life was gradually becoming good again. I was slowly getting past the death of my mother and Escanaba had replaced Manistique as the place that felt like home. I was starting to make friends, finding my favorite places and developing a routine. Contact with my Catholic school friends became less frequent, and in fact I had grown into someone they no longer knew. The truth in retrospect is that we could have had like experiences culturally and socially, but we no longer shared them together. So with the decade a little more than half over things were new and exciting, but we were about to enter a period of materialism and cultural nothingness. But sometimes monotony can drive one to seek that which is inspiring, and so it was with me. With the three years that were about to follow being a musical and cultural void, I would begin to seek the present in the past and that process would have a hand in shaping me into who I am now.

CHAPTER FIVE

The world opened itself to me when I got my driver's license, and with its issuance I began to feel less like a boy and more like a young man. It was another step in the march toward independence and with this document I didn't need to rely on my dad as much. If I wanted to go to the mall I could make the run whenever I had the urge, if I wanted to shoot some baskets or play tennis at Royce Park, I didn't have to wait till it was convenient for Dad to take me, and with this new sense of freedom I began to cut loose from my father. I still worried about him if he didn't come home when I expected, and I would still watch TV with him on some evenings, but most of the time I was off doing the things a teenager with a license does. The summer of '77 arrived and the time had come for me to get my own vehicle. Dad and I had been sharing his truck and it behooved both of us for me to have a car of my own. My brother Tony had two that were for sale. One was an big, ugly, blue station wagon, and the other was a 1964 Olds Dynamic 88. I dug the Olds and bought it for one-hundred dollars. It ran good but needed a paint job. Uncle Elmer was a painter and had the equipment in his garage to spray it. I went with a lime green, which wasn't that unusual at the time. Other customizations that had to be made in the spirit of the times were lining the dash with carpeting and putting chrome tape along the side of the vehicle. All I needed to make the transformation complete was an eight-track player, but with the money I had already spent, that would have to wait.

Shortly after getting my car I took a drive to my Uncle Pete's cottage outside of Manistique. It was my first trip of fifty miles or more that I made alone, and when I arrived everyone seemed surprised to witness this step of my coming of age. I could tell they were worried about me being an inexperienced driver and their prime concern wasn't to visit but rather to get me on my way before dark so I'd get home safely. My relatives were beginning to see me less frequently and therefore didn't know my capacities, and looking back I'm sure I would do the same to someone I had known as a child but wasn't around to witness the maturation process. Besides, I had grown awkwardly and gangly, which didn't add credibility to my nearing adulthood. I must have looked like a stretched out version of the little kid they used to know. Uncle Lou was at the cottage, helping Uncle Pete with some siding work. He came down from the scaffold and congratulated me on getting my license, then handed me a twenty-dollar bill. I remember beaming when he gave it to me. Right or wrong, I'd been waiting for that twenty since '68 and I was glad to know that he indeed cared for me as much as he did Suzie. Looking back now, I wish I would have never spent that twenty dollars, but then again, he gave that money away so his teenage nephew could have some fun on him.

During that first year when you have your own car there seems to be an added significance to the song of the summer—the song that may not necessarily be your favorite but seems to be heard every time you turn on the radio. In that summer of '77 I'd cruse the main drag with the radio playing songs like *Sir Duke, Strawberry Letter 23,* and *I Wanna Get Next To You.* The song I recall hearing the most, though, was *Smoke From A Distant Fire.* 1977 was the last year I listened predominantly to AM radio, and perhaps that lent more reverence to the title *Song of the Summer.* The listenership would become more specific and compartmentalized with FM; you listened to a station that played your music. As with so much that seems to be an advancement, a refinement, or an improvement, you eventually look back at what *was* with fondness. There is something in not having everything at your fingertips, but instead having to wait for it that makes it more special, and so it was with waiting to hear your favorite song on a station that played Sinatra, The Letterman, and Henry Mancini along with the music that you called your own.

The first TV mini-series I watched in its entirety was Alex Haley's *Roots*, which traced Haley's genealogy back seven generations to an African named Kunta Kinte. The story began by focusing on Kinte, who was captured and brought to America by slave ship and renamed Toby, then followed his lineage through subsequent generations. The series aired for seven nights in 1977 and captivated Americans from all walks of life. The all-star cast starred LaVar Burton as the young Kunta Kinte and John Amos as the thirty-something version, Ben Vereen as Chicken George, O.J. Simpson as a tribal chief. It also featured James Earl Jones, Leslie Uggams, Ed Asner, Lou Gossett Jr., Lorne Greene, Sandy Duncan, George Hamilton, Lloyd Bridges, Burl Ives, and Maya Angelou. It prompted many African-Americans to seek their lineage, some of whom legally changed their names back to that of their ancestors, a concept I employed with one of my characters in *The Potomac Circle*.

There are certain periods we go through that stain the fabric of our lives, and for me one such era began while I was seventeen. I was at an age where even the most contemporary parents can be a source of shame, and with a father that was forty-five years older than me my dad was less than contemporary. Since he'd retired he was spending a lot of time at home, something I had craved just a few years earlier, but now I wanted time when I could have the house to myself. Aunt Celia was seventy and had begun making trips to her daughter's in Indiana that would last several months, so my dad was my only impediment to having a free run of the place. I'd be alone with my music blasting, and I'd see him pulling up and I'd sigh. Furthermore, he was developing emphysema and with that he'd have long, loud coughs with a deep, productive finish. We had gone to church on Sundays as a family until Mom died, and after that Dad and I would continue to go together, but with his condition I stopped going with him to Sunday mass, never telling him why. Instead I went alone and sat on the other side of the aisle. Three or four times during the service I would hear the distinct sound of his cough, as could everyone else, regardless of where they were seated. I cringed with embarrassment as I waited for the coughing to cease, hoping the distance I had put between him and myself would keep any of the girls I went to school with from finding out he was my dad. Also, with him spending much of the time trying to fill the hours of the day, combined with how he was playing a less important role in the day to day needs of my life, he was becoming softer and more sentimental. I'd been getting work as a laborer, so I decided to put a fifty in the card I got him for his sixty-third birthday. When he opened it and saw the bill he began to cry. I couldn't handle it. He had always been strong and decisive, and not only was I slowly seeing his body deteriorate but now he was crying with a joy that probably relieved a doubt that he was still significant. I hugged him, but made an excuse to get out of the house as quickly as I could. In the fall of that year I began to think about flying to Hawaii after graduation. I couldn't afford it, though, so I asked Dad if he'd loan me the money, to which he said yes and that maybe he'd go, too, but looking forward to being an independence-seeking eighteen year-old I said, "Forget it then, I won't go." As a child my dad had been my hero, the man I waited impatiently for when he drove home from work on Friday evenings. He was the one who could do no wrong. Now, there were times where he was an encumbrance. It would take almost a year to get through this phase—the phase I look back at with self-hatred—and as I look back I'm thankful that he didn't die while I was acting like such an uncaring ass. The following January he would take off for the winter, leaving me with the freedom I wanted, but also providing time for me to reflect upon what he meant to me and experience what life would be like without him around.

By 1977 the music scene was experiencing yet another change. When Elton John announced that he was gay, his reign ended overnight. Songs of his that would normally go toward the top of the charts would now top out at #34 or something of the like. In retrospect, it's funny that many of us didn't realize Elton's tendency—with his frilly clothing and flamboyant sunglasses—but back then I believe that most of us assumed just about everyone was straight. With John dethroned and disco running out of creative fuel, acts like Journey, Fleetwood Mac, Boston, Bob Seger, and The Steve Miller Band, were poised to take prominence, the latter two experiencing comebacks from previous success. *Rumours* and *Night Moves* were two naptime favorites of mine. In the days of LPs you could take the record-support arm of your record player and position it over the record, and if you did this, the album would play through and then the record player would shut off. But you could also leave the arm off to the side, allowing the recording to play over and over again, which was what I'd do with the LPs whenever I napped.

Some of the fads of the mid-seventies were pet rocks, shag carpeting, and mood rings, but without a doubt the one that drew the most attention was streaking. Small towns throughout America experienced sudden surprises during parades, sporting events, campaign speeches, and seemingly any event where the perpetrator could generate shock and disruption. After the fad had established itself as legitimate, Ray Stevens came out with the novelty song *The Streak*, which quickly shot up to #1 on the Billboard charts. Outside of the aforementioned outlandish streaks, there were some, myself included, who had to do it once but in a less conspicuous way. These people streaked through neighborhoods that were not their own and did so by the light of the moon; the thrill coming from the mere chance of being noticed and clothes that were left two blocks away. I did mine with a couple of friends a few years after the craze had been in its heyday, running around the block of an elite neighborhood in Escanaba. We were all apprehensive at first, not that we weren't going to do it, but it took some time to actually proceed. We peeled off everything but our tennis shoes, the trademark attire of streaking, and made a run for it. On my mind most was that we'd get caught by the police, actualizing the old joke about the streaker that got caught by the fuzz. I ran half-heartedly, ready to jet behind a house or shrub if the wrong viewer materialized. Still it was a thrill, just by not knowing who by happenstance could be looking out their window. In the end we made it around the block without experiencing an obvious encounter. Now, if the topic comes up in conversation I can say that I had done it back in the day and not mention the conservatism in our deployment.

In March of '77 I lost my little friend of ten years. Pierre had been with me through all the turmoil of my youth. He was at Aunt Irene's when I was making a transition of being motherless and had been my only buddy in those early days in Escanaba. I believe my dad took the loss as hard as I did, for he'd been in both our lives for ten years. Even Aunt Celia had gotten attached to him. I recall Dad coming home from the vet. I asked him if Pierre was going to be okay, but he just shook his head no. As I sat alone that evening I looked at his empty bed and his half-full food and water dishes. No one had had the heart to do anything with them. Pierre's body had been cremated, but I wanted a memorial. I found a small matting of hair on his bed, put it in a jar, then dug a hole in the back yard with the post-hole digger. I dropped the jar into the ground and covered it with the fresh, damp dirt. I wished I would've pet my dog for the longest time before Dad took him to the animal clinic. Yet, I know animals have feelings and I know they sense things, and I'm sure he sensed his fate and appreciated the time I had spent with him in his final days.

I began my senior year in the fall of '77. I had already decided that I would attend Bay College in Escanaba after I graduated, not for any particular curriculum but simply because it would be the next step. When I began my last year in high school I had nothing in mind but making the most of it. Being a senior I got to attend first through fifth hours, not fifth through ninth as I had as a freshman, and it was cool to get out of school at a decent time and have the rest of the afternoon to myself. As I went from class to class that first day I found familiar faces, the result of being a fourth-year student, and one of the faces I recognized belonged to Ann Marie. She looked as angelic and innocent as she did as a sophomore.

Another advantage of having my own wheels was that I could get a steady job. I had done some work for a cousin of Dad's, helping put a couple of roofs on some waterfront cottages that she owned, and some other odd jobs as well, but I wanted steady employment. One of Dad's friends, Jim Bushey, was a patron of a bar that he frequented. He worked for Red Owl Foods, a union grocery store that was notoriously hard to get into. Jim got me an interview and I was hired. So on October 21, 1977, I officially began my working career. I showed up for my first shift wearing a white shirt and tie, bellbottom jeans and platform shoes, the latter two representing the popular style of the time. One of the cashiers had a motherly way about her and was quite helpful at getting me to feel at ease. She had a son, Dan, who would stop in to see her from time to time. I had recognized him as someone I saw in high school and I began to talk with him whenever he'd stop by. Dan LaFave and I became best friends. He lived about five miles out of town, and it seemed that I was always over there or he was at my place. I preferred the former, as he had a good looking sister. To his credit or stupidity we would sometimes hang out at his place on Friday or Saturday nights so I could be around Cathy. She was three years younger than me, so she hadn't reached the age of mobility that we had. I would schmooze with her and try to talk her into kissing me, while Dan would roll his eyes and try to coax me into hitting the town. I continued to talk Dan into staying home on either a Friday or Saturday night until his sense of humor did me in one evening. Dan, Cathy and I were sitting at the kitchen bar, chatting about whatever topic came up. I sensed I was close to getting Cathy to kiss me, and in fact felt that it might happen that night. Dorothy, their mom, brought a plate full of homemade cookies and a glass of milk for each of us. I was washing down a mouthful of chocolate chips when it happened, right then and there, Dan had to say the most outrageously hilarious line of the night, and as I tried to keep from spitting out my milk, out it came from my nose. The first thing I did was check to see if Cathy had seen me; a question answered by the look of disgust on her face. I knew any chance I had with her was over, done in by the strange combination of humor and dairy. We would eventually go to a Styx concert in Marquette with Dan and his girlfriend. We had a good time on the way up and the concert was cool. Dan had driven and Cathy and I were in the back, and when I made a move it was obvious that she had only accompanied me as a friend. I sulked for the rest of the ride and listened to the sickeningly sappy Lionel Richie tape Dan was playing. About five years later I ran into her and we went to a movie and then out for a few drinks. We saw *Pale Rider* at the Delft Theater then went to Don's Bar, but the time had passed—for both of us. We talked for an hour or more after the film, then I took her home and would never see her again.

There were four of us who hung around together: Jerry, Terry, Dan, and myself. Of the group, Jerry was the dork and we were always pulling pranks on him, if he wasn't pulling them on himself, like the time we were already getting served and on our third drink when the bartender asked him, "Did I check your ID yet?" to which he replied, "No." So he dug his license out and the barkeep said, "You're not eighteen yet," to which he replied, "I'm not? So when *do* I turn eighteen?" Needless to say we were all kicked out. Jerry never seemed to catch on to what we were doing, no matter how many times the gags were perpetrated. The big thing back then was to drive up and down Ludington Street, the main thoroughfare in town. It ran from the highway through the business district and to Lake Michigan, which was a little over a mile. Then we'd loop through Ludington Park and back down Ludington Street to the highway. Most cars didn't have bucket seats back then, but the sofa seats where three people could ride in the front. So with this type of seating, it was common for young lovers to sit next to each other. Dan and I would set it up where he'd sit in back alone, Terry would drive and I'd force Jerry to sit in the middle of the front seat while I sat to his right. When we approach a red light I'd bend down and pretend to be tying my shoe, crouching low as I did so I'd be out of sight to anyone in the car next to us, and at the same time Dan would lay down on the back seat, leaving Jerry and Terry looking like a couple of love-struck homos. The other two never caught on to what we were doing; Terry would just complain about me having to tie my shoe all the time.

I was the tough guy of our bunch, even though I wasn't that big. In eighth grade I was the smallest boy in the class, and at five-foot two I had begun to get picked on. By my junior year in high school, however, most kids didn't want to fight me, not so much because I was that tough, but because I was gritty and nobody wanted to chance losing to someone who only weighed one-hundred forty pounds. To make it even more humbling for anyone who would lose to me, I looked young for my age; a clean-faced kid who couldn't grow a facial hair if he tried. So on another occasion while driving down the strip, this time with me at the wheel, a car cut me off and I hunted him down. As he pulled over I got out of my car, slammed the door and marched up to him, only to see Jim Burbe, the wrestler who had made All-American. I didn't know him well enough to make small talk and the slamming of my door had already made my intent clear anyway, so I did the only thing I could—I apologized. I remember the shame I felt as I walked back to my clan. I had stormed out as Mr. Tough Guy and retreated back to my boys thoroughly humiliated. Escanaba was a tough town, at least back then, and there were fights almost every weekend, and Dan had once said that he liked hanging with me because he felt safe and I had taken pride in that. Now I'd been humbled and compromised, and from then on I was never looked at in the same light by those three friends. Perhaps, in terms of personal growth, it was for the best.

Dan's older brother was in the army and he had a fiancée back home who was our age. She'd spend time at the LaFave's and would occasionally do a thing or two with Dan and me. The first time she did she asked for a ride as I was about to pull out of the mall. I opened the door of my Skylark, leaned forward and pulled the seat back, forgetting about the banana split I'd just bought and set on the back seat. She sat on it. I apologized and helped her clean it off with an old sweatshirt I had in the car, but somewhere in that episode she developed a crush on me. A week or so later she asked for a ride home, which was about seven miles out of town. I had no sooner gotten the car in park when she lunged at me, pressing her mouth all over mine. I knew she was going with a friend's brother, but she had caught me unprepared and I didn't want to be perceived as a bad kisser, so I said, "Let's try this again," and pulled her into me. We made out for several minutes before a porch light came on and we said goodnight. By the next morning I wasn't feeling good about what had happened and began to avoid her. One early evening about a week later, just as I was about to head out to do something, I saw her car pull up to my house. Aunt Celia was in the living room and I rushed down to tell her to tell the girl that I wasn't home and that I'd wait in the basement until she left. Aunt Celia hated lying, but to my surprise and relief she agreed. (Looking back she probably agreed to keep me from having sex.) I went downstairs. I could hear the conversation clearly from down there, and when my aunt relayed my message the unexpected happened. She said that she'd wait for me. I stayed in the basement while she watched TV with my aunt and it was an hour and forty-five minutes until she left. My aunt razzed me when I came back up, something else she didn't normally do. For as religious as she was I think she got a kick out of the situation.

In the meantime my eye was still on Ann Marie. At school I would look for her in the halls. In the evening I looked for her car in the procession of high school kids cruising Main and take a close look at the cars parked near the tennis courts at Ludington Park. On Sundays I would sit several rows behind her at St. Joe's Church. Even though she was as humble as anyone I'd ever encountered, I still felt like an unknown commodity in Escanaba, so through the logic of a teenager I felt inferior to her, even though I knew she had passed up the accolades of social hierarchy. I knew myself well enough to take it slow; a few common greetings and clichés until I built up enough confidence to really talk to her. I felt envious of those who had gone to school with her since kindergarten, for if I had known her I wouldn't have felt intimidated. But thoughts like that were neither here nor there and with all the wishful thinking aside I still trembled whenever I contemplated making a significant move. After three years I still felt like the new kid in town where she was concerned. Also, without having my mom around and my dad being forty-five years older than me I didn't feel I could talk about things such as love or feelings of inferiority. Furthermore, there are insights and advantages that contemporary parents bestow upon their children that my dad couldn't provide me, such as giving you style tips, or knowing other kid's parents and thus giving you inroads to friendships with other classmates. In saying this, though, I have to say that of course I wouldn't want to have had anyone else for a dad.

I remember one basketball game in particular. It was our senior year and we were playing a road game in Marquette. I was sitting in about the tenth row and directly in front of the Escanaba cheerleaders, and as the hometown Redmen were getting the best of us I caught eyes with Ann Marie. For the longest time neither of us looked away. Finally she smiled and went back to her cheering. I had often pondered why I had never become popular in Esky, like I had been in Manistique. Granted my dad's occupation before he'd retired had put us in upper middle class, but since he'd retired our budget was considerably less. I felt self conscious about the clothes I wore as they were of department store quality and not as stylish as those worn by kids with well-to-do parents. But my hair was mid-length, keeping with the tone of the seventies, I had a car, and I was entertaining to people that I was brave enough to talk to. Unfortunately, Ann Marie wasn't one of those people in that latter category. The attitude I had kept me from entering many doors that should've been open to me, like playing on the basketball team or going to the prom. As for basketball, I knew I was better than three or four of the twelve kids on the team, but I was still haunted by the effects that had caused me to avoid the limelight in any way. To be quite truthful, if I had been on the court in front of a crowd, or been at a dance with a girl who I didn't know well, I would not have done well. My body would've been trembling on the court and I would've been at a loss for words with the girl on the dance floor. This was a one-eighty from what I used to be. When I was in Catholic school I'd volunteer for lead roles in school plays and the church readings for the daily masses we'd attend. This fear of the spotlight made me think to my upcoming graduation where I'd have to go up on stage in front of a couple thousand people, and for a while I actually contemplated trying to catch pneumonia so I'd be excused from the ceremony.

After that basketball game in Marquette, my friends and I went for a bite before heading back to Esky. Now there were two things that happened in my life that made me a less aggressive person. The first happened in or around 1976 as my dad and I were at camp. We were taking a walk through the woods looking for birds when we came upon a raccoon. I asked Dad what I should do, and with him being an old French-Canadian of farmer and trapper descent, he told me they were good eating. I was carrying a 4-10, not a powerful gun, and I aimed and shot. The raccoon dropped out of the tree and onto the forest floor below. It was the series of events that followed that would take away my desire to ever hunt again. From out of the woods came another raccoon. He scurried up to his dying mate, frantically nudging her and making crying sounds. I'm still not sure why I did what I did next, but I pointed my barrel at the second raccoon and shot. It dropped, and in pain began rubbing his mask with his little paws. It killed me to watch this. I would never shoot another living thing again. The second experience that made me less aggressive happened after the Escanaba -vs-Marquette basketball game. There was a natural rivalry as we were the only class A schools in the Upper Peninsula and there would usually be fights between student fans after the game. Outside of McDonald's our entourage got into it and we each found a foe. I clasped onto the down-filled coat of my opponent and threw him to the ground, tearing his coat as I did. The image burned into my brain as I looked at my adversary on the ground with feathers floating around him. He didn't come back at me; he rolled over, pushed himself up and called me something derogatory as he walked away. I had my victory but I didn't feel good about it. I sensed he was a good kid, but moreover, there was something about the ripped coat that got to me. My dad had bought me a similar coat for my birthday. By the end of 1977 when this had happened Dad's health was declining further, and I thought about the effort he had made to go out and get me a winter coat that I would like. So thinking in a linear manner, I wondered how that kid had come to get his coat. Was it a gift from someone who cared about him? Had he saved his own earnings to purchase it? The more time passed the worse I felt. I wished I could've found the kid and apologized to him. I wouldn't be my last fight, but any subsequent ones would be entered into with a combination of need and discretion. As I pondered the consequences of my actions I found the complexities of the maturation process. I now had to consider things from the standpoint of conscience and decency. As a youth you have someone else monitoring your actions, letting you know when you were right or wrong and leaving you free to act without as much thought. Now that was no longer a fallback. I was about to have adulthood throw at me with the expectation of understanding and compliance.

I came of legal drinking age in January of '78, and shortly after my birthday my dad took the aforementioned trip, going to Colorado with some friends to spend the rest of the winter. I enjoyed this sudden freedom and the right to make my own decisions. On occasion some of us would go to the bar on our school lunch hour and have a few beers—just because we could. One time I decided that I was having too good a time to go back to school and skipped the rest of my classes. The next day I was called into the attendance office and was asked what had happened, whereupon I told the woman that I was sick. She told me that I needed a written excuse, so I asked her for a pen and paper and proceeded to write one on the spot. She said, "You can't do that! It has to be from a parent or legal guardian." Now there are some moments in life that you just wait for and then enjoy the hell out of them once they arrive, and so it was when I told her, "Actually ma'am, I'm of legal age and I live alone." The look of indignation she wore was enough to make up for all past transgressions and suppressions brought upon me by supervisors from any school I had ever attended.

For as much as I liked the freedom I had, it was good to see my dad when he returned from Colorado. I had missed him and felt bad about the way I had slighted him the previous year. Even more, I realized his age and his health and made it a point to spent more time at home with him. We'd watch sitcoms or sit at the kitchen table and play cards, or we'd play the game where you fold a piece of paper into a triangle and flick it with your finger trying to get it to dangle over the edge of the table without falling off. If it fell it was a change of possession, but if you got it to hang over it was six points. Then your opponent would put his index fingers together and point his thumbs upward to form a goal post and you'd hold the top of the triangle with one finger and "kick" it with the other for an extra point. To my surprise Dad seemed to like that game. I was normally a competitive person, but I silently rooted for him to score. Before long, though, I was back to spending most of my time with my friends. Although I worried about my dad, I hadn't thought of him worrying about me until I got myself into a thicket one spring night in 1978. It had been a glorious day, reaching the mid-sixties by the afternoon. I was going out to a friend's hunting camp with Terry, and on the way in I got my car stuck in a mud hole created by all the water from the melted snow. We tried pushing the car out, but as we realized we were up to our knees in mud we knew we didn't have a prayer. It was a moonless night—so dark that the only way I knew I was on the half-mile dirt road that led to the cabin was by the different sound my footsteps made when hitting grass as opposed to gravel; so dark that at one point I had gotten within three feet of a deer before it bolted off and nearly stopped my heart in the process, as I was also aware that it was bear country. We got to the camp and no one was there. That left us five miles away from the nearest house, which was a drag because it had gotten cold enough to make my muddy pant legs freeze. By the time we got to a phone it was after four in the morning. My dad drove out and picked us up. I expected him to be upset, and he was, but he seemed more relieved than anything. As we rode back into town I imagined myself waiting for him and not hearing anything until four hours after he was expected to be home, and I realized how torturous it had to have been for him.

I graduated from high school in May of 1978. During the ceremony I found out something about myself regarding my fear of the stage. Even though I had to go up in front of that two-thousand plus crowd, I didn't have any fear. What I learned was that my stage fright wasn't as bad when I was in a situation where I didn't have a choice. During the school year I was terrified when I attended a class where I might have to read aloud because I was dealing with an if or a mere possibility, but when something absolutely had to be done, I could come through. The same would happen some years later with my fear of flying. I was a wreck until the jet took off, but once the wheels left the ground I knew I no longer had a choice and I was fine.

I was eighteen when I first realized that I remembered more of the sixties songs than most people my age. I had gone to a smelt fry at the home of one of Dan LaFave's friends. Don Gray, the host, and most of the people at the party were in the range of being seven to ten years older than we were and the music for the party was that of the late sixties and early seventies. I was singing along with all the tunes, as we were all drunk and singing out loud, when someone asked, "Hey, how does this kid know all of these?" referring to me. When everyone concurred that it was at least noteworthy that I knew the lyrics, I realized for the first time that most of the people my age didn't. I should mention, too, that this happened in the days before oldies radio and for the most part the songs being played hadn't been heard since a few years after they had charted.

I can't recall the call letters, but the first FM station I listened to regularly was FUN-104 out of Escanaba. The transition from traditional FM to contemporary late-seventies was awkward, as taped DJs announced rock bands with proper voices, saying, "That was Ted Nugent with Cat Scratch Fever," as smoothly as they would have said, "And that was Vivaldi with the first movement of his trumpet concerto in C." To be quite blunt, the DJs' voices weren't hip and they didn't match the music they played. Furthermore, everything was taped. There were no call-in requests, no dedications, no birthday wishes, and there was no spontaneity. Yet, its destiny to be the future carrier for popular music was undeniable; it just needed time to grow and develop.

Disco was still the sound of the night scene and there was one discotheque in Escanaba, The Station Bar, which was located across the street from the police station. We would go there on Friday nights to dance and hit on the girls, listening to the music of KC & The Sunshine Band, Donna Summer, and The Bee Gees. Ironically, the Disco culture's biggest moment came right as it was about to meet its demise, with the release of *Saturday Night Fever* starring John Travolta. Songs from the movie flooded the top of the charts and dominated airtime on FM stations. But bumper stickers proclaiming "DISCO SUCKS" were beginning to be seen, disco records were burned in center field at a White Sox game, and the sentiment was growing that the music was a joke. By 1979 Disco had come to the end of its reign; doomed by the repetitiveness of its sound and creativity quelled by perpetuated emulation. Just as quickly as it had come onto the scene, it was over. Looking back now through the filter that only time can provide I can say there were some good songs that came out of the era, such as the inaugural Disco song, *T.S.O.P.* by M.F.S.B., or *Love's Theme* by Love Unlimited Orchestra. The era was in the books as a part of musical and cultural history. We had lived the scene that has come to be mocked by *Saturday Night Live* and Hollywood, with us in our bellbottom pants, silk shirts, and platform shoes, surrounded by those swirling dots of light and propelled by an unchanging cymbal-driven beat.

This decade of transition was about through. We saw the war in Vietnam come to an end and with it an end to the disconnect between young and old. Of course there will always be generation gaps, but perhaps none as profound as the one between children of the sixties and their parents. Music had evolved as well, or devolved, depending on your taste. In ten years it had shifted in three directions: from the light sounds that took us out of the sixties, to disco, and to the sound that was formed to be the antithesis of disco and which would evolve into heavy metal. I felt ripped off in growing up when I did, as far as music and the part of our culture that was influenced by it was concerned. The sixties had been so vibrant and tumultuous and in my mind it would have been the perfect time to be a teenager. Yet, the seventies had taken me from a boy to a young man. They had brought me extreme sorry, saw me slowly work through it, then molded me into the embryonic version of the adult I now am. The decade showed me a variety of paths that would lead into the eighties—different paths with different outcomes. It had centered those of my generation who were a few years older than me and saw them make the transition from rebellious youths to adults with respectable jobs, mortgages, and children. The world was changing rapidly. Innovation was occurring at an unprecedented rate and life was moving at a pace unfathomable to previous generations. There was talk that before long most people would have computers in their homes, you would have phones that you could carry around with you, and cars would be able to pass other cars simply by hovering over them. I was skeptical—it seemed all so futuristic—but I couldn't wait to see for myself.

CHAPTER SIX

As a young adult I entered decade number three. I had survived those dangerous years of recklessness; that is learning to drive, being a novice at drinking legally, answering dares, feeling invincible, and all the other foolishness that comes with being a teenager. Now I was beginning to think like an adult and was ready for all that would come with that designation. The last eighteen months had been stagnant and I was ready for something to happen. I had been working midnights for the past half year and it was isolating me from social interaction. Music had become boring and predictable, a result of the intertwining of the arts and culture, so the world around me seemed rather dull. People my age were either into the head-banging sound, which I found to be inartistic, or they could be generally classified as Parrot Heads. There's a fairly reliable pattern where one can make a contrast between Parrot Heads and those of us who began finding our present in the past, i.e. sixties relics like myself. They like Buffett while we preferred Dylan; they went to The Caribbean and tanned on sunny beaches while we traveled Europe by rail. They are simple comparisons: cocaine or marijuana, polyester or cotton, synthetic or earthy, tanned or natural. Now I have no problem with Buffett and I do enjoy some of his songs on occasion, but his music doesn't personify who I am and I usually don't relate as closely to those who admire him as I do to the members of the hippie generation who grew parallel with myself, that is, keeping a reverence for what inspired them, yet still becoming a contributor to the advancement of society.

1980 brought a movement to revitalize music and take it toward the direction of its roots. New wave rock was touted to be the rave and punk bands like The Clash and The Sex Pistols (with the notorious Johnny Rotten and Sid Vicious) led the charge. I didn't see much that was *new wave* about it, but it provided definition to popular music after a rather vague period that began at the end of disco. The sound was filled with energy and the vocals sounded quite British. It featured songs with basic chord progressions without drawn out guitar solos. But just as this was being heralded as the sound of the next generation, another new sound was on the horizon. It involved speaking lyrics in a rhythmic or syncopated style and was being called rap. However, the only successful group to be heralded as an up-and-coming rap band was Blondie, whom, with the exception of their song *Atomic*, were without a doubt more new wave than rap. The musical forecasters had described what this music would evolve into after its incubation period, and it didn't sound like anything I would care much to hear. In fact, it seemed to have the same repetitiveness that had limited the listeners' tolerance with disco. Rap seemed to be a flash in the pan in 1980, and it wouldn't really be heard again until the middle of the decade. In the meantime new wave didn't seem to be catching on either, at least not as a movement. Some of the bands were successful but new wave didn't promulgate into a full fledge invasion as had been promised. As for myself I can't say I disliked the sound, but it still wasn't anything that I could latch onto and call my own.

So 1980 found me stranded on an island without music, and that's when the sounds of my youth made their revival. At first it was the pop stuff, the catchy tunes that had survived the filtration of bad music that only time can provide. It was the music of the early Beatles, Herman's Hermits, Pet Clark, and The Rolling Stones. But even though songs from that first wave brought back memories and were generally a lot of fun, by their very nature I tired of them quickly. I needed music that was rhythmic, yet meaningful and inspiring, and when I found it, it was like all the passion and intensity of the late sixties exploding, and in the process infiltrating me with all the color and freedom and excitement of that movement, and once again, everything was new. I began buying everything I could get my hands on from that genre: Jefferson Airplane, The Beatles later albums, Jimi Hendrix, Crosby Stills and Nash, The Moody Blues, The Doors, Country Joe and the Fish; obviously I could go on and on. I looked at the styles in the photographs, styles that had been dubbed as antiquated by my peers, and cloaked in those styles I saw the coolest and most interesting people. I saw people with a reason. I saw individualism and nonconformity and folks who believed that real life wasn't found in one's hometown but on the road. Ten to fifteen years after the fact, I found the music that matched who I always had been and would further shape who I would become. So the past became the present and the zeitgeist of the sixties filled my world.

My favorite song became *Dear Prudence* by The Beatles. As a boy growing up in Manistique, AM radio stations didn't play album cuts and the only songs I heard were ones that were released on 45. Consequently, I didn't get to hear *Dear Prudence* until my revival. When I shifted my focus from reacquiring 45's to buying albums, it was in the unreleased cuts of those albums that I found the gold mine of sound I had sought, and with it I experienced the freshness of newness. Right around that time we had a new employee join us on our night crew. His name was Doug. He was a cool individual; he had long hair and played in a band, taught part-time at our local community college, and for our small Northern Michigan community I found him to be diverse, as he had married a girl of Chinese decent while attending the University of Hawaii. He was nine years older than me and had experienced the era that provoked this renaissance while in his late teens. Furthermore, while I had other friends and acquaintances his age, Doug had been more culturally aware during that period and had been a true hippie. Consequently, he became something of a guru—pointing me in the direction of the sound that was still underground to me. He told me stories of the sixties that further prodded my intrigue and brought me albums to listen to, some of them quite obscure, like *The West*

Coast Pop Art Experimental Band. My first wave of album buying helped refine second-round purchases. I didn't really care for Moby Grape, for example, but I loved the sound Jefferson Airplane created in *Surrealistic Pillow*. I remember how the groove within me flowed when *After Bathing at Baxter's* arrived from special order. I ordered *Crown of Creation* the next day.

I asked another older friend which song most exemplified the sixties to him, and after a brief period of consideration he said *Incense And Peppermints* from The Strawberry Alarm Clock. I told him I liked his choice, then said that mine was *Light My Fire* by The Doors, partly because I remember the live bands playing it often during the Friday night concerts that resonated from the upstairs window of the downtown dance hall and into our backyard. Of course we began to discuss each other's picks, and in the course of that conversation I pinpointed 1967 as the year that the sixties came to represent the sixties in the way that I most often refer to them, and I believe that it's fairly common now that when people talk about the sixties as an ideal, they're referring to the period from '67 through '69. By the time 1967 came around I had become aware that more was going on with music than just the song. With the unique instrumentation and all the color, I'd made a differentiation between the psychedelic sound and other music. Now, for as much as my renaissance was fed by the direction music took with the release of *Sgt. Pepper*, I do regret that it ended the garage band sound. Whereas *Pepper* and the psychedelia that followed was deep, esoteric, and introspective, garage songs like *Gloria, Dirty Water, I See The Light,* and *Pushin' Too Hard* were upbeat, raw and catchy, with baselines that had survived the fifties. They had a place in my revival as well and I wish the movement would've had more time to add to its collection for the sake of posterity. However, like always, the music had followed the culture which in turn had followed the times, and the mood of the nation had become more serious with each year that passed.

Despite all that I was rediscovering, everything still revolved around The Beatles, as they had been placed upon a pedestal by myself and by history. Two things that made them a phenomenon were their artistic foresight and the diversification of their music. They evolved not with the times, but unlike anything we as a generation had seen, the times evolved with them. Culture followed their length of hair, the clothes they wore, and in some ways their philosophy. Other bands copied their sound and tried to keep pace with them but they were always one step ahead. They had gone from fun loving songs like *She Loves You* and *Please, Please Me* to psychedelic masterpieces such as *Tomorrow Never Knows* and *Within You Without You*, back to *Yesterday* and *Here, There, And Everywhere*, all the way to *Helter Skelter* and *Revolution #9*, to ballads like *Rocky Raccoon,* and *The Continuing Story Of Bungalow Bill.* The music was creative and the lyrics flowed from introspective to invigorating, such as in the song *It's All Too Much*, with love shining all around the girl with the long blonde hair and eyes of blue. The Beatles had survived all the pitfalls: complacency others had fallen into, Paul getting busted in Japan for marijuana, John Lennon stating that the group was more popular than Jesus Christ, and competition from other groups. Since this is a book about culture more than anything else, I have to say that The Beatles were the most profound and lasting element of the culture in which I was raised.

In the summer of 1980 I took the first vacation without my dad. In the late seventies I had gone to Detroit with Dan LaFave for baseball and football games, but this time I was heading all the way to Florida. I had become friends with Dan's brother Dave as well. He was recovering from injuries sustained in a car accident and had time on his hands and he decided to come with me. I was driving a 1972 Buick Skylark at the time. It was a good car, but my dad didn't want me to take it. He had found a deal on an old Mercury so he had a spare car, and he let me take his truck, which was good because we could camp in the back and save on hotel costs. The list of states visited had been holding at four, and I was not only about to add seven, but four that were quite different from the Midwestern state in which I lived. I went to pick up Dave at his house. Cathy came out to see us off and right before we pulled away she said the words that would leave a cloud hanging over not only my vacation but my life for the year that would follow; a cloud that would turn black in the weeks that would follow. "Did you hear Ann Marie was hit by a car?" I froze. "She's in a coma and they don't think she'll make it."

I had to try to keep it on the back burner; there were two of us taking this trip and I felt a responsibility not to ruin it for Dave. Besides, there wasn't anything I could do to change the situation and it had been over two years since I'd seen Ann Marie on a regular basis. I managed not to think about it until nightfall. We stopped for the evening as we entered Kentucky and stayed at a KOA campground. It was July and there were many campers. Some were playing Frisbee; others were lounging by their fires. I went for a walk while Dave began to arrange our camper. It was my first time alone since hearing the news and it felt right that I was in such a peaceful setting. I walked to the top of a ridge that overlooked a quiet interstate that ran some one-hundred feet below. As I was looking out over the vast woods across the highway, John Lennon's *Imagine* came into my head. It would become one of three songs I would forever associate with Ann Marie, and in that introspective moment I felt that I was with her spiritually. I spent as much time as I could up there—until I reminded myself again that Dave was on a vacation, too, and I found the wherewithal to keep my grief to a minimum and hope for the best.

I began enjoying the trip. We took a leisurely pace the next day; toured some caves and visited the birthplace of Abe Lincoln. The mountains were beautiful and by the time we got to Tennessee I was getting a feel for the South. It had been in the low seventies when we left Escanaba, but already we were adding fifteen degrees to that. I was doing most of the driving, and upon entering Georgia the naive twenty year-old succumbed to the tales of Georgian sheriffs pulling over cars with northern plates for the most insignificant of reasons. I drove fifty-five until we got to Florida. And then there we were. I had never been so far from home and I liked it. As we stopped at the welcome center and got our free orange juice—compliments of the Florida Orange Growers' Association—I gazed at all the palm trees and realized how much more of the world was still out there waiting. That night was sticky-hot and it was hard to sleep in the back of the truck. At one point I got out to use Nature's facilities and found myself staring down an alligator, which was returning my stare from some fifteen feet away. After I made a safe return to the truck, I again felt inspired to be in a place so different. At the conclusion of the next day we saw a roadside pull-off on a channel in Fort Lauderdale where some ten others were setting their stakes for the night. Now that the activities of the day were complete, Ann Marie was on my mind again and I wanted to be alone. I popped in a tape of *The White Album*, cued it up to *Dear Prudence* and settled atop my sleeping bag. The next morning we both got out to stretch our legs a little, but I hadn't slept well and went to crash for a while longer. Dave had a regimen of exercises that were part of his rehab, so he got back in, too, and began doing push-ups until I reached over and punched him. "What the hell'd you do that for?" he asked, to which I replied, "Moron! Two guy crawl into the back of a truck and then the thing starts bouncing up and down?" He laughed and then I started to laugh, too. It felt good to laugh, and like the rest of the vacation, good times were entwined with my gloom. It was unbeknownst to me while we were staying in Dayton on the last night of our trip that Ann Marie had succumbed to her injuries. Cathy greeted us as I pulled in to drop off Dave. She smiled and welcomed me back, then told me the news.

Ann Marie's death would have a profound impact on me. Even though we never did have that conversation I had once hoped for, I loved her. Yet, because we had never gone out and few people knew how I felt, I didn't feel it was proper to show my sorrow in public. There was now a void in my life. I went into a depression. I felt the desperation from realizing that I couldn't change what had happened, and because I further understood the fragility of life I realized my own mortality more than ever. A feeling returned that I hadn't experienced since my mother had died. It was the realization of never—ever—seeing someone's soft smile or warm gaze. I vowed to take on some of Ann Marie's role in life and make the world better in her stead, and I believe that to this day I have never been a better person than I was during the year that followed her death. At her funeral I sat toward the back and watched as classmates who had known her longer and better laughed and joked before the service started, while I fought to keep from crying like a child. I visualized our last encounter; a wedding reception. She was sitting across the table from me. It was smoky in the hall, and through the haze we caught eyes. We stared at each other for the longest time, not saying a word, just smiling and gazing until one of her friends came and ended the moment. Had I known that night that I would never see her again I would have told her how I felt. I would have poured out everything and not felt ashamed, for there was no one who could measure up to her.

After all the formalities were over and time began to pass I developed a routine to kill the hours of the day. I was working part-time nights and had way too much time to think. In fact, I couldn't stand to think anymore and my depression took me to sleeping fifteen to seventeen hours a day. I felt bad for my dad. He was concerned about me; he'd ask if something was wrong and if he could get me anything, but outside of that he didn't know what to do. I tried talking to him once but he didn't understand the depth of what I was going through, and as I sensed his lack of grasp I said no more. I realized that I needed to show him that I was okay, though, so I began watching M*A*S*H reruns with him every weekday evening. (During that time Aunt Celia's health was beginning to fail and she was taking longer stays with her daughter in Indiana.) In watching television with Dad I began to get those glimpses of normalcy I'd experienced after my mother's death. As like before, they came intermittently at first but slowly became more frequent. However, I wasn't pulled out of my melancholy state until Ann Marie's sister Michele came to work at the store and provided the transition I needed to put the past behind me and

104

resume living life.

In December of 1980 I was watching Monday Night Football when Howard Cosell interrupted the chatter between Frank Gifford and Dandy Don to announce that John Lennon had been shot and was in very serious condition. Weirdly, the former Beatle had been friends with Cosell; I remember him being interviewed from the press booth during a previous Monday night game. Shortly after, Lennon succumbed to his wounds. Don McLean had sung about the day the music died, referring to the deaths of Richie Valens, Buddy Holly, and the Big Bopper in a plane crash back in 1957, but the embodiment of the death of music had never been closer to me. I watched all the newscasts the next day and had never seen so much of a thirty minute broadcast devoted to the lead story. The ABC broadcast took the final five minutes of their program to catch everyone up on the rest of the day's news. The voice that sticks in my mind, though, is from WLS radio in Chicago when the newswoman profoundly stated, "And John Lennon becomes the first Beatle to die." It was the arrival of an inevitable; the specifics of which previously unknown but wordlessly anticipated. It was so untimely for Lennon to die just as he was returning to music after a lengthy hiatus. The release of the *Double Fantasy* album brought an excitement that the former Beatle was back on the scene. The cuts played on the radio were catchy and new and I looked forward to what would follow. But it was not to be. Lennon's death put an end to the unending speculation of a Beatles reunion as well. I waited for the other members of the group to comment on the loss of John. I wanted to see how it affected them because to me they would always be inseparable, regardless of where life's paths had taken them as individuals. There were mixed reports about Paul's reaction. One reporter said that he was visibly shaken while another said that there was a touch of sarcasm in his comments. The rift between the two primary songwriters that led to the breakup of the band had bothered me and I hoped that the reports of Paul not giving John his respectful due were erroneous. Fourteen years later I would see Paul opening his concert at the Pontiac Silverdome with a tribute to John.

Similarly, I was watching TV in my living room when the broadcast was interrupted by a special bulletin reporting that President Reagan had been shot. We didn't know the severity of his wounds at first and my initial reaction was that we were about to experience another Kennedy type situation. But soon reports began coming in of him cracking jokes before heading into surgery. He would come out of the assassination attempt as strong as he'd been before getting shot, but even stronger politically. Unfortunately, his press secretary, James Brady, and two officers didn't fare so well. I had been a Democrat all my life and had voted for Jimmy Carter over Reagan in the previous election, but Reagan's charisma in dealing with the tragedy began to win many of us over. (In the next election some would be categorized as Reagan Democrats, I would become a Republican, and though not a straight-ticket voter I still lean Republican to this day, largely from the influence of Ronald Reagan.)

A movement that came into the forefront during the eighties was political correctness. The concept was fine, both initially and theoretically, but like many movements that survive the fledgling stage, it went too far. In the beginning, however, it addressed habits that we had as a culture that were obviously offensive to women and those of minority races and religions. For instance, I remember being at a friend's house in the late sixties. She had grabbed some grapes out of a grocery bag and was about to eat them when her mother said, "Don't eat those before they're washed! Mexicans pick them with their hands!" Political correctness put pressure on people or even ostracized them when they made racially or ethnically tasteless comments, and the world of today is a little better because of the reforms of this effort. I believe it went too far because the battles weren't being chosen properly, similar to how environmentalists lost some credibility when they blocked timber harvesting in Oregon because one spotted owl resided there. With political correctness, it got to the point where you couldn't hear an interview without long pauses after every asked question as the interviewee filtered his answer for anything that could be misconstrued. On *The Tonight Show* in the headlines segment Jay Leno featured a press release from the New York Yankees. He said that The Yankees had a fax checker that would automatically default the word black to African-American. The release came out saying that on such and such a date Yankee players would be wearing an African-American number 5 on their sleeve along with an African-American armband in remembrance of a former player who had died. I've evolved to where I don't care for hyphenated distinctions of Americans. I believe it's time to look past color and be Americans. Yet, I'll still use they hyphenations until the involved parties themselves decide that they're no longer needed. On another occasion a network was asked not to show *Planet of the Apes* during Black History Month. It's hard for me to find legitimacy in the arguments of conspiratorial theorists who believed the network was showing this film to belittle African-Americans. By the time we got to the mid 2000s, political correctness had become part of our thought process, but it is becoming more tempered and practical.

One of the things I regretted in the summer of 1981 was that I had not chosen to attend a major college. Ann Marie was still on my mind, as the one-year anniversary of her death was approaching, and I thought about how cool it must have been for her to attend Michigan State University. My buddy Doug had been hired to teach at Lansing Community College, so I figured the time was right for me to head down to East Lansing. I thought I'd find a job and after I got settled in I would try to get accepted into MSU, but if nothing else I wanted to get a taste of being around a Big Ten Campus. Steve, a friend from high school, was going down for his senior year. He wanted to get out of the dorms and rent an apartment, but he needed someone to share expenses. It seemed like everything was falling into place, so I put my two-week notice in and headed down to East Lansing with him. The campus looked different than I remembered from a trip I'd made to see my cousin Louise in '74, but I was older and looking for different things now and they all seemed to be there. The setting was magnificent, the girls were beautiful, and the banks of the Red Cedar River gave me a place to meditate. Everything seemed perfect—until I got to know Steve a little better. He was a pain in the ass and was holding me back. I remember tiring of him in high school, like when he gave me crap for breaking when a cat darted in front of my car. I thought he had matured, but he hadn't. After two weeks we still hadn't found an apartment but were staying in an unoccupied sublet on Hagadorn, which was cool because it was free, but we were beginning to push our luck. One morning we were about to check out a listing from the paper. We got in my car and I was about to head to Okemos when he said, "Take a left here first." (I had a feeling what he was about to do, although there had never been any discussion of it.) I took the left. After that it was a right, followed by another left, and then another, and this continued until we pulled up to the bus depot. I had been right. I put on my surprised face and tried to hide the elation I was feeling. I listened to him say that he wanted to take a semester off, but I knew it was because there was tension between us, so I did feel somewhat guilty that I had interfered with his education. But I was finally free to do what I pleased without a cumbersome tagalong. Doug was also taking night classes to get his doctorate in philosophy and was living in married housing, even though he was going through a divorce. He had an extra room and said I could stay for a week while I looked for a place of my own. Things had gotten so much better within a day as I was staying on campus at MSU with a good friend. When we both had free time we'd toss a football around, and often neighbor guys would join in, too. With Doug being a good and respected friend, though, I didn't want to overextend my welcome, so for as much as I enjoyed it where I was, I found a place in Holt, which was about twenty minutes away. The place wasn't much more than a shed with a bed, but it was cheap, and without a job or anyone to share expenses I did what I had to do. The cold nights of November forced me to make a choice—sleep shivering or breath the gray-ish-blue smoke that the heater emitted. The smell made me sick and after a couple weeks I could no longer deal with it. Furthermore, I hadn't found work and my money was getting low. It was time to go home. I left before Thanksgiving, but I had gotten what I wanted; a taste of life at a major college.

It wasn't long after I got back that Aunt Celia passed away. Both of us had mellowed over the years and we appreciated each other for what we were, and I was glad for that. I was worried about what would come of the house, though. I'd been living there for eight years by that time and was content with staying there. Furthermore, with my dad's age I didn't want him living alone. My aunt's oldest daughter, Bernice, had talked with her sister Marilyn in Alaska and they decided we could continue living there with the contingence that one day the house would go up for sale and when it did we'd have to move. That possibility was at the back of my mind, but for the time being there was stability and life was allowed to go on the way we had known it.

It was between late 1981 and early '82 when I began to bond with my second and third oldest sisters. Jeanine lived in Iron Mountain and was nine years older than me, and Donna lived in Rapid River and was seven years older, but we were all the same age as far as our interests were concerned and in regards to our recollection of the past. On days off I'd go visit them, but basically we were getting to know each other. Jeanine was cool. She was popular and lived a fairly posh life, while Donna more domesticated and religious, but I found both interesting in their own way. Often I'd bring various tapes of music that I recorded and we'd sit and chat with the sounds of the sixties in the background. Growing up where they did, they were mostly familiar to radio-played music, so some of the album cuts I brought were just as new to them as they had been to me just a few years earlier. (I remember that Jeanine refused to believe me when I told her that much of The Beatles' music had been influenced by LSD.) We'd go out to lunch, or to the beach, or Jeanine and I would play tennis, or I'd romp with their kids, and when the afternoon was over I'd go back to Escanaba. My sister Mary had moved across the street from us in '79 and I had spent a considerable amount of time over there, as did my sisters Connie and Jackie, but there was a different dynamic at play there. I lived a different life than they did; the core of who I was differed from who they were, and the visits to Mary's house served the killing of time more than anything else. After a couple years of visiting Jeanine and Donna, though, the novelty of them being my sisters wore off, and I found that from time to time they'd treat my like a little brother, Jeanine especially, disregarding me in certain social situations or trying to tell me how to live. I found myself explaining my goals and objectives—often to skeptical ears—as if to prove that I wasn't a stupid kid. I hated that. As I said before, I treasure my individuality nearly as much as anything and I trust my own judgment more than advice from others. The visits grew less and less frequent.

The Big Chill was the movie of the eighties for me and another of my three all-time favorites. It began with the reunion of a group of friends, brought back together by a funeral of one of their own, and followed by a weekend of memories, camaraderie, regrets, arguments, affairs, and person-to-person juxtapositions. I found reality in the film with the inclusion of all this because it gave a plausible depiction of relationships. I thought how cool it would've been to be a part of a similar dynamic. *The Big Chill* had an impact on me because of where I was in 1983. I was working nights so I lacked human contact and I missed having such a group of friends. Furthermore, the music they flashed back to was what I'd been listening to for the last couple years and it painted the movie in colors to which I could relate.

The initial broadcasting of MTV in my hometown came in 1983 and with it I noticed a distinct change in the sound. Between the onset of new wave and the popularity explosion of MTV was a period where we thought that the eighties pop charts would be dominated by Hall and Oats and Michael Jackson. Both acts released many singles and were selling a lot of records, but neither had a sound that I liked. MTV defined the culture of the eighties in many ways; I can't imagine the decade having definition had the music continued in the direction it was going in 1982. When people refer to the eighties sound, they're really referring to the period after the onset of music television. The synthetic decade of big hair and plasticine attire had begun. The 1980 talk that new wave would be the next direction that music would go was now proven to be false. Although there were flashes of talent, it wasn't enough to keep the movement going and music waited in limbo for something to take hold of it. Music videos not only provided a visual interpretation of songs, it showed a fun or melodramatic or whimsical side to them. I believe that the production of videos also stirred the pot of creativity. This sound was unique, new, and good, and it would evolve throughout the eighties while staying within itself. Today, more radio stations play eighties music under the designation of oldies than they do seventies music. Retro nights are popular in nightclubs as well, where not only the music is revisited but the attire of the decade, too.

It was 1984 when I fulfilled my dream of going to California. I left Escanaba via Greyhound and began my first substantial western heading. I had booked a central route for the way there and would loop through the Southwestern states on the return trip; consequently, my list of states-visited was about to grow by eleven. I began to feel diversity of the land when I crossed The Mississippi, and would feel it again and again as I passed through the vast plains of Nebraska, hit the foothills of Wyoming, viewed the monument formations of Utah and traversed The Rockies, went through the Mojave Desert, and finally when I got my first view of the great Pacific Ocean. California was everything I expected. The days were warm and dry, the streets of the cities in The Valley were pristine and lined with palm trees, but mainly, there was always something happening.

I first realized that I had an accent somewhere in my late teens, but I didn't become aware that the accent from the Upper Peninsula was something others belittled until I began my travels of the mid to late eighties. If I got far enough from Michigan, people would ask if I was from Canada. Somewhere not long after I realized that there was this quasi-intellectual evaluation based upon my accent. I began to make an effort to eliminate everything that fed those perceptions. First went the *eh?* and then the *Holy Wah!* I eliminated all the local colloquialisms. Next, I had to remember to say the *G* at the end of *ing* words. This was harder because unlike the words I eliminated, they were still words I used, and of course when stringing together a sentence you don't stop and evaluate every word. The hardest thing to do, however, was to get rid of the singsong cadence with all the highs and lows. For those who may not be familiar with our accent, at times it can sound Indian or Pakistani. I have to add that many people think that I'm doing the Upper Peninsula a disservice by distancing myself from the accent I was born with, and in some ways I agree with them. My dad had the accent, although his was perceived to be more French, and many people I know and respect have it, too. So it comes down to this—if you have that or any accent and you embrace it as a part of who you are, keep it.

When I again vacationed in California the following year I decided to attend *The Tonight Show*. I drove from my hotel in Thousand Oaks down to the NBC studios in Burbank on the morning of my first attempt, only to learn what the process was for getting tickets, then understanding that it would require me to arrive much earlier. The next day I got to the studios three hours before the ticket window opened and took my position. The way the process worked was you'd get in line to get a complimentary pass, and if you were fortunate enough to get one you'd go back in the afternoon, line up early again and wait another three hours to see if there was enough room for you to enter after the invited guests were seated. I got my pass that second day but didn't get to the afternoon phase on time, but I was learning the procedure. It was beautiful on the morning of my third attempt—quintessential Southern California. The dew coating the blacktop path that led from the parking lot accentuated the greenness of the finely trimmed grass, lit in an Impressionistic manner by the newly rising sun. The man behind me was a former Bostonian who had moved to Los Angeles ten years earlier. He was a kindly old fellow, a unique blend of East Coast awareness that had been softened by the California lifestyle. With him were his wife and a friend of hers, and as we were only allowed to obtain two passes and seeing that I was alone, he asked me if I could get an extra one. We all got our passes, and then we were off. I took a ride through some of the canyons of the San Gabriel Mountains before returning to hotel. I saw the old fellow again as we were lined up in phase two and I waved, but I wasn't about to lose my place in line and had to leave the greeting at that. Upon entering the studio I was glad to see that he, too, had made it in. An attendant led me to my seat. As I looked around I was surprised to see how little seating there actually was. (On a later tour of the NBC studios they explained how they never show the whole theater on the show and how they use camera angles to make it look much larger.) Ed McMahon warmed up the crowd before the cameras rolled, then delivered his classic "Heeeere's Johnny!" prompting Johnny Carson to push his way through the stage curtain and begin his monologue. Shelly Winters was the main guest that evening, but the cool thing was that, unbeknownst to me, Cat Adams from Escanaba who had been the female vocalist winner on *Star Search* was also appearing that night. Enter hindsight. If I'd thought of telling the seating attendant that I was from the same small town as her I probably could have gone backstage to say hello, where who knows who I could have met.

I had never been to a professional basketball game. I was driving toward L.A. one evening when I heard the Lakers would be playing the Rockets at The Forum, so I drove to Inglewood, found the arena and entered one of the parking lots. On my way to the ticket window I came upon a scalper offering a ticket for thirty dollars. I asked him if it was a good seat and he of course assured me that it was, so I bought the ticket and found myself to be about forty rows up. The players were still shooting their warm-ups and I went to the reserve seating attendant and asked her if I could walk down to the front row to get a few pictures. She said that I could and I did. After snapping off a few, I noticed that a few other people were on the court and walking past me. I turned to see if the attendant was paying any attention to me and when she wasn't I took off and followed two men who looked to be with the press. Soon I was directly behind the visiting team's basket and had 7'4" Ralph Sampson pass within two feet of me after making a practice lay-up. Following him was Akeem Olajuwon (he hadn't yet begun going by Hakeem) and across the court were Magic Johnson and Kareem Abdul-Jabbar. Strangely enough, I wasn't really star-struck until I saw coach Pat Riley walking toward the Laker bench. I guess that even though I was in the midst of all those famous players, I knew they were going to be there and had expected to see them so there was no shock factor, whereas for whatever reason I hadn't been in that mind-set with Pat Riley.

I first got into Techno in Los Angeles, and I believe that it was only being there and having a taste of The Valley that bent my ear toward the new sound. Having been out of high school for seven years and focusing on the music of the sixties had begun to make me feel out of touch with modern music, so being in the land of this sound's conception led to my sudden openness. Beyond the borders of music, though, I was digging the yearly trips out west. I loved being in any state west of The Mississippi, and especially California. Furthermore, as I had taken yet a different route when I took the train on my second visit, I was adding a lot of color to my map of states visited. On the trip out west I had initially boarded Amtrak in Milwaukee and gotten as far as Flagstaff, Arizona before a train ahead of us derailed and we were bussed from Flagstaff to Los Angeles. As we got on the Greyhound I was seated next to a fine looking black girl and we began to chat. She was pleasant, and when I got a sleepy she offered her shoulder as a headrest. We both fell asleep. When I woke my head was on her breast and when I straightened myself out I saw a puddle of drool on her boob. *This will be fun to explain* I thought as I rolled my eyes at a stupidity I had no control over. But she kept sleeping and by the time she awoke it was dark. I couldn't tell if her shirt was still wet, I let it go, and she made no mention of it.

The beginning of change in geopolitical structure happened in 1985 as new Russian president Mikhail Gorbachev ushered in the age of *perestroika* and *glasnost*. The philosophical changes in governing imposed by Gorbachev and newly given freedoms granted by him would set the stage for events that would take place in another four years and would profoundly change the map. As an American who as a child was shown where the fallout shelters were, I was keenly interested in what was happening in The Soviet Union. There is mystery in the unknown, and so it had always been with our great competitor. Although there were cities in America with large Russian immigrant populations, there was little the average American knew about the communist nation or its people. Their borders were tight to citizens of the Western world and news from within was closely scrutinized by their government. Films like *Dr. Zhavago* depicted Russian citizens to be living in a state of communal poverty. But even though that portrayal was of the early nineteen-hundreds, we knew that the riches of the vast nation weren't going to the people but rather toward military proliferation. I remember Ronald Reagan's commercial during the '84 campaign that spoke metaphorically about a bear in the woods. The bear, of course, was The Soviet Union and the success of the commercial showed how much the American people were still leery of the Soviets. So we eagerly waited to see what the man with the birthmark stain on his head would do to end oppression in his country, make it less of a mystery, and in the end make the world a safer place.

CHAPTER SEVEN

I began the second half of the decade with a trip down to Florida to visit my dad, but it was what occurred on the way home that will stay with me forever. I said goodbye to him and departed by train, heading up the eastern corridor toward Washington D.C. I had caught eyes with a couple of girls—sisters—while gallivanting throughout the train, but it wasn't until we got to within 100 miles of the capital that I got up the nerve to talk to them. Courtney had black hair and Stephanie was blonde and both were gorgeous. I asked if they wanted to grab a slice of pizza, they did, and we went to the concession car and chatted as we snacked. They had a little sister who found us, which turned out to be good for me as nothing would've happened with both sisters there, and not long after, Courtney took her younger sister back to coach. Stephanie and I were having a good conversation but our setting wasn't the best, so I asked if she wanted to go to my compartment. As we continued to talk I noticed how deeply she seemed to be looking into my eyes, and though I feared the possible negative outcome of the action I'd been contemplating since her sisters had left, I leaned in and kissed her. There was no negative reaction. Because she didn't know me well I felt awkward. We didn't stay in the compartment long, as she was worried about what her mother would think if she couldn't find her. She gave me her address and I tucked it into my suitcase, then I cracked the door open to make sure the coast was clear and we flung ourselves into the hall and tried to look innocent. Already my heart was aching as I knew we'd soon be arriving in Washington where she and her family would get off, while I'd have to endure a four-hour layover before continuing north. We went back to the coach. I was trying to be casual in front of her mother so I asked if there was anything interesting to see within walking distance of the terminal; something I wanted to know anyway. Her mother told me to check out the National Air and Space Museum. I had asked a porter the question earlier and he had told me the same thing, so that became my plan. I felt the oncoming of the sadness that comes when you know you'll probably never see someone again. It reminded me of that scene in the sleigh at the end of *Doctor Zhivago* as Lara takes the balalaika from Yuri and looks into his eyes with painful longing as she realizes she was bidding him a farewell that would be final.

We said our goodbyes on the train without giving any indication that we had done anything more than chatting while having pizza and soda. Again I tried not to give anything away and simply gave Stephanie a light embrace and whispered that I'd write while taking in the scent of her hair one more time. Courtney gave me a tight hug and kissed my cheek, and I remember looking innocently over her shoulder to Stephanie. I left the train as they gathered their bags and walked down the corridor toward the terminal. I'd been right; twenty steps and I was already missing the girl that had come into my life so suddenly and who was destined to leave just as quickly, but the mood of the day was about to change dramatically. Upon entering the depot and proceeding toward the museum I noticed a gathering of people staring at a television that was mounted on the wall. The news was as ironic as it was horrible. It was while going to the National Air and Space Museum that I learned that the space shuttle Challenger had exploded, killing all seven astronauts. I changed my plans and stayed glued to the television. The special report showed the sequence of events, but what I remember most was the hauntingly unemotional professionalism in the voice from mission control in Houston as he stated in monotone articulation, "Obviously a major malfunction." For the rest of the way home my thoughts were split between Stephanie and the

117

disaster. It would be an understatement to say it was a day that would stay with me forever.

By the time I got back from my vacation the routine of working at night and sleeping most of the day away was beginning to get to me. I'd been doing the night shift for over six years and enough was enough. Still, despite my sentiment, there hadn't been an end in sight until I got word that our store was about to be sold. Now as a company we had been sold many times, oft times to non-grocery based companies such as Gambles and Wicks Lumber, but this rumor had just a few of our stores that were located in Northern Michigan going to a small company from Gaylord called Glen's Markets. The sale went through in May and things began to change quickly. The unionization that had been holding me back was dissolved with the sale and I was free to advance based on my performance. I remained on nights for a couple of months, but when the dairy department began throwing away hundreds of gallons of milk each week due to over-ordering, my time had come and I was named the new dairy manager. Moving to days changed my life instantly. I was around people again. I was part of the hustle-and-bustle rat race and I loved it. When I worked for Red Owl Foods our average tenure was eighteen years. Few people left because it was a well paying union job, and few people were hired because of a union negotiated three-to-one part time to full time ratio, seasonal help excluded. Consequently, we only had perhaps seven or eight new hires a year counting the summer and Christmas temps. Without having the hiring restrictions that the Teamsters had negotiated, Glen's was able to staff about thirty more people than we'd had at Red Owl, so suddenly there were many new faces. One of them was brought to me one afternoon by the front end manager. "Duane," she began, "this is Greg and he just sliced his hand and I don't have time to take him to the emergency room." I dropped what I was doing, took him to the hospital and waited as he got stitches. Greg Haddock and I became friends, along with two other new hires, Todd Hess and Mike Beaudion. We began doing the things that I'd been deprived of while working the night shift. We organized football games, we played Nerf basketball in my living room, we chased girls—sometimes successfully and sometimes not—but we always entertained ourselves. It felt refreshing to be around people who enjoyed life and made an effort to be interactive with it. They spent a good bit of time at our place. My dad liked them and they were respectful to him, which was important to me as he was now over seventy. There was one bar that we would go to. It was owned by an old man and tucked away in a corner, so it didn't get a lot of attention from the police. I was the only one who was of legal drinking age, but this bar served us all and it became our hangout. We had a good time each time we went there, but one night in particular stands out. I had never had a cheerleader before, not to mention one that was nineteen when I was twenty-six, but on one warm summer night Todd and I took Amy and Christy to the beach after the bar closed. He ended up with Amy and I with Christy, but it could just as easily have gone the other way as each girl seemed hot for either of us. I awoke the next morning with sand on my sheets, but that was okay. The encounter had purified me of all lingering effects from seven years on the night shift and my assimilation back into mainstream society was complete.

My dad was wintering in a small apartment complex in Ocala, Florida when I went to visit him in May of '87. His health was fair enough for him to stay on his own, but he now bore the look of an old man. Although I didn't admit it to myself at the time, I knew that because of his emphysema he was in the final few years of his life. Even though he couldn't do half the things he used to do, I took more of an appreciation in what he could do. There was a restaurant about five blocks up the road that the retirees frequented. We were both hungry and decided to go there, and for a reason I can't remember we decided to walk, which was something that would take Dad's breath away. As I made what I now think of as *The Walk* with him, I quietly cherished being at the side of this man whom I had known to be so strong when I was a child—intuition correctly telling me this would be the last walk we'd take together. Yet it wasn't a sad experience; sadness would be saved for later. I just slowed my pace to match his and smiled and occasionally spoke, pointing out something along the way or reminiscing about shared experiences of the past. I had a good stay with my dad, and after three days I headed west for New Orleans.

I had taken the Greyhound down to Florida and would be taking Dad's truck back to Michigan for him, as he'd be riding back in two weeks with Bert Auger, a buddy of his from Escanaba who also wintered in Ocala. If I would have known the discomfort that ride would cause my dad I would have insisted he come with me then and there, as the cold air conditioning that Bert liked wasn't at all good for Dad's ailing lungs. But I wasn't aware of that as I rolled down Highway 10 on the morning that the national speed limit of 55 ended. I waited till I saw the first sign, then throttled up to 72 mph. Soon I was immersed in the warm morning haze of Gulf Port, Mississippi, driving with the Gulf of Mexico to my left and stately mansions and an unending line of palm trees to my right. There are many photos in our minds that don't have corresponding camera-taken pictures as memory floggers, but yet they remain clear in the smallest detail as though we held the photo in our hands, as so it is with my recollection of Gulf Port, Mississippi in May of '87. The French Quarter of New Orleans was equally impressive. Even though Mardi Gras was three months removed, Bourbon Street was crowded and alive with street musicians, jugglers, mimes, and a man blowing fire from his mouth. The outdoor cafes had live jazz and I stopped at several of them. I took a riverboat tour and visited Jax Brewery, but the 95° heat eventually sent me to my hotel's swimming pool. I stayed another day and then began my northward trek. It had been a good trip. I'd seen some new sights, one of them Graceland, added three Southern states to my list, and it was good to have seen my dad.

January of '88 brought the purchase of two more Red Owl stores by Glen's. One of them was in Sault Ste. Marie and I was asked if I'd be interested in transferring. I thought it over for a week. First and foremost, my dad would be one-hundred eighty miles away and I would worry about him as his emphysema was continually progressing. He was still able to drive so he could go where he wanted, but by now he had to take a small oxygen tank with him. Still, Aunt Betty and Uncle Elmer lived next door and in the end that made me feel secure enough to take the promotion and move to The Soo, as it's most commonly called. It was hard to leave my friends behind, too, but it turned out that they would make regular visits and I'd go back to Escanaba on every other weekend. The Soo was notorious for its winters and true to form it snowed *and* was below zero every day for the first twenty two days. Nonetheless, I liked the town; it had a different flavor than any other city in Upper Michigan. It was a national border town, and its sister city, Sault Ste. Marie, Ontario, had close to one-hundred thousand people. Also, it offered a multiethnic aspect that was new to me, as there were large populations of French, Italian, and Chinese. It seemed I was farther from home than one-hundred eighty miles as I walked through the mall and heard different languages being spoken, my pocket filled with multicolored Canadian currency, and street signs written in English and French. My senses had been stirred and would be stirred more when I met Marie LaJune from Montreal, who was now living in the Canadian Soo. I began to cross the border nearly every evening, which of course drew the suspicion of the border guards and as a consequence my car was searched frequently. Marie was beautiful, but in the end her self-destructive habits were too much for me. In April I had the privilege of living in a city that won an NCAA championship as the Lakers won in double overtime, so in the four major sports the championship schools were Notre Dame (football), Kansas (basketball), Stanford (baseball), and Lake Superior State University (hockey). But we were just getting into summer and there would be much ahead. It turned out that nature delivered the strangest summer I'd ever seen. It began with record high temperatures that would continue throughout the season. Then there were forest fires in Ontario that gave the sky a strange grayish-orange glow, a phenomenon that would last for nearly two weeks. Strangest of all, though, was the tent worm, caterpillar moth fiasco that culminated in the great blackout of '88. I remember it that way because there were multitudes of these creatures which would go towards light, and they would cover the lights in our store, making it seem dark enough inside that one would think we were closed. These bugs were everywhere and they were also very soft, which made for disgusting situations, like when a cashier would ring up a head of lettuce or cabbage and roll it down the belt and there'd be three squashed bugs on it by the time it reached the bag boy. But eeriest of all was the knee-high pile of live, squirming bugs we'd get when sweeping the sidewalk. I recall one of the older locals telling me that they were cyclical, I can't remember the interval, but they were gone as quickly as they had come.

1988 was an election year. I recall watching an episode of *Gomer Pile U.S.M.C.* back in the early seventies. Without elaborating upon the details, by sheer happenstance Gomer shakes hands with the President. As soon as I saw this, shaking hands with the President became a goal of mine. The closest I've come to achieving it was at an Al Gore campaign stop at Lake Superior State University. I knew he was an up-and-coming politician from Tennessee who didn't have much of a shot at winning, but he was young and the possibility existed that he would someday be the leader of our country. With that in mind I went to his rally. When he finished speaking he came down from the stage and began to greet people. Soon a line formed and I knew that I'd be able to get that handshake. Well, I did, but it was without recognition or acknowledgment. He shook my hand while looking over my shoulder and speaking to a guy behind me, never once making eye contact. In the end I had shaken his hand, and we all know how close he would eventually come to being president, but on that day Mr. Gore and other celebrities came down from the pedestals I had put them on and landed a little closer to you and me. Gore didn't make it out of the primaries, losing to Michael Dukakis, who in turn lost to George Bush's promise of *A Kinder Gentler Nation* that beheld *1000 Points of Light.*

In the meantime my Aunt Celia's daughters had sold the house in Escanaba, so my dad would have to move. He found a downtown apartment on a side street adjacent to Main so the location was fair enough, but his health was getting worse and it seemed strange for him to be starting anew at his age. I began to feel guilty about being so far away from him, but Aunt Betty and Uncle Elmer were still just a few blocks away. I went to see him in his new place. It was a nice apartment and I tried to project a positive view about it, but I felt bad that my favorite person was so alone. He only stayed there for a couple months before an emergency visit to the Veteran's Hospital in Iron Mountain, which is about fifty miles from Escanaba, where the doctor advised him not to stay alone any more. Elmer and Betty had an extra room downstairs and said he could stay with them, and he did. It was hard for me to see him there because he was usually in his pajamas and his room had a convalescent look to it. Consequently, enter the period that I now look back upon with regret as much as any in my life. My dad was a salt-of-the-earth sort of guy and never said an unnecessary word, and now his disease and subsequent depression from being compromised made him even quieter. I had a hard time having a two-way conversation with him. Even though I was twenty-eight—old enough where I should have been more responsible—I had a lot of restless energy and I would only visit with my dad for half-hour intervals. Then I'd need a break and would go off to see my friends. I felt bad that I didn't have more to talk to him about and that he didn't have the energy to engage me in conversation. I still don't understand why I couldn't just sit quietly beside him.

Back in Sault Ste. Marie I was scheduling myself to have every other weekend off, at which time I'd go back to Escanaba. In the first part of December I was transferred to Roscommon, Michigan, which was one-hundred fifty miles south. I hated it there and regretted taking the promotion; plus, I was sixty miles further from my dad. One day I got a call from Aunt Betty. She said, "I think it's time. You better come right away...and you should bring your suit." I knew my dad was dying and I had known for some time that it would come soon, but certain words bring clear and unfettered realization. And so it was with, *and you should bring your suit.* I was going home to say goodbye to my dad. I was going to look at that face I had seen so many times, more than any other face on the planet, and I was going to look into his sweet, caring eyes and realize that I was seeing them for the last time. I packed what I needed, called work, then began the longest two-hundred ninety mile drive of my life.

I arrived at the Veteran's Hospital in Iron Mountain. Dad was alert when I got there and he smiled when he saw me. Aunt Betty and Uncle Elmer were in the room, as was my sister Jeanine, who lived in Iron Mountain and would come see her Uncle Roy on the different occasions that he'd been admitted. I greeted my dad and we all chatted together for fifteen minutes. The others were hungry and were going down to the cafeteria and they asked if I wanted to join them. I said I wanted to spend some time alone with my dad and that I'd be down a little later, so they went out and I stayed. I can't remember exactly what I said to him but at the same time it's a moment I'll never forget. Dad knew he was dying as much as I did and I embraced him and said everything I wanted and needed to say. I told him that it was his work ethic that made me what I was, and that I loved him, something that neither of us said freely. A nurse came in and Dad introduced me as his pride and joy. We talked and held until he was getting too tired. Then I joined the others at the cafeteria. With my dad's emphysema being in such an advanced stage he wasn't getting enough oxygen to his brain and when we got back from lunch he was a different person, and would be for the remainder of his convalescence. I believe that he'd been fighting to keep his cognizance until I arrived so we could say our proper farewells. Once that was done he gave up the fight and let himself slip into the state that fate had waiting for him. He died several days later, in the middle of January, with me at his side and holding his hand. When I was a little boy Dad would often call me his chum, and now I had lost my chum and I was alone. It was around eleven at night when he died. I had to stay at the Veteran's Hospital for an hour or so and sign some papers before I could go back to Escanaba. I recalled the sequence of events in the couple of hours that preceded his death. I had been asleep in my hotel room when I got a call from the hospital, telling me that Dad didn't have much longer. Because he was in a state of incoherence, all I could do was hold his hand and talk to him. This went on for an hour or so before a nurse came in for my dad's final moments. He held a stethoscope to his chest, telling me that we were getting close. Then finally and in an unceremonious way he lifted his stethoscope, looked to me and said, "He's gone." It was a couple of seconds after that that I did something that to this day remains inexplicable—I looked up at the TV to check the score of the basketball game. I have since tried to figure out what would have prompted such an untimely action. I have asked myself all the questions: was it a diversion from the reality I was facing? Was it simply a trained and involuntary action drawn from habit? You hear from recounts of near-death experiences how a soul will stay in a room momentarily, hovering above and observing before moving along to its next destination. All I can think of is my dad doing this and seeing me watching the fucking television! I don't know if I'll ever be able to forgive myself for that.

This was still on my mind on the ride home when one of the most profound things in my life happened. Some may say that it was sheer coincidence; I say it was a sign from God. The fifty-mile ride from Iron Mountain back to Escanaba was bound to be dreadful. The radio had been on when I started the car and I immediately turned it off. I just wanted it to be quiet so I could reflect. About halfway home the reflecting was getting the better of me so I decided to put the radio back on, just to occupy my mind. When I did, the song that was playing blew me away. Dad had never been a fan of the music of my generation; he didn't even care for mellow songs like *Yesterday* by The Beatles. On one occasion, though, I was listening to Melanie, and as he walked past my room he began to sing along with, *What Have They Done To My Song.* It stopped me in my tracks. He smiled as Melanie sang the next verse in French and he again sang, "Ils ont change ma chanson, ma, c'est la seule chose que je peux faire et ce n'est pas bon, ma." I asked him how he knew this and he said he used to sing that song when he was young. Back to the ride home. One can imagine the comfort I felt when I turned on the radio and heard that song playing, after I hadn't heard it on the radio in ten or so years. Hearing that song at that moment was astounding. I took it as a sign that my dad was okay.

I remember sitting on my sofa one evening, thinking about the farewell I'd had with my dad and looking at it from his perspective. He had raised me on his own after Mom died and he had taught me about life. On his deathbed he had to have been resigned to the fact that there was nothing more he could do and he could only hope that I would continue on in a positive direction. That must be such a helpless feeling, especially in a world with so many traps and vices.

Life went on as it must and for the first time I was in a world without my dad. From the time I was thirteen I had realized that the day would come, and I guess Dad's death was easier than my mother's because I was prepared, but there still was a vacancy that remains to this day. I took solace in the richness of the life my dad had lived, and by spring I was ready to put the lamentation behind me. I got out of Roscommon and took a transfer to St. Ignace, which was only fifty miles south of The Soo and one-hundred miles closer to Escanaba. I felt better about my job and I formed a circle of friends with whom I had a lot in common, most notably Dale Hess, who is still a close friend to this day. By April I was ready to hit my beloved road again; a little trip across southern Canada, over to Niagara Falls, and then up to Toronto on the way back. It was good to be behind the wheel and checking out the countryside for whatever wonders were to be seen. It was then I knew that I would be okay. Two months later on a warm June night I set out to retrace the trip I had taken back in '75 with Dad and my friend Tom. It had been fourteen years since I'd been to Quebec and now I was old enough to appreciate it properly. Sure I had thought it was cool as a fifteen year-old, but now I understood the history of the area and I had that sense of *from whence I came*. I followed the same route: through Blind River, Sudbury, and North Bay, spending the first night in Mattawa. The motel I stayed at had a quaint setting. Though it was late when I arrived, I couldn't resist spending some time in the warm June air. I walked up the slope that led to the highway and drew a deep breath. The light from the parking lot was bright enough to illuminate the green grass that stood in stark contrast with the damp, black pavement of the driveway. Off to the right was a red and white telephone booth, the kind we used to have in the states, and it looked perfectly right on the outskirts of this rural Canadian town. Sometimes when one travels it's the simpler things they remember, and so it was with me—at that moment I couldn't have been in a more perfect place. I scoped the grounds the next morning, as it was also the same hotel we'd stayed at in '75. Everything looked familiar, though I had only spent one night there almost a decade and a half ago. I walked down to the river and could picture Tom and I tossing large rocks into the water for us to step on so we could get the proper angle for a photo of the river bending downstream. I looked around a little more, then checked out of my room. Towns in that part of Ontario are comfortable and friendly by their very design. The people are approachable and not only tell you what you need to know, but tend to ask you about your journey as well.

I headed east down Highway 17. As I entered Ottawa I found it to be the same as I remembered; very clean for a big city. I chuckle at another memory of entering Ottawa. I had been converting just about everything since I'd crossed the Canadian border: distance in kilometers into miles, speed limits posted in kilometers into MPH, and figuring out the exchange rate in currency with every purchase. So when I saw the city limit sign saying *Ottawa: population 300,000,* instinctively I wondered, just for a split-second, how many Americans that would be. Marie LeJeune, the girl I had known from the Canadian Soo, worked in Hull, which was on the Quebec side of the river. I thought it would surprise her if I stopped in, so I asked directions and was told that the Shop Lane Bridge would take me to the other side. I drove up and down, back and forth, but couldn't find anything close to a Shop Lane Bridge. Now being French, I felt very small in accordance with my ethnicity when I finally spotted a sign pointing to the Champlain Bridge. I crossed it and found that the street signs that were previously inscribed in French and English were now only French. I eventually found Marie at the restaurant where she worked, but she was under the impression that I had traveled all that way just to see her, and when she told me that I had taken things too seriously I got mad at her and left. I mumbled to myself as I drove down the road, but in the end it didn't matter, in fact it was better, because she was not one of the steps I was in the process of retracing.

I crossed back into Ottawa on route to Montreal. Montreal is a diverse and cosmopolitan city with a vibrant *centre ville*. I parked and went for a walk, purchasing postcards and a couple tee-shirts along the way. One particular corner where people were conjugating caught my attention. I went to it and sat on a bench, just watching everyone walk past me. It felt cool to be in a large city again. As I watched an interesting array of lives intersect with mine from my park bench vantage point, I considered moving to Montreal; something that would never happen but would provoke thought and lead to a different move. After a couple hours downtown it was time for the road again. Quebec City was about three hours away and I wanted to get there and take a look around before it got dark. When I arrived I found much that I remembered from 1975. Quebec, after all, is a timeless and historic city and fourteen years weren't about to corrupt it. I passed through the gates that separate what has been preserved from what is modern and into the only walled city in North America, down the winding hill past The Vendre Dome and into the heart of the continent's most European city, with its old, Norman style architecture. From The Citadel that looked out over the Saint Lawrence Seaway to La Chateau Frontenac, I reflected upon the time I had made those same steps with Dad, and in thinking that, he was a little closer to me. Afterwards I wanted to take an evening ride through the city, but oddly enough both of my headlights were burned out. Instead, I took a walk across the street from the uptown hotel I had checked into and to a McDonalds, and suddenly, the old once again had become the new.

The last place to visit on this trip of reminisce was the basilica at Ste.-Anne-de-Beaupré. It's funny how some things become your own, no matter how far away they may be, and so it was with this cathedral and the Stations of the Cross that ascended the hill across the street. My dad had been there with my mom shortly after they were married, and the trip we had made in '75 probably served the same reminiscent purposes for him as this trip did for me. I walked the stations and then went into the cathedral, knelt in the back and said a prayer for my dad in a place where he felt in unison with a land and a people who were his own. I stayed another day; then it was time to go. The ride home was mostly quiet and reflective. The trip had served me well.

Back in St. Ignace I found myself one mile away from the historic wonder of Mackinac Island. I had been there once before on a class trip in '74 and I remember how different it seemed to be in a world without automobiles, where even cops rode bicycles. The bikes, horse and buggies, and horseback were the modes of transportation. I recall eating at an outdoor restaurant and having a fly land in my food, then looking onto the street at the piles of horse excrement and knowing that at some point of the day that fly had probably visited one of them. But fifteen years had passed and now it was a little less rustic but more interesting. It was more renown nationally, whereas it used to be a Michigander's little secret. The movie *Somewhere In Time* starring Christopher Reeve and Jane Seymour had been filmed there, and they had done a photo shoot for one of the Sports Illustrated swimsuit editions. So when I took my first trip back to the island I found it to be quite different. Now there were swarms of tourists as opposed to a nicely gathered crowd. Many summer employees in gift shops were from France, Germany, and England, and the laborers in the hotels and restaurants were from Jamaica. Another change was that there were a lot of attractive girls. It wasn't the same island—it was better. No longer was it simply a place to go to see the historic fort and the Arch Rock, but somewhere where one could have a lot of fun. Greg and Mike were still living in Escanaba and I gave them a call and told them we had to do an overnighter; it would be the first of a handful of times we made such a visit. To get there one can take a ferry from either peninsula; we departed from the upper. I remember that first ride over and how we messed with the tourists who had come from far away and were unfamiliar with the island, telling them with straight-faced sincerity about the swinging bridge on the backside of the island that connected with the mainland twice daily. There was a flurry of activity as we neared the island harbor. Horses with trailers were lined up on the dock as workers loaded supplies onto them, tourists filed out toward the weekend that awaited them, and the main street was filled with a hustle-bustle that extended up the hill and toward the fort. Seemingly, the village became even livelier after the departure of the last boat to the mainland. One could tell where the happening places were by the number of bicycles out front. I likened it to the old west where riders tied up their horses before entering a watering hole. We decided to go to Horn's Bar first. We'd learned that the trick was to get a booth, as the place became standing room only very early into the evening, so we got there around seven and procured one. It worked. One group of girls came and stayed for around twenty minutes, offering to buy us each a drink if we'd share our table, and then another group came right in behind them. We split our time between Horn's Bar and The French Outpost, hitting on the girls just as one would at the hippest joint in New York City. After all the bars had closed we walked with three girls we had met, down the road that rimmed the shoreline and bent its way past the quiet houses of seasonal inhabitants. Mike and one of the girls split off and went down to the beach while Greg and I and the other two continued walking toward The Grand Hotel and back toward The Murray Hotel where we all were staying. Somehow by the time we got back the two girls had lost interest in us, which didn't really matter except for the fact that Mike had the key to the room. So we hung around the lobby for a while and then paid a visit to the vending machines. I needed ten more cents for the item that would satisfy my drunken craving, whatever that might have been, but I remember being fixated on it. After a half-hour or so we went up to the girls' room to see if Mike happened to be there. He wasn't,

130

and I recall being greeted by something to the extent of an unen-thusiastic "What are you guys doing here?" To Greg's chagrin I asked if either of them had a dime for the vending machine, and then we were on our way. We finally caught up with Mike who beamed sickeningly over his conquest. Nonetheless the weekend was good, and so it would be with each subsequent visit.

1989 proved to be a year of change in the world. On November 9th travel restrictions were lifted in East Germany, prompting thou-sands of East Germans to cross to the West German side. There were celebrations in the streets and by nighttime the Berlin Wall would fall. I was working with a girl from Germany at the time and it was interesting to hear accounts she would pass along from her relatives back home. The events in Berlin would be a precipitator for political and social change that would sweep through Eastern Europe. Czechs and Slovaks demonstrated for political reform in Czechoslo-vakia. In December of '89 Romanians had overthrown Communist hardliner Nicolae Ceausescu. To this day I clearly recall the defiance on the face of this seventy year-old ruler as reformers held a revolver to his head. But his execution was just another revolution of the roll-ing rock that could not be stopped. Before long Communists were ousted in Bulgaria and Albania as well. These changes set the table for reforms that would soon happen in The Soviet Union and would mark the end of the cold war. Quietly looming in obscurity, another change in political hierarchy took place when Sheik Abdullah Azzam was killed by a land mine in Pakistan. His successor in his war to save Muslim lands from the infidel encroachment would be Osama bin Laden.

The decade was nearly in the books and it had taken me from a young man to someone entering his prime. Death had beaten me up about as much as it could, as it had taken three people I loved and my little dog Pierre. But I was hardened from my experiences and ready to face whatever its adversary, life, would throw at me.

CHAPTER EIGHT

Before going into the nineties and then into the next millennium I want to reiterate that this book is about the world as I saw it, at whatever age I happened to be at the time. Thus, even though rap and Brittany Spears, for example, are about to come into cultural significance, there will be little or no mention of them and certain other elements of the times that may not be of interest to a baby-boomer. It's just as parents of those who are my age didn't relate to The Rolling Stones or The Doors. To those who are younger, I hope that you won't look at this book as a documentation of history—that was never my intention—but see this as a cultural exposé and an inside look at an average life from the previous generation. With that said, onto the nineties.

I didn't particularly care for our district manager. He was smug, effeminate, and quite frankly I didn't think he was that sharp. Still, he had ultimate authority and didn't tolerate opposing opinions of any kind. In the crisp weather of early spring I had thrown my arm out while making practice throws from the outfield to the plate. I could barely lift my arm higher than my shoulder and it was so sensitive that it would hurt to open a bag of chips. I asked for a few days off, but this district manager would have none of it and said I'd have to take a vacation if I wanted time off, so I took two weeks. I called Greyhound and got an All Aboard America pass, which would allow me to go anywhere in the country within a fourteen day period. The list of states-visited was still in the back of my mind and was lacking any states from the northwest, so I headed toward Washington. I went as far as Livingston, Montana before taking a break. Livingston was a beautiful little town; one of those unexpected treasures you find when making travels. I stayed the night, then spent a night in Seattle and another in Portland, taking time for daytime sightseeing in both cities. I then headed south for Los Angeles. I had added North Dakota, Montana, Idaho, Washington and Oregon to my list, I had seen two great cities of the northwest, and from those cities I observed the towering peaks of Mt. Rainier and Mt. Hood. My Aunt Gen lived in Tucson and I went to see her after leaving Los Angeles. I was only planning to stay for several hours, but when she asked how many days I'd be staying I didn't have the heart to tell her I was thinking hours not days, so I told her it would be just for one night. With that, though, I had time to do something in the area and we decided to take a ride to the Mexican border. I walked over into Nogales, Sonora while Aunt Gen waited on the American side. It felt as though I'd walked into a third world country as I strolled about the open-air markets along the sand streets. There was a butcher with long, black hair who was cutting meat off a hanging side of beef. The differences in our cultures were evident as he took his cut and handed it to a customer, then with his hands covered with blood and grease he pressed his hair down and pulled it out of his face. I noticed that flies hovered around his head and landed as soon as he stood still. Yet, none of the people at his venue seemed to mind. The clothes being sold in the market were hung on lines and covered with dust, looking like those that would prompt an American mother to yell at her child for being a slob. Houses rose up along several hills behind us and were gaudily painted in pink, canary yellow, and turquoise. For as poor as the area was it was interesting to observe the contrast, especially as the change had been immediate and I could still see the American side from where I stood. I drove my aunt's Cadillac back to Tucson, stopping at an old Mexican mission along the way. I said farewell to my Aunt Gen the next morning, not knowing that I'd never see her again. As I look back I'm glad that I decided to stay and share those experiences with her. At the time the decision to stay the night was purely altruistic, but with time I appreciate what I too had gained. From Tucson I went to Vegas and then to Denver before heading home. My shoulder was still sore—it would be over a year before it felt right again—but I was ready to get back to work. Yet, the road had stirred my desires in the same way Montreal had one year earlier and I began to rethink why I was living in such a small and uneventful town.

One of the inequities of this existence is that we're unable to fully experience everything of which we get a taste. If you've had a dash of New York culture, for instance, it tends to make you want to feel everything that goes along with it: the crowded streets, girls with their crude Bronx mouths, compacted neighborhoods where everyone is known by yourself, your parents, and your children, the occasional trips into Manhattan, or going to Yankee Stadium. I can take a two week vacation and go there to get that flavor, but that just leaves me wanting more. I could even move there, but it still wouldn't give me enough time to *get* what the city is all about. And if I did spend a sufficient amount of time at that locale, it would force me to abandon everything else I have to urge to savor to the utmost, for instance, small-town Nebraska with its white picket fences and neighbors that barbecue and invite you over to eat with them, and kids that aren't too complicated and who have a genuine respect for their elders. The same curiosity for distant places can be derived from music, like in the lyrical picture painted in the song *Under The Boardwalk,* or from movies shot in exotic locations. One particular movie setting that inspired me to see New York was *When Harry Met Sally* because the urban life was portrayed so well in the filming. With this, I'm thankful for the writers, directors, and musicians who bring such scenes to us so vividly. So back to the broader point. I think we begin life thinking that we can do everything, then enter adulthood with only a subconscious understanding that we can't, and it isn't until times of significant reflection where we take that realization out of our subconscious and put it into the forefront. Once we put it there, we lament the inadequate amount of time we have. Having said all of that, maybe

I'm wrong by making the assumption that this concept is pertinent to everyone. Perhaps some only need a taste of the great unknown to satisfy their curiosity and thus have enough peace of mind to take that taste and then leave it as an experience of the past and go forward from there. However, different people in different life situations have different desires. Those who have the quintessential nuclear family may be quite content with every aspect of their lives. As for me, I always have been the restless one and I wanted to have a taste of just about everything. For example, I grew up in the days of drug experimentation and LSD or "acid" was very popular. I always wanted to try it but was leery of having a bad trip. Still, it haunted me; I wanted to try it once. Then some ten years ago I would do opium on occasion, and on one particular trip I got so high that I couldn't move my arms or legs without putting my body into a quasi-manual override and had to specifically think about lifting up an arm or putting one foot in front of the other. In the end it was a different type of high and I still hadn't done acid, but the experience satisfied my curiosity. I haven't done opium since, but I had tasted that part of the culture. So this will stay an unanswerable question: not that we should be able to experience everything, because obviously we can't, but can we get to the point of compromise and contentment in satisfying the desires we had when we were young.

Another dynamic that comes into play is that we tend to glorify certain eras or events we were aware of but weren't able to experience, then make them out to be more than they would have been. Take Woodstock as an example, and for the purpose of specificity let's look at it in a fictional scenario through the eyes of a sixteen year-old. Will this example hold the lone possible outcome? Of course not; it's simply the way things might have happened and is an exercise to highlight that which is often overlooked. So here we go. Let's say that he went to Woodstock with one of his friends, his brother who was eighteen, and one of his brother's friends. The drive from Michigan to Upstate New York is long and the two older kids peck at the two younger boys most of the way there. They arrive at the festival and the kid is awed by the number of people and particularly the number of hippies, for his parents won't let him grow his hair out. He hears music and everybody's digging it. He thinks it's cool that he's at such an unbelievably grand event, but at the same time he is sixteen, apolitical, and would rather be seeing The Monkees or Herman's Hermits than Richie Havens and Jimi Hendrix. Yet, his enthusiasm heightens when two naked hippie chicks run past. He spends most of the day listening to the concert. Some of it he enjoys but he ends up getting bored. It's been raining all day and his brother had to park so far away that they sleep on the wet muddy ground instead of going back to the car. The kid wakes up cold and hungry and can't find anything to eat; their food, too, is in the car and three miles down the road. He wants to go to it anyway but his brother's friend is calling him a pussy and says he'll punch him if he doesn't shut up. So he does. And on it goes with his interest ebbing and flowing. They get home and the kid tells his friends what a groovy experience it was. Is he lying? Only partially. It's a lie of omission. And in the end would it be cool for him to look back upon, ten, twenty, thirty years down the road, after he's matured enough to understand what Woodstock was all about? Definitely! In fact it would make him a local icon to have attended an event that fermented its way into history. So with this possibility I have no intention of implying it wouldn't have been worth doing, but rather to look at it as a whole and add perspective to the earlier consideration of regretting what we aren't able to experience.

I was getting restless with living in small-town Northern Michigan and was ready for a change. I was at an age where a more progressive atmosphere suited me and I needed to be in a place where I could grow. The music that followed the toppling of the Berlin Wall and the fall of communism paralleled that of sixties-movement music and I found it to be a driving force in seeking what the world held. My goal was to go out east, but I wasn't sure exactly where. There were cities I enjoyed, but most of them were too small, like Rutland, Vermont and Manchester, New Hampshire.

I needed to live in a city large enough to be diverse, not necessarily ethnically, but in terms of holding my attention. I bought a wall map of the United States and a Rand McNally *Places Rated* survey. The survey listed the top metropolitan areas and ranked them in eight categories, the ones relevant to me were: jobs, cost of living, recreation, climate, and transportation. I studied the statistics for the cities I was interested in and narrowed the field down to ten. I taped the map on the wall in my spare bedroom and highlighted the ten cities. Every week I would make a list and rank the prospective cities from one to ten. Sometimes the order would change a little, but as time progressed I was getting an idea of where each city stood and had soon narrowed my list down to five: Burlington, Vermont; Provo, Utah; Orlando, Florida; Wilkes-Barre, Pennsylvania; and Rochester, New York. I had accrued five weeks of vacation time per year and had time to travel, and during a year and a half period I made eight trips to New York, Pennsylvania, and Vermont, but my findings never matched the image I had in my head—the image that I knew existed somewhere. Ultimately, and perhaps by default, I settled for Orlando. The selection process had taken a couple of years, but after receiving my bonus in March of '92 I was out the door and on the road. The idea conceived in Montreal had materialized. I found it easier than expected to say goodbye to my friends, which made me realize I was doing the right thing. Dale in particular had been a force in convincing me that it was a good move, and he'd been party to many a conversation about what was lacking in the small towns in which we lived and worked.

As it turned out, had I picked any of my other final four candidates I may still be there, but then again I wouldn't have made it here, and Petoskey has been instrumental in molding me into what I've become. Orlando, however, I found to be quite plastic. Most residents showed little interest in anything intellectual; they were more interested in hitting the beaches in the day and the high-energy dance clubs at night. The materialism of the eighties had dissipated on a national scale, but it still seemed prevalent in that part of Florida. Furthermore, the terrain was flat and bland, the grass had a polyethylene look to it and the water tasted like sulfur. Half the locals were rednecks who didn't like the transplants, and many of the transplants had aggressive, self-serving characteristics that left me with no desire to befriend them. The only people I felt comfortable around were black. One of them was James Brown. He was eight years younger than me and always wanted to race— and I would always beat him, which wasn't supposed to happen with me being white and all. Tony and I worked together and we both played a lot of basketball during the day, but never got around to playing together as he lived in Longwood and I lived in Sanford. There was a cashier who worked at the Winn Dixie whom I thought was cute. I guessed that we didn't have too much in common, but she was the epitome of a Southern Bell and I found that intriguing. She seemed shy and I was out of my element in Florida but after weeks of consideration I asked her out. We went to see *My Cousin Vinny* at the cineplex. It was one of the funniest movies I had seen and I laughed loudly, causing other patrons to turn and look at me while my date shrunk in her seat. I brought her home and told her that I had a good time—she told me to have a good night. I never went out with her again and after a week of casual greetings I felt uncomfortable shopping at Winn Dixie and found another super-market. The episode seemed to befit my whole Florida experience. Overall, living there wasn't what I thought it would be. The job I had taken was all encumbering and I didn't have free time to do much of anything. After six months I tried a different company, but my first shift went from a scheduled eight hours to fifteen. I hadn't found anyone to really hang out with and was bored much of the time. It was time to head north again.

Before leaving, though, I wanted to take advantage of what the state had to offer. On a couple of occasions I had heard early morning explosions and was told that it was from the space shuttle breaking the sound barrier. I realized that it wasn't much of a drive to Cape Canaveral and there happened to be a launching toward the end of the week. I went to a vantage point that wasn't part of The

Kennedy Space Center but where many people went to watch liftoffs. I listened to an AM station that was activated only in correspondence with NASA activity. It was chilling when they gave the final warning to pilots, telling them what the restricted area was and that anyone entering that area between such and such a time would be shot down without warning. It was a brilliant liftoff and a spectacular sight to behold. Greg came up from Fort Lauderdale before I left and we went to Epcot. When I first moved to Florida and before I found work I would take my van to Daytona Beach. I spent the night on the beach several times, until the time the high tide caught me off guard and I woke to the sound of water under my vehicle. Although I've never been much of a beach person, I had liked all the activity at Daytona. I made one last trip there and then I left Florida.

I took everything that would fit into my car. When I went down I had owned two vehicles—a car and a van—and I'd made two trips. By the time I left I had sold the van, so I had to make decisions about what would come with me and what would stay behind. We were only a month removed from Hurricane Andrew, so I sent many items of clothing to the relief effort. Outside of that I loaded my car with what was most important to me. I took I-95 and followed the coast up to New York, where once again I tried to set something up. Once again I came up empty. There have been few times in my life that I've felt as depressed as I did on that last night in New York. I had planned for two years for a successful relocation and it had fallen apart. I remember talking to Dale that night from my hotel room, and him trying to cheer me up but clumsily dancing around the word *failed*. I decided to return to Escanaba and regroup there, but as I was driving through Northern Michigan I recalled making day trips to Petoskey while living in St. Ignace. I had thought highly of the town and figured it would be worth a look. I imposed a time limit on myself; I had to find a job and an apartment in two days. I did, and Petoskey became home and still is to this day.

Petoskey was a cultural oasis compared to Florida and my interest

139

for things different than what I had been exposed to grew. It was set beautifully on Little Traverse Bay, upon which the land made a horseshoe, culminating in the city of Harbor Springs being in direct view across the lake. There were rolling hills, an ample number of parks, art galleries, lavish developments, and historical districts, as well as an abundance of tourists which provided a steady infusion of new people with new stories and experiences which kept the city from ever approaching a stagnant status. Many of the locals had a Bohemian air about them, something that was lacking in Florida, and after traveling around the country I found myself feeling at home a mere forty miles from where I began my search.

I had arrived in Petoskey just before Labor Day weekend. Up the road some forty miles was Mackinaw City and every year they had the Labor Day Bridge Walk, the only day of the year that people could walk the five-mile span of the Mackinac Bridge. 1992 was an election year and President George Bush would be making a short campaign speech on the St. Ignace side and then walking the bridge with Governor Engler. I left Petoskey at five-thirty in the morning so I could get a good spot to observe the speech. Still, I had a hundred or so people in front of me. Even though it was cool to hear the President of the United States speaking in a town where I used to live, I could barely see the top of his head. Only the profoundly white-haired head of the first lady, Barbara, did I see clearly. When the speech was over, though, and we all headed for the bridge, the athlete in me came out and I dashed and weaved and got as close as the barrier rope held by National Guardsmen walking side by side, separating us common folk from the dignitaries. Beyond the rope were Secret Service agents. 353 feet above us atop the towers were sharpshooters. They were also atop the tollbooths and in boats on both the Lake Huron and Lake Michigan side of the bridge. At one point a youngster whom I'd guess to be fifteen ran under the rope and was corralled by the Secret Service agents. They escorted him back and told him not to try it again. When he did anyway, I got a stark understanding of how serious the job of protecting the president is as they told the youngster,

"If you do it again we *will* shoot you!" The bridge authority had opened up the two northbound lanes for southbound pedestrian traffic, leaving the southbound lanes open for two-way traffic, the lane closest to us heading north and the other heading south. From where I was I could see the president quite clearly, and about half-way through this five-mile walk I found it interesting to observe the faces of the passengers as they passed the president, as I was only about twenty yards behind him. You could tell that some of them were aware of what was going on, but I got a kick out of those who obviously didn't. I could imagine them driving from some point in Ohio or Indiana and crossing this bridge in the middle of nowhere, wondering why there were 70,000 people conjugating in such an obscure location, curiously looking out the window as they drove by at ten miles per hour, only to see the President of the United States. To take things full circle, Mr. Bush had begun the traditional Labor Day campaign push in the small town of St. Ignace, Michigan, and would end up losing the election to Bill Clinton largely because of six words he had uttered on his '88 campaign, "Read my lips. No new taxes."

I quickly became attached to my new town. Its culture seemed to transcend geography. It was refined and genteel, and had many events and activities for a city of six thousand. On summer Tuesdays and Fridays they have afternoon concerts at the gazebo in Pennsylvania Park which feature an eclectic list of performers: jazz quartets, folk soloists, brass ensembles, locally established rock and roll bands, and an occasional country performer. The concerts are a community event and draw people of all ages. Some people sit on the benches parked in front of the gazebo, others play Frisbee or sit on picnic tables with their lunches or ice cream cones, and parents flank their youngsters as they frolic along the railroad track that runs diagonally through the park. The environment inspired the creative side of me; a side that was influenced by my mother but left dormant for nearly twenty years. I developed a taste for World music, and particularly the haunting sounds of Eastern European gypsy rhapsodies. They took me back to a different time, a time that neither I nor anyone who had been alive in my lifetime had experienced firsthand, but one I could imagine vividly, and I came to love classical music as I came to love the concept of life in Old Europe. I can picture the sound of a harpsichord emanating onto the streets of Warsaw from a half-opened window, a young Chopin playing in the bottom floor, his sight level with the feet of passing pedestrians. I found inspiration in all these melodies that were new to me and my desire to travel Europe was stronger than ever. I contemplated the trip. My fear of flying was intense and going by ship was about eight times the cost of flying. In early '94 Greg told me that he was going to Germany to stay with his fiancée's brother for a week. I told him that I could probably do the flight if I went with him. We took off from Miami International on May 1st. I put my fears and superstitions aside and flew over the Bermuda Triangle on May Day. Greg had changed his plans when I confirmed I'd be going along and we flew into DeGaulle in Paris. As we neared the continent I looked at the computerized map that showed the plane's position in relation to the globe and I felt the imminence of landing on foreign soil. Soon multicolored fields of France were in sight and from there it was no time before I felt the wheels hit the runway. I was realizing a dream I thought I'd never achieve. I was in Europe.

We took the Metro and headed for the train station, where we would take the train to Brussels. I felt the reality of experiencing Europe in the same way of the people I had previously envied whenever I heard their stories. As we headed toward downtown Paris I observed the graffiti on white painted walls, which made it seem like I was going through New York instead of *The City of Light*. But there was a European cosmopolitanism amongst the passengers on the Metro that offset that perception and brought me back to the newness in which I was immersed. The initial glimpse of downtown Paris brought Europe to my soul, but Paris would be seen on the backside of the trip and we boarded the Eurail and were soon on our way to Belgium. The landscape between Paris and Brussels was much like that of Northern Michigan which made the ride mundane, or at least anticlimactic. Yet I looked forward to getting into Belgium. Just as I had begun counting the different states I visited when I was young, I now wanted to see how many countries I could see. Before long the train was slowing and we were in Brussels. The station we chose to get off at was in the Turkish part of the city, which offered a perspective of its own. Here I saw things that were unique to the Muslim culture. After getting a taste, we made our way out of the Turkish district and into the heart of Brussels, but we didn't have a lot of time and after four hours we were off again and heading toward Germany. It was evening when we departed and the faint lighting cast long shadows, making the continent seem even more Old World. The people on the train were cool. There was a group of soccer fans and we hung around with them in the hall for a while before settling into our seats. We changed trains early Sunday morning in Hannover. There was a restaurant in the terminal and a German breakfast sounded good. It was there we first encountered the strange apricot tasting drink for the first time. We had earlier noticed how tall the Germans were, and with that in mind we dubbed this drink *vitamin fortified euro-juice.* Greg and I had the same breakfast, but for whatever reason his cost twenty-two Deutchmarks while mine had cost eleven. We took a short walk to a statue of a war hero on a horse. (I hadn't paid attention to who it was.) The wind whipped bitterly cold for May first and I hoped it wasn't a precursor of what was in store for us. We boarded the next train and soon were riding the rails again. I elbowed Greg awake as we pulled into Göttingen, Germany, where he would stay while I'd continue my tour of Europe by rail. I hurriedly told him to have a good time and said I'd catch up with him in four days as he scrambled to gather his gear and get off the train. I fell asleep shortly after we pulled out of the station and awoke an hour or so later to the eerie sight of a fog-cloaked Nuremberg at dawn. Visions of the Nazi industrial complex filled my mind, and suddenly it was very clear that I was alone and very far from home. I would experience that far-from-home feeling the next morning at the hotel in Munich as the restaurant waitress tried to translate the menu to English and said, "Und ve take little creatures from zee sea and ve chop them up and ve put zhem in your eggs." Unfortunately, these little creatures did not sound appetizing and I had French fries for breakfast.

After I ate I went onto the streets to have a look around. I recall observing a dog and thinking how he didn't know that he was in Germany or if he was in France or Spain or America; he was just a dog. It reminded me of a picture I'd seen back in America that appeared to be from the early nineteen-hundreds. It was of a small boy holding a fish he had caught. He was dressed in tights and ankle-high button shoes and wore a big straw hat. I recall thinking how his attire dated him but how the fish looked the same as it would now, or as it would have looked when the Romans were invading The Holy Land. And the fish has no philosophy or prejudice to abide by, so its five-hundred year old ancestor would not only look but act exactly the same as would its relative born five-hundred years from now. I continued to observe the dog as I contemplated my itinerary.

I went into Austria and toured Salzburg, the beautifully old city where *The Sound Of Music* was filmed. I recall sitting on a bench in a piazza, trying to engage a girl in conversation. She seemed to be put off by me and responded to my questions with one word answers. After a few minutes she asked what part of England I was from, to which I replied that I was American and not British. Suddenly I had her undivided attention and she began to ask me many questions. I tried to be interactive with Europeans whenever I could and it was gratifying on each occasion. From the piazza I roamed around for several hours, had an Italian meal before leaving Austria, then went into Italy. My original goal was to see the Côte d' Azur, but I decided to change plans when the trains quit running at one in the morning at Bern, Switzerland, foiling my intention of traveling through the night. I went to a hotel near the depot but the rooms were two hundred twenty-five dollars American. Another European tourist told me of a cheap hotel down one of the side streets, but when he became overly adamant that I follow him I grew leery. I told him I was good and he angrily went off alone, and from his temperament I felt my hunch had been correct and that he was looking for homosexual sex. I decided to wait at the station until I could board my six a.m. train. My luggage was too large for the lockers so I had to carry it with me. I looked down the corridor and saw a maniac drop-kicking the temporary wall of a shop under renovation. He saw me watching him and came up to me, showed me his ring, which had spikes protruding from it, then took a swing at me with that hand. He was stupid and I wanted to floor him but I recalled the movie *Midnight Express* where an American got incarcerated in a Turkish prison, and decided that hitting anyone on foreign soil wasn't a good decision. He took off his sunglasses and put them on upside-down, made some unintelligible noise, then noticed two cops with police dogs which immediately and instinctively went off on him. The cops yanked heavily on the leashes of the enraged canines as the maniac bent down and got face to face with the dogs, barking back at them before running back down the corridor. I climbed the stairs to the upper level, only to see a bag lady urinating on the floor. Whores were soliciting me and I was getting bored with walking around. Furthermore, the temperature was dropping as the night progressed and the cold air flowed freely through the large arching entrances. About halfway through the night I met a German girl named Hannah who had a dog named Luther. She, too, was waiting for a six o'clock train, although to a different destination, and we hung together until our trains arrived. I was tired from staying up all night, and as I alluded to, I had changed my mind about going to the French Riviera. I decided to take the train to the first town in Italy, get out and look around for an hour or so, just to be able to say that I had been to Italy, then head back toward Munich. The trip through Switzerland was beautiful, especially as we rolled past the rolling hills of Lago Maggiore, which to this day is the most splendid place I have beheld on this earth. (I would later use that setting for one of my short stories in the book *Fictional Numbers*.) We crossed the border into Italy. Apparently Italian customs was putting a big emphasis on keeping Tylenol out of the country, as they questioned me for ten minutes on why I had it and what I intended to do with it. Eventually I convinced them that it was for headaches and assured them that if I got one I would be careful in taking the medicine, and we were on route again. However, when I got to that first town I found they only had one train go through each day, so I rerouted myself over to Milan and then to Verona, with a three and four hour layover in each city. I tried to eat in Verona but the food at the station was dry and the water tasted like Alka-Seltzer. By three in the afternoon I was very tired and took a compartment where I thought I could get some shuteye. In keeping with my luck of the past day, an Italian businessman took the seat across from me and smelled so bad that it was unpleasant to breathe, ergo, I couldn't sleep. I headed back to coach. When I had toured Salzburg I had begun that morning by checking out of the Best Western in Munich, and I ended this touring loop in the same hotel thirty-six hours later without having slept for one minute.

I liked Germany more than Italy and it felt good to regroup. I caught up on sleep and spent most of the next morning in laying back. I went to the depot across the street from the hotel and had breakfast at Burger King, a breakfast which of course included vitamin fortified euro-juice. I bought an American paper at the newsstand and learned that my Red Wings had lost their playoff series two days earlier to a inferior San Jose team. I casually strolled through the shops of the terminal until just before noon, when it was time to check out of the hotel and make my way back toward Göttingen and reunite with Greg. I made it there around six that evening. However, his fiancée's brother didn't have room for me, so we hung out for a while and explored the town, then I took a room at a hotel. That evening I did some walking on my own down a wooded path, not so much to any place in particular, but to wherever the path took me. The trip was nearing an end and it was a time for reflection. It was there that I seemed to see Europe at its purest, for I wasn't so much a tourist at that point as a man utilizing a walk as a catalyst for thought.

146

I was restless that night at the hotel. I wanted to send out some postcards before I left Europe and I remembered seeing some for sale on the front desk and went to get a few, but when I stepped into the hallway the lights were out, as though I was staying at someone's house and they had all gone to bed. I felt my way down the stairs and snagged a few anyway, thinking that I could pay for them in the morning. When time for checkout came I tried to explain to the girl what I'd done, but with her lack of English and the little German I spoke there was irreconcilable confusion. I left the money on the counter for the cards I had taken, but every time I turned to leave she would say, "Sir, your postcards," and then, "Sir, you forget postcards again." Obviously she thought I was stupid, so to simplify things I took more postcards. It reminded me of the "little creatures from the sea" episode. I hooked back up with Greg and after a breakfast and one last glass of vitamin fortified euro-juice we were on our way to Geneva, Switzerland. We changed trains again in Heidelberg, Germany and had time to roam around. Looking back, I found Heidelberg to be as interesting as Paris or Brussels, and in general I found Europe at its purest in places visited without burden of expectations.

Geneva was cool at night, in fact it was the only time I experienced European night life. It's funny how universal things are when you get past your preconceptions and see things for what they are. In the Geneva night I saw well-dressed couples out together, guys hitting on girls, friends hanging out together, and the misfits who tried hard to be cool but only looked uncomfortable; nothing unlike Chicago or Omaha or Petoskey, or the similar observation I'd made on Mackinac Island. We took a look around Geneva the next day. It was interesting in some aspects, but unfortunately I had expected more from the city. I guess if it'd been one of those places I hadn't heard of I wouldn't have been disappointed, but in the end it didn't live up to the hype bestowed upon it. My outlook was positive, though, and we headed for Paris.

Going through the Burgundy Valley was inspiring. Off in the distance in the middle of nowhere was a castle, one of many I'd seen on this trip but have yet to mention. These castles reminded me of just how old Europe is compared to America. Yes, we do have ancient Aztec ruins and other archeological sites that probably outdate some of these edifices, but because I'm of European decent I get a sense of my own history in observing these structures and I wonder what Feudalistic role my ancestors played. We rolled into Paris just before five. We only had four hours of daylight and it would be our only night in the city, so the rest of the evening was a scurry. We made a quick hotel check-in and went to find the bus that went to the Eiffel Tower. It was at that point that the rudeness in which the French are so generally viewed became a reality. We were standing in line where the passengers for bus 61 got off, and the dumb bastard driving the bus said, "You can't get on here!" I didn't know what was going on and assumed we had the wrong bus. I said, "Shit," to which he said in his snotty little girly accent, "That's right... sheet!" The moron got back behind the wheel, literally pulled ahead twenty yards from where we were, stuck his head out and said, "Okay, you can get on now." We would see that same rudeness later in the evening when a waiter at a sidewalk cafe snorted and threw down the menu when we told him we weren't ready to order. In the end, though, the bus got us to a stop near Eiffel Tower, we got our meal at the restaurant, and the quintessential nature of the two characters gave us fodder for laughs. It was Greg's idea to get off the bus a few blocks away from the Eiffel Tower. It was a majestic sight that deserved proper viewing; that is, to be seen from an approach. When we got to the tower my claustrophobia kicked in and I told Greg to go up and that I'd wait at the base, to which he said, "So you're telling me that you travel three-thousand miles, get to the foot of one of The Seven Wonders of the World and that you're not going up? That's just stupid!" I knew I didn't have an argument and I joined him in the elevator. From the top of the tower I saw the complexity of the structure of Paris and pinpointed many of the city's famed landmarks. I thought about The Seven Wonders and was glad that Greg had prodded me into making the ascension, even if under the threat of embarrassment. With the tower toured, a boat ride down the Seine seemed obligatory. The Eiffel Tower had been spectacular in stature and fame, but it was floating down the river where I took in the true feel of the city. The bank to our left was an event in-and-of itself and reminded me of Bourbon Street in New Orleans, with jugglers, poets, and musicians. To the other side were buildings like Notre Dame and The Louvre. Furthermore, everyone on the boat seemed to hold the city in the same reverence as us, which formed an unspoken bond amongst the passengers. The last thing we'd have time for was a stroll down the Champs Elysees to the Arc de Triomphe. If the Eiffel Tower was spectacular and the ride down the Seine was inspirational, I would characterize the Champs Elysees as regal. And so it was. I was standing in the middle of the arch built by Napoleon, realizing my vacation was essentially over as soon as I turned from it. I looked up at the stars that were coming into view with the onset of nightfall. As I gazed upward I experienced a realization that perhaps I was standing on the same ground where Napoleon once stood and was seeing the same sky as him. I began to reflect. I had seen the Alps and fabled cities, history and the realization of a goal. The first three hours of the trip were just about perfect and had set the tone for the vacation of a lifetime. I had done something I had always wanted to do, and now it was time to go back to the states and my new town to see where life would take me from there.

As often happens, one goes from the dramatic to the ordinary and conforms to the latter without thought or recognition, and so it was with me when I got back to Michigan. As inspiring as the trip had been, there I was once again putting vegetables on the shelf, sorting through them one by one and culling out the ones that were inferior. Perhaps that's the way it should be; one wouldn't enjoy the magnificent if not for the mundane. I picked up where I'd left off as far as my interests were concerned. Tourist season was around the corner and with it came an influx of new faces: the vacationers, the seasonal residents, and the Mexican, Jamaican, and Lithuanian workers who annually came into Petoskey in the summertime. It was going to be my second summer here, and as a kid enjoys the second Christmas he or she is old enough to comprehend more than the first, so it was with me going into my second tourist season. After a long and grueling winter (I had parked my car and canceled the insurance from January to May to save money for the trip to Europe) I was ready to get out and have some fun. I got the car fixed and reinstated the insurance, lubed the wheels on the rollerblades, and aired up the basketball.

The first time on the basketball courts of Petoskey I noticed how the recent wave of poor sportsmanship in the NBA was creeping into small town America. Kids on the court next to me were trash-talking, boasting how much better they were than their opponent and what they were going to do to them next time down the court. It had always irked me to see those multimillionaires in professional sports barking and beating their chest, seeing that I had grown up in an era where the players were still gentlemen. Coaches didn't throw chairs and players didn't choke coaches, and in football no one gathered in end zones for choreographed dances. Now I was seeing the influence of modern professional sports come into our neighborhood. That and other social influences of the time had proliferated itself into a poor work ethic and a lack of respect for elders amongst some of the teenagers of the nineties. I recall experiencing it while walking the streets of Bar Harbor, Maine. Bar Harbor is quite similar to Petoskey, and in fact there was a local shop that had an outlet in Bar Harbor. As I strolled the street I saw the runner on the window: Bar Harbor... Charlevoix... Harbor Springs... Petoskey... Saugatuck. I was so used to seeing these names that I walked several more paces before it hit me that I wasn't in Michigan. I turned back and went into the shop. There was a kid of perhaps eighteen sitting behind the counter and I with a smile I told him where I was from. With a disinterested look he replied, "So, like can I help you with anything?" But to be fair, I think every generation looks at the following one as degenerate, at least to some extent. We were looked upon that way in the era of the great generation gap, with our frumpy attire, long hair, and long-haired music, as my dad used to call it. They detested the sexual revolution and deplored the fact that we were unraveling the culture they had woven. With this in mind I tried not to criticize these youngsters even though I felt the same disinterest toward their culture as that which was bestowed upon mine. And to again use a full circle analogy, I believe these kids will mature into adults who will experience the same sentiments toward the youngsters of the next generation.

The nineties produced the third of my all-time favorite movies, *Shawshank Redemption*, which had the best story line of the three. I loved *The Big Chill* for sentimental reasons, and truth be told, had I first watched *The Sting* at the age of twenty instead of fourteen I would've foreseen the scam and not been elated when Newman and Redford began to rise and smile after they had apparently shot one another. But *Shawshank* was a genuinely well written film that kept me interested from the beginning to its gratifying conclusion. There were many other movies that I have enjoyed throughout the years: *The Godfather, Jesus Christ Superstar, To Sir With Love, Close Encounters of the Third Kind,* and later, *1969* and *Deep Impact* to name a few, but the three I've singled out are above the rest and not one can I place above either of the other two. Also, I've come to enjoy Steve Martin as an actor, especially when he plays a serious role, like in his portrayal of a lamenting dad in *Father Of The Bride*. There's a part toward the end of the film that chokes me up every time. It's the night before the wedding and he can't sleep. He hears his daughter shooting baskets in the driveway and he goes out to join her. As they're talking it begins to snow—the first snow in Los Angeles in years—and his face turns serious. His daughter asks what's wrong, then guesses his look stems from thinking that the snowfall will make the wedding even more expensive. But while looking into her innocent eyes with the white flakes falling gently onto her hair, he says his expression comes from knowing the moment will be one he'll never forget. I see myself in his role, as I'm at an age where I'd be giving away a daughter had I had one, and I appreciate the emotion a father would feel. There are so many great moments that come to us through film, so many scenes that make us think or remember or laugh, and I believe that a good film holds the possibility to let us realize what we want from life and in turn, if we act upon the sentiment, make us better people.

One never knows when they're at the halfway point of their life, but by the mid-nineties I knew I was at least nearing mine. Whenever one thinks such a thought a self-evaluation seems to follow, and so it was with me. I looked at my accomplishments and noted my travels. I critiqued myself on where I'd fallen short of my expectations, most notably becoming a father. Overall though, things were going well for the country and myself. I was at the height of my professional career and I had found a town in which I felt comfortable. With the images from Europe forever stapled to my memory, my list of goals had moved from the fringes to the center and I was becoming less of a gypsy and more of a traditionalist.

CHAPTER NINE

I'm constantly amazed by the vastness of our nation. There have been many songs written about the glorious wonders we have from sea to sea, but we sing the lyrics and hum the tunes the way we recite *The Pledge of Allegiance,* without appreciating that which inspired the words. To live in a country with natural wonders such as Yosemite, The Grand Canyon, The Badlands, Mammoth Caves, and The Petrified Forest is special in its own right, but it might be the lesser wonders that make this such a great land to travel. I'm referring to the magnificent sights one never hears of until he stumbles upon them. I was driving through upstate New York, for instance, when I saw a pull-off alongside the road. People were taking a trail from the side of the road to a small bridge that crossed the highway. I decided to park and check it out for myself. Upon getting to the bridge I found there was a distance of 150 some feet, if I remember correctly, between the road and the river below, and upstream was and old hydroelectric plant whose buildings lined the upper bank of the stream while maintaining the aestheticism that nature had bequeathed. I've found that every state, be it Nebraska or New Jersey, California or Michigan, has something to offer. I remember sitting at the base of The Gateway Arch at two in the morning, gazing up at the stars through the loop of the edifice. I had been there earlier in the day and it was teeming with sightseers, but at this later time, even though this structure was world famous, I had it all to myself. During the course of our lifetimes we accrue places we call our own. As children we are only familiar with our hometowns and we establish sites within them that are unique to us, such as The Jungle Tree of my youth and Horseshoe Hill in my teen years. As we age, the territory in which we're knowledgeable expands through the familiarity brought about by frequency of visits. For example, if we're traveling football fans, we may become nearly as familiar with other Big Ten campuses as we are with the two in Michigan. I have now been to Niagara Falls ten times, so when I go there I know beforehand what I'll gain from the visit and I proceed directly to my favorite post. I have been fortunate enough that I can say the same for most U.S. cities. Consequently the nation becomes more of my own. Then we can sit back in our old age, and like when we were children, we can once again be embedded in our hometowns, content with the memories of where we've been.

With Europe behind me, so was my urgency to travel. I had seen most of what I wanted to see and I was the prime age for moving up the business ladder. Clinton was doing a good job with the economy and things seemed to be in place for me. I was in middle management with a company that was lacking high-caliber personnel in corporate positions. For my age, I had more experience and diverse training than most and I was loaded with confidence. I was paying a social price for the ambitions I had, I worked a lot of hours and didn't get out much, but it all seemed to fit that mid thirty-something mold. I would satisfy myself on occasion in nights of indiscretion with one of the cashiers, and later would have a relationship with one of the other girls I worked with. That would last a couple of years, but we really had nothing in common except for the need for companionship, and eventually the lack of common interests put us back on the separate paths that we had been on before we met. I remember the last memorable moment we experienced together. We were coming back from Maryland when we witnessed a midnight rainbow served up by a break in the storm clouds and a full moon. It was a phenomenal thing to see. But even as we were returning from our vacation I could sense things were coming to an end; hence, I knew this rare and spectacular sight we were beholding wouldn't get its proper due. I wish that it could be recalled with someone from time to time as the years pass. There's fulfillment in sharing significant moments with someone you know will be there for the rest of your life. The lessons I learned were that the need for companionship can sometimes disguise itself as love, and our desires can blind us from the obvious drawbacks that our friends can see but we can not. Ironically, as we abandoned that relationship because we weren't in love, I fell into a place where I didn't want love and I cherished my individualism and freedom more than ever before.

It was in those years that I experienced another musical revival. I had always appreciated Bob Dylan for his lyricism, but he hadn't had a big role in the resurgence I'd experienced fifteen years prior. The only albums of his that I owned were compilations of songs I had already known and it wasn't until I bought *Highway 61 Revisited* that I respected Dylan for the genius that he was. I would listen to *Desolation Row* over and over again, which was something in-and-of itself as the cut was over eleven minutes long. I had never heard such word imagery before, exemplified in such ways as taking modern day peasants and giving them names of the historically significant. From the Spanish style guitar work to the brilliant lyrics the song captivated me like none other, with the possible exception of *Dear Prudence*. Here are a few samples; they are sequential but not continuous:

Cinderella she seems so easy, it takes one to know one, she smiles,
And puts her hands in her back pockets, Betty Davis style.
And in comes Romeo, he's moaning, you belong to me, I believe
And someone says, you're in the wrong place my friend, you'd better leave.
And the only sound that's left, after the ambulances go
Is Cinderella sweeping up on Desolation Row.

They are spoon-feeding Casanova to get him to feel more assured
Then they'll kill him with self-confidence after poisoning him with words.
And the phantom's shouting to skinny girls, Get out of here if you don't know
Casanova is just being punished for going to Desolation Row.

Praise be to widows Neptune, The Titanic sails at dawn
Everybody's shouting, which side are you on?
And Erza Pound and T.S. Eliot are fighting in the captain's tower
While calypso singers laugh at them and fishermen throw flowers.

As it would turn out, nobody would have more influence on me as a writer, not Hemingway, not Hugo, and not Steinbeck.

By the mid-nineties music had become more situational for me and remains so to this day. For instance, if I'm driving down Woodward Avenue I find a Motown station. I like The Beatles in the spring, Jefferson Airplane and The Doors in the summer, Simon & Garfunkel in the fall, and The Moody Blues on rainy days. I always bring Crosby, Stills & Nash to Blissfest and listen to *You Don't Have To Cry* on Saturday morning when I rise, and every year on the anniversary of my dad's birth I listen to *Curtains* off the *Captain Fantastic* album and think commemoratively of him with the lyrics, "Cultivate the freshest flower this garden ever grew." *Exile On Main St.* has a late night New York City underground sound to it that fits periods of creativity.

Meanwhile, I noticed that the offspring of our baby boomer generation was coming of age and I witnessed that we had delivered an unprecedented influence. It would have been inconceivable to think of us as eighteen year-olds dressed in knit pants and wearing fedoras while listening to the music of our parents, such as The Ink Spots or Tommy Dorsey. In fact it wasn't until I was in my early forties that I bought a Bert Bacharach CD. But the children who came of age in the mid to late nineties were mirror images of what we once were. These eighteen to twenty year-olds could tell you more about The Beatles or Dylan than someone ten years older than them. They grew out their hair and dressed in loud, frumpy clothes and spoke with sixties phraseology. (The only discernible differences were that our tie-dyed shirts were done by hand with dyes, rubber bands, and strings, while theirs were factory fabricated, and that the word *groovy* had disappeared from the lexicon.) It was a resurgence for me as well, and there was a vicariousness in observing the long-gone image of my younger self through them. I hadn't been enamored with the culture amongst young people over the prior decade, with their idolatry of what I considered to be pointless noise-making bands like Megadeth and Motley Crew and the plastic-wrapped sound of Madonna, and it seemed good to see a resumption of what was more grounded and earthy. Beatles' music was being heard everywhere again, but with it there was a dynamic that hadn't been in play in the sixties, stemming from the fact that more was known about the band members as individuals. While they were current they were simply The Beatles to us; a great band comprised of four vibrant personalities. But with this second wave of popularity people began to identify themselves with leanings toward John or Paul; something that I don't remember being prevalent when the group was together. In the sixties the music they produced was generally thought of as Lennon/McCartney songs, a joint and equal collaboration as stated on each record label. It wasn't until we grew older that we learned about the agreement they had where songs would be credited that way, but in fact many if not most of their songs were predominantly written by either one or the other, usually the one who sang lead, with only tweaks and suggestions by the other. Looking at it now we can see how each song had the unmistakable fingerprint of its author. *Yesterday,* for example, was melodic and refined, and John Lennon had no more of a role in its making than Pete Best. Conversely, edgy songs like *I Am The Walrus* and *Tomorrow Never Knows* were clearly John's. By the nineties this wider knowledge of these two unique personalities offered a litmus test of one's musical tastes and we often considered ourselves more inspired by one than the other. To be clear, everyone agreed that The Beatles wouldn't have been what they were without both and indeed all four members, but if we had been influenced in some way by the band, as most people on the planet had, then, for a diehard Beatles fan, finding whether your main source of that inspiration was John or Paul became nearly as necessary as finding out the origin of your ancestors.

After the breakup of the band Paul had more success as a solo artist than John, and with that, an opinion regarding the need of balance provided by a writing partner. I believe that John Lennon needed Paul McCartney more than Paul McCartney needed John Lennon, but The Beatles needed John Lennon more than they needed Paul McCartney. Keep in mind that the proposed paradox is subjective and of course I'm talking micro-measurements, and again, the band obviously needed both individuals. As a solo artist John did write some brilliant songs such as *Imagine, Working Class Hero,* and *Happy Christmas War Is Over,* but he also had some material that needed those tweaks from Paul to keep from fringing out too far. In The Beatles, however, I believe that John's creative edge was more important than Paul's melodic brilliance. I say this because perhaps the most remarkable thing about the group was that they were always one step ahead of everyone else, and I attribute much of that to John's experimentation in both sound and lyrics. (George Martin as well played a huge role in keeping The Beatles progressive.)

The more time passed the more ordinary the ex-Beatles became. When *Imagine, Another Day, My Sweet Lord,* and *It Don't Come Easy* came out they sounded like they could have been Beatle songs, but by 1997 when Paul came out with *Flaming Pie* it was obvious that the freakish superstardom had passed him. I say this because the songs were good, but something about them wasn't the same—something that I couldn't identify until I heard Paul himself broach the subject, saying that he felt that they were great songs, but as far as the public was concerned, they weren't Beatle songs.

Just as some from our generation chose to keep listening to Johnnie Ray or Bobby Vee instead of The Beatles and The Doors, not all of the young people had followed in our musical footsteps but instead listened to rap, hip-hop, and high energy dance music. I try not to be judgmental toward the younger generation. Part of this is because I went through the criticism that our generation received over hair length and choice of music. Still I grumble to myself when hear the sound of heavy thumping bass that can picked up three blocks from an approaching vehicle even when the windows are up. At the risk of sounding old I wonder how it can be enjoyable to listen to something that has everything on the car rattling. Having said all this, there are four songs that still prompt me to turn up the bass level whenever they come on: *Spirit In The Sky* by Norman Greenbaum, *Carry On* by Crosby, Stills, Nash & Young, *Rock On* by David Essex, and *Lucky Man* by Emerson, Lake & Palmer. Granted, I don't take it up to window-rattling proportions, but when I listen to these songs my awareness rises and I become a shade more tolerant of the youngsters.

My Aunt Gen had received my mother's accordion after she passed away. When Gen died it came back to me. I tried fiddling with it but couldn't make sense of the cord keys. One summer Tuesday I went to a concert in the park, which happened to feature a polka band. I dug the sound and watching the fun everyone was having and it inspired me enough to give the accordion another try. With the discovery of the indented key I was able to find a basic three-cord progression, and then another. With that I was able to play ten or so songs. During those days Aunt Irene's health was declining and I'm glad to say I was able to make it back to Manistique and play a couple of songs for her. She was too weak to respond much, but I know she enjoyed hearing me play my mother's instrument. She passed away in January of '96. She had been high on the list of my personal *1000 Points of Light* and my memories of her will forever be fond. With her death I had lost most of my Gorsche aunts and uncles. Uncle Ferd had died when I was a boy. Uncle Lou died of a heart attack shortly after I'd seen him at the cottage. Uncle Seb, with whom I played many a game of cribbage, had passed as well. Also gone were Uncle Pete Gorsche, Uncle Lawrence and Aunt Luella, and Uncle Francis. Within another five years we would lose Aunt Dorothy, who had been married to Uncle Ferd, and Uncle Pete Berger. The same was true for the LaMarche side; the only ones I have left are Aunt Betty and Uncle Phil.

In '96 I bought my first new car and took an apartment in a historical district with a view of Lake Michigan. My new residence was in a neighborhood of stately homes, and unbeknownst to me I was living across the street from the nephew of Ernest Hemingway. (I wouldn't learn his relationship to the famous writer for nine years.) There were more cardinals than robins in the tree outside my bedroom window and I seldom spotted a mosquito, a popular nemesis in other Michigan towns in which I had lived. I was two blocks away from downtown and Pennsylvania Park, and two blocks in the other direction from Sunset Park. I began to experience the Bohemian side of Petoskey, as I was in the heart of the artistic district, and this new setting would further stir my creative side. On Friday and Saturday nights I'd sit in the same bar where Ernest Hemingway sat, listening to live bands and not knowing at the time that I'd soon be in the same profession as him. One difference was that when he frequented that bar there were no live bands, but instead the establishment served as a speakeasy. Also, even though he went in the days of prohibition there would usually be something in his coffee, as a local Hemingway historian told me. I had quit drinking the year before which made for another distinction between the lives we led. Still, we both socialized in the same setting and I find that to be rather cool. (Though I justify it to now be over ten years since I quit drinking, I'll still have a bottle of champagne on New Year's Eve, a Guiness or green domestic on St. Patrick's Day, and perhaps a few drinks on either Mardi Gras or Cinco de Mayo.)

Past the backyard of the building where I live is a small downgrade and beyond the bottom of the hill is Penn Plaza Park, a space open to the public beyond the old train depot that has been converted into a strip office complex. The park is quite scenic, with the lake to the front, the old railroad lines to the rear, and lush green grass and shade trees all around. On summer Sunday mornings a group of five women and one instructor do yoga and I find it intriguing enough to watch them for long intervals. One girl is better than the instructor; her lines are perfect and she is as steady and unwavering as a Soviet-Block gymnast. She is strong and has the look of someone who could bear a child in the morning and be to work at the factory for her afternoon shift. Three of the other girls are very good, although the instructor will go around and adjust their body parts, posturing their legs and arms into the proper positions. The fifth girl interests me the most. She isn't as good as the other girls and doesn't seem to care to be the best, although I can tell that she tries to do things correctly. She doesn't keep her body rock-solid still like the others and often looks around as if her curiosity for the world around her preempts the importance of the exercise. She gives eighty-five percent whereas the others give one hundred. I believe that eighty-five percent can be a good lesson for many of us. Obviously there are exceptions—if a doctor is removing my spleen I hope he'll give one hundred—but I see people who are so one dimensional that they quickly become a bore to anyone who doesn't live in the same realm of interest. Going back to a comparison between the first and fifth girl, I can imagine the first one going home after the session is completed and thinking about the class, anticipating the next one, and working on her positions throughout the week, while the fifth girl was already antsy to move onto the next activity of the day before the session ended. I liken myself to her; when I was a boy my dad had many times asked, "Can't you sit still for one minute?" The answer was no and although my curiosity is now tempered with age, I still have a restless heart and I feel for people who don't have the desire to experience every possible thing.

I first gained knowledge of what would be my second biggest life-changing event on May 18th, 1999, when the company I was working for informed me that they would accept my letter of resignation effective on June eleventh of the same year. To set this up, I must backtrack. I held the position of grocery manager, and due to an inability to hire a sufficient number of capable workers, I was overwhelmed. A year earlier I had begun to experience some chest pains and was concerned about my health, and when corporate wanted to add untraditional responsibilities to my position I turned in a letter of resignation. The situation was resolved by the store manager, though, and he said not to worry about these new pressures; he would find a way to divert them from me. So he didn't accept my resignation, but the letter had already gone into corporate and that set the groundwork for what would happen one year later.

We were having some problems at the store with workers being treated unfairly, and when the girl I'd been seeing was dismissed, I'd had enough. Earlier, I had been a member of the Teamsters for nearly ten years, and I gave them a call in regards to organizing in our store. When I talked to another employee about this he informed me that they had already contacted another union and that their efforts were already a couple months in the works. He encouraged me to join their movement instead, so I did. Not long after that corporate got wind of what was happening and sent a mole to one of our meetings. Now they knew all who were involved. A short while later I got the letter. I did not accept their acceptance of my resignation and told the corporate representative that the letter was no longer valid and applicable, but he said, "It doesn't matter, we accept it anyway." And with that I knew with whom I was dealing. I continued to schedule myself beyond the June eleventh date that they had set for my departure, only to find my name crossed out, but I wanted it made clear that I wasn't leaving on my own volition. When June eleventh came I was told I would not have a job beyond that day. At the end of my shift I made rounds to say farewell to my coworkers. The district manager was there and he came and told me that I had to leave and that I would no longer be welcome on company property. So I left, but I had covered my bases. It was a federal crime to fire someone for participating in the formation of a union and I had them dead to rights. Their contention was that I left of my own will, and with my initial letter the implication had to be that they would have known I'd be leaving for a year, had their contention been sincere. But there were many flaws in their case, the main one being that they made no attempt at training anyone to take my position. Also, there had been a food safety program which corporate required management to attend. It was a costly program and I completed it about a month before I got the letter. The sentencing question is why would they pay me to take this course and then send me to take my certification if they had know I was leaving. I called the human resources director, and under the guise of being interested in the extended health insurance program, I said, "You probably know that I was fired and I'd like to know about the COBRA program." In her response, she offered no correction to the term "fired." I won't burden you with more examples, but the short story was that I had a lot of evidence against them. The union filed a suit with the National Labor Relations Board on my behalf, and a day before the hearing the company offered me an acceptable settlement. I signed the paperwork, which included a provision that I could not reapply for employment for the rest of my natural life, which was more than fine with me—I had never worked for more incompetent, conniving and dishonorable bastards. With a stroke of the pen, over twenty-two years in the grocery business came to an end.

Twenty-two years is an adequate amount of time to tire of one's work. Jobs are either construction or maintenance. If you ever see a finished product you're in construction; if the routine in never ending it's maintenance. A contractor building a house, for example, has much to do, but from the excavation to the building of the foundation and everything after he gets to the point where he can step back and look at the house and feel the satisfaction of knowing the job is completed. I on the other hand had worked in a business where I never saw the fruits of an ultimate accomplishment. Whatever I did and no matter how much effort I put into the aesthetics of the task, it would have to be redone the next day. Some people are programmed for such work; I wasn't, which made leaving even easier.

June 11th had fallen on a Friday. Despite losing my job I was in the mood to celebrate that night. I went down to The Noggin Room, a small pub in the basement of the Perry Hotel, and listened as Irish folk singer Sean Ryan sang *He Went To Paris*, a Jimmy Buffett song about a man who had experienced tragedy but went on to make the most out of his life, then reflected upon it in his old age.

As I listened, I decided then and there that I was going to take the summer off. Tourist season was just beginning, and in my previous occupation it had been a time I could never enjoy, as it was our busiest time of the year. As I sat back and listened I couldn't remember ever feeling so free. I would continue to be free for the next three years.

I'd been working on a novel for about nine months and with this decision I could give it my full attention, so from there my schedule revolved around writing, socializing, and catching up on all the things I hadn't been able to do being in a business where I worked when everyone played. With this new direction, though, I'd get up around noon and go out for a breakfast of pancakes, Coke and cigarettes, then work on the book until around five, when it was time for dinner and a nap. In the evening I'd go down to the Mitchell Street Pub or The Noggin Room, and sometimes The City Park Grill. I'd hang out till about two, and if there wasn't anything going on after the bars closed I'd return home and work on the book till about five a.m. During those years I'd set Saturday nights aside for after-hours parties, which began around two a.m. and culminated with breakfast for all who survived the night, usually at the Flap Jack Shack. The hosting of this event was alternated between Hobie, the Saturday night bartender at the pub, and me. Each venue would have its own flavor; music at my place, both live and on CD, and cards and foosball at his. Sometimes somebody would bring a guitar and I'd pull out my accordion and we'd have a little jam session, if you want to call anything with an accordion in it a jam session, but we were having fun and enjoying life. I was living an avant-garde existence in the height of nocturnal Bohemianism. On weeknights I'd enjoy being at a table filled with friends, letting the conversation go from topic to topic, with the stimulation of debate sans the necessity of resolution. It seemed there was always a table available for such conversations. I was chatting recently with Pete Kehoe about a soundtrack for this book that he and Michelle Chenard would be doing. We were talking about reminiscing and flashbacks and how conversations about the past bring back such fluent memories. I mentioned the *and* factor; that is how someone starts talking about something, concludes his or her thought, then someone adds and..., and suddenly there's a continuance to the remembrance and the conversation proliferates.

In the spirit of this new freedom I began to grow my hair. (I had actually started a week before I left the store while using my last week of vacation, on a trip to Niagara Falls with my friend Cathy, getting a haircut in Buffalo.) I had pushed the limits on hair length with corporate America, but there was only so far I could go. Now I decided I wouldn't cut it for at least a year. The same went for my beard, although that only lasted six months. Still, I hadn't been allowed to grow a beard since I had worked for Red Owl, which was fifteen years prior. I was only twenty-five at that time and my beard had come in patchy, so I was pleased to see that through the years of prohibition I had developed the ability to grow a full, fast-growing beard. Another cool thing about the beard was that it came in black. With many men gray in the beard is a precursor to having gray hair, but apparently I was the opposite. My hair had developed the salt-and-pepper look years earlier, and I felt the grayish hair with a black beard was distinguished looking. I kept the gray for a bit, then decided to dye it a light brown for a more youthful look. After around eight months of growing my hair and having a subsequent two-month growth of beard, I saw my reflection in a shop window and thought how I looked like someone famous, but I couldn't put my finger on who it was. My hair was mid-length light brown with streaks of gray that were beginning to come back through, and parted in the middle, which was something I hadn't done in many years. Furthermore, I had a much more maturely shaped face than the last time I had grown my hair long back in '77. The issue of who I looked like bugged me off and on for a few days; then I went into The City Park one Friday evening and got my answer. The Jill Jack Band was playing. (I have since become friends with Jill and Billy, the lead singer and lead guitarist, but I we didn't know each other at the time.) I caught her eye as I walked in and in the midst of her song she interjected, "Look, it's Eric

Clapton." Exactly who I'd been thinking of but couldn't place. Even though I knew my hair looked better at mid-length, I continued to let it grow. The only thing that bothered me was how I was perceived by older people, namely those of the World War Two generation. I recall one episode in particular. I was walking and had come to an intersection. The light was red, and there was a car with an elderly couple who were waiting for the light to turn green. There was no one else in sight, neither cars nor pedestrians. My hair was past shoulder length and I was wearing a bandanna. When I passed in front of them on the crosswalk I heard the doors lock. I was crushed—they didn't trust me. I often think of people who are not treated fairly, perhaps someone with thick glasses or unappealing looks. In my mind I take them back to their infancy, with a father and mother so proud of their child, and I think of how they would feel to know that people disliked or mistreated this child that means so much to them.

It didn't take long for the book to take shape. I would read what I had written and genuinely be impressed. I'd have my friends take a look and they, too, told me I had talent and that by all means I should continue. The desire to write for a living got in my blood and I spent an increasing amount of energy working on the book, but still leaving enough time for concerts in the park, day trips, and socializing—all the luxuries I hadn't been previously afforded. Around that time I decided to go by my middle name. I had used my middle name in the early nineties, but just with close friends. I always felt that my first name, Duane, clashed with my last, and now that I was hoping to be an author I wanted a more synergistic sound. I experimented with the concept with some of my local friends. Others I knew but who weren't close enough for me to explain the change resisted at first, but I was meeting so many new people that in no time everyone was calling me Jacques.

Life is fragile. It's nothing new to say that we don't know when the end will come or what age we will be when it happens. Death is also a horrible thing to witness—to see a human being alive and vibrant, then lifeless just fifteen seconds later. I was going to my sister Darla's place for a party for my niece and godchild, Jessica, who had graduated from high school and would soon be on her way to Princeton. While driving north toward Marquette on U.S. 41 I saw a car parked on the southbound shoulder; I had one car in front of me and there was one coming toward us. Suddenly I saw a kid, twelve or thirteen years old, running up the northbound embankment. As soon as I saw him I braked. I saw it coming; he wasn't looking, just running straight onto the highway. I pulled over and so did the vehicle in front of me, even though neither of us were close enough to be involved in what was about to happen. The boy got about halfway across the highway before he saw the southbound car approaching and his momentum carried him right into the path of the oncoming car as it tried to stop. The rest I remember in slow motion as if part of a movie. When the boy realized the position he was in he froze. There was screeching of brakes and then impact, which sent the boy crashing into the windshield, where the inertia ricocheted him off the car and flipping twice before he hit the pavement. His dad and mom and another younger child were behind the car that was parked across the road and they had watched it happen. I felt so bad for the dad as he frantically ran onto the road toward his boy with a crying scream. Fifteen seconds. That's all it took from the time I saw it develop to the time it was done. I remember looking at the boy's tennis shoe which his body had been knocked out of and was sitting alone on the blacktop. I thought how that morning the boy had tied that shoe, and perhaps he had combed his hair or tucked in his shirt, oblivious to the futility of doing such things on that particular day. Fortunately, this story does have a decent ending, as the boy did not die. I was haunted all night by the images being replayed in my mind. I knew the boy was still alive when the ambulance came, so I called the Marquette County Sheriff Department. The officer was reluctant to disclose anything over the phone, but when I told I was witness to the accident and that it was troubling me he said that the boy had suffered many broken bones, most severely a broken pelvis, but that there was no paralysis or brain damage. From that time on, though, I became more aware of how small decisions that may seem inconsequential can change a life.

It seems like most people I talk to have had that one strange occurrence in their life. Some stories are explainable while others raise an eyebrow. I had one such episode happen. I went to mail a letter in the lobby of our local post office. It was after midnight; no other car were parked out front. As I went in I saw a woman who looked to be in her early thirties, but she was dressed in the attire of the nineteen-twenties. She was standing a a table where one can affix stamps or write return addresses or the like. I dropped my letter in the slot, and she was leaving as I turned toward the door. I had long hair and a long, bushy beard and probably looked intimidating to a lone woman, especially with it being after midnight. I didn't want to have her feel uncomfortable so I counted to five before leaving to give her some space. I looked to see where she was when I got outside, but she was nowhere to be seen. There had been no vehicle out front other than mine and there were long stretches straight ahead and to my right and left. I took the five-step walk to my right and looked in the only direction I where my view was obstructed. Again, nothing. Her eighty year-old attire along with her unfathomable disappearance sent a chill through me. I'd noticed that she wasn't distracted when I entered; it was as if I wasn't there. She just did what she was doing without a sound. I won't be so presumptuous as to say I know what I saw. As I contemplated it throughout the years I always considered logical explanation. Perhaps she *was* frightened by my late night presence and immediately hid in the hedges. (And when she saw me looking for her she probably thought *I was right about him.*) As for her garb, maybe she'd been at a costume party. Then again, maybe I saw someone whose existence on this earth was of another time.

All in all the nineties had been a good decade for me personally. I had gone from being a young corporate up-and-comer to a Bohemian author in waiting. There was an earthiness in the younger generation that reminded me of ourselves, yet they had a worldliness that we lacked at that age. But all was not good for every

American. There had been three notable tragedies in the decade: Waco, Oklahoma City, and Columbine, but for as terrible as each of these incidents was, I felt more detached from them than the shooting at Kent State. (I was only ten when the latter had happened and it was only another news story at the time, but by the time I was fifteen it became part of the tribulations of my generation.) The incidents of the nineties were acts of violence that didn't involve us as a generation—stories we followed attentively but not interactively. With Kent State, the bullets weren't just aimed at the four students but at all who opposed the war in Vietnam.

As we neared the end of 1999 our attention was on the approaching millennium. Some made predictions of the end of the world based upon biblical interpretations. Films portraying cataclysmic events topped the box office. Movies like *Deep Impact* and *Armageddon* depicted the end of the world scenario by means of an asteroid impact. Warnings of Y2K breakdowns had people stockpiling water and food supplies as if preparing for a nuclear attack, which, by the way, was one of the possible unintended consequences. Some predicted that at the stroke of midnight, Russian computers that hadn't been updated wouldn't comprehend 2000 and would initiate a launch sequence of its missiles. There would be failures in anything overseen by computers. Bank records would be lost and no one would have access to money. Nonetheless, I attended a millennium New Year's Eve party and celebrated as the world waited for the chaos that was to follow.

CHAPTER TEN

The prognosticators were wrong—2000 came upon us and the Earth was still in tact. Russian missiles did not destroy the land, bank accounts weren't lost, and the food supply lines kept up with consumer demand. So I took the fifteen-hundred dollars I had stashed and put it back into my checking account and took solace in the fact that I wouldn't need to buy bottled water or non perishable food for the next several months. Additionally, the future shock some had warned about some ten years earlier had failed to do any psychological harm. The grass was still green, M*A*S*H was still on television, and life was as normal as if we'd just rolled into 1987 or any other year.

I had completed life's midterms with the termination and had entered my period of renaissance. My first book came out in June of 2000 and my life was about to change again. I sensed the book was good, but I never anticipated the reception it received. People I didn't know were calling to congratulate me and I was being asked for autographs—not just signed books, but autographs. It was embarrassing to a degree, but with the book as a catalyst, the coolest adventure of my life was about to happen. There were two girls in this period of time who, through their artistic nature, inspired me as a writer. I'll begin with Kerry. It was a Sunday night. I was at The City Park Grill for open-mic night with two of my friends when we met this girl from California. She was an actress and a playwright and had a Brigitte Bardot look. We took to chatting with her and eventually began playing a rendition of *The Dating Game*. I was bachelor number two. At the end of the game I had expected her to choose the friend of mine who was known to get all the girls—but she chose me. Thus began a summer that was split between Petoskey and Harbor Springs and would culminate with a cross-country trip to California.

Kerry was cool. She had been in a few low budget Hollywood productions and an episode of Seinfeld, but she was genuine and unpretentious. Her parents were spending the summer at Harbor Point, an exclusive, old money section of quasi-mansions that were called cottages, located on a small peninsula in Harbor Springs that jettisoned into Lake Michigan. Her parents had been put on heart-smart diets and Kerry had come out to implement them and ensure that they were followed. She had bought a book from me that Sunday night at The City Park and I signed it and added my phone number. Within a couple of days she called to say she enjoyed the book and I asked her out. We went to the Noggin Room and got to know each other while we listened to the background sounds of Sean Ryan's Irish folk music. Our date was a success and we would go out again two days later, and from there we began to see each other on a daily basis. She invited me to Harbor Point. I had fairly long hair at the time and felt rather conspicuous asking to enter such posh surroundings while I waited at the gate for entry confirmation. Once inside I felt as though I was in a French impressionist painting. I had crossed the mountain to the morning side and into a place where I previously hadn't been allowed. I walked down the narrow sidewalk that followed the contour of the shoreline and wound its way to cottage number 49. She scratched out a late meal featuring some sort of healthy vegetarian lasagna. It tasted like paste and I hoped that I would never be placed on a heart-healthy diet, but I enjoyed the setting and Kerry's company and therefore I enjoyed the meal. After eating we walked down to the lake. We hung around the dock until the sun set, then went into Petoskey, and upon returning we went back to the dock and hung out till four in the morning. And such was the tone of the summer. She hesitantly asked how I'd feel about fathering a child for her, jokingly saying that if I didn't she have some trucker in Montana impregnate her on the way home. To her surprise and delight I said I was up for it. When mid August came and it was time for her to return to California she asked me to make the trip with her and her two dogs, Rocko and Gizmo. Rocko was predominantly a spaniel and was quiet and well behaved. I could get him to do things that Kerry couldn't, no matter how much she would coax, like go in the water of Lake Michigan. Gizmo was some kind of small-dog mix and the only part of that mix I can remember is Chihuahua. I would tease Kerry that Gizmo wasn't so bright, as he was always doing stupid things, but he was a good dog and I loved them both.

I awoke on the morning that we were supposed to leave with an excruciating pain in my knee that resonated throughout my leg. I had never it experienced before and there's something about first time pains and ailments that make one worry, as you don't know how long the affliction will last or how it will progress. The thought of a 2,500 mile ride under such circumstances was daunting and I was about fifty-fifty on whether to go or not. I knew a trip I'd remember for the rest of my life was just an hour in front of me, so I popped a couple Tylenol and hoped for the best. We stopped at a Big Boy in Cadillac for breakfast, and Kerry, being the unabashed Californian that she is and despite my objection, asked the waitress to bring a bag of ice for me. I rested it on my lower thigh as we ate, as by then that was where the pain had promulgated itself. Whether it was the ice that helped or not I don't know, but the pain went away about an hour later and never came back.

And there we were—the writer and the actress traveling across country with two dogs, Rocco the wise and Gizmo the stupid. The experience became real once we were out of Michigan. We spent the first night in Iowa and woke to the quintessential Iowan sight of eight-foot corn stalks behind the hotel. Kerouac had written that the most beautiful girls lived in Iowa, and that may be true, but what I remember most about the state is all the cornfields. It was somewhere after leaving the hotel that we began talking in various European accents. If I had known that neither of us would be able to stop I would never said a word, but before long it was too late. Kerry (an actress remember) was very good with it, and I wasn't bad myself, I must say. We went from Italian to Polish to Swedish to Irish, sometimes in the same sentence. It was cool at first, like when we were going through the straight, unending roads of Nebraska and Kerry turned to me and in a Russian accent said, "Me want quickie." But by the time we were in Utah we were pleading with one another to stop. Unfortunately, as we advocated for this, we did so in accent.

I had traveled by land from east to west many times, but never with someone whom I cared about or found to be as exciting as Kerry. Nebraska had always been a chore, but I found myself noticing beauty in the land that I hadn't before observed. When we reached the foothills we stopped at a rest area and Kerry took a picture of me with the dogs, which would become the back cover shot for my second book, *The Potomac Circle,* a book which I had started before we left but would be colored in by many of the events given to us by the road. Looking back now I think of the song *Two Of Us* by The Beatles and think how it captured the essence of our experience. We were contemporary and cool and were in the middle of a bond that neither of us may feel again. We spent a night in Nebraska and the next one in Park City, Utah. Park City was beautiful and the people were friendly. I took the dogs for a walk around the hotel grounds the next morning and let the clean air fill my lungs with the best of Mother Nature in the backdrop. I remember thinking how peaceful it all was until some jerk with a cell phone was talking loudly and pompously to a business subordinate. I couldn't resist, I neared him and prompted the dogs to start barking.

I don't want to turn this into *My Summer Vacation* more than I already have, so I'll wrap it up by saying that we visited the salt flats before leaving Utah, enjoyed Montana, and did a little gambling in Reno before heading across the border to California. Kerry told me that she'd be spending a few days in San Francisco with her sister before heading home. It was shortly after crossing into California when she revealed that she couldn't handle good-byes and preferred to make them abrupt and, from what I was about to learn, somewhat impersonal. She told me she wanted time to sort everything out before getting to San Francisco and that it would be better if I got off in Truckey, which is about twenty miles west of the Nevada border. If blindsided is too harsh a word, it's suffice to say that I wasn't prepared to be dropped off in such an unceremonious manner. She called Greyhound to see if they had service there, and when she found that they did she exited into the city to find a place for me to stay. Everything was happening quickly. I didn't know what the bus schedule was, but a cheap motel seemed to make sense. For the most part the motel we found served as permanent housing for Mexicans, and the fact that I was a vacationer made me feel a little out of place and added to the surrealism of the situation. I was a little mad at Kerry for her fickleness and was ready to say goodbye to her then and there, but she wanted to hang out for an hour or so, and with the larger picture in mind I refrained from objecting. We had sex in the afternoon with the dogs watching us and the sound of Spanish permeating through the thin walls.

We went to find the bus depot, which as the luck of the preceding few hours would have it was three miles away. I learned there was a bus heading toward Chicago that evening, but not until eleven and it was only three. We headed back toward the motel, but I had her drop me off at I strip mall in front of a Starbucks. I don't remember why. We talked for the duration of the cigarette I lit and smoked as I stood outside her car. I recall watching her car until it was out of sight, not knowing if I'd ever see her again.

I walked back to the motel, which was actually a conglomeration of three unit shacks, and which would later provide inspiration for one of the settings in *Falling From Delaware*. In the middle of this group of shacks was a laundry room. I had time to kill before my bus left and figured it wouldn't hurt to do a wash. As I waited I experienced the dynamic of social interaction within the microcosm of this Mexican community. I could see how, if I had stayed, some would welcome me into their world while others would not.

I was home for a week or so when Kerry called and told me she was pregnant with my child. I remember laying in bed that night with the light of the full moon penetrating through the cracks of the Venetian blinds and onto my face, thinking how cool it was that I was about to become a father. I thought about all the things I would do with my child, all the fun we would have, and how I could use my experiences to help shape him or her for the world. Kerry was thrilled too, as you remember she had asked me shortly after we met if I would be willing to do this. With news of the baby we began to talk about me moving out to Los Angeles. Meanwhile, she had two friends who were trying to convince her otherwise. One was Charlie Diercop who played the tough guy in *The Sting* with Redford and Newman and played the role of sergeant for five years in *Police Woman* with Angie Dickenson. I remember talking with him on the phone. He was dignified as he spoke to me, but I could tell he perceived me to be something that wasn't good for Kerry. The other man after her heart was a professional wrestler from New York who grappled under the name Mad Mike. I chuckled when Kerry told me, before the talk of me moving out there, how he asked her why she'd want to maintain a relationship with someone who was so far away and she told him that I was cute. Then she showed him my picture and in a gruff voice filled with resignation he said, "Oh damn-it Kerry, he is cute." Now I've been called cute before, but I didn't expect it after the age of forty and definitely not by someone named Mad Mike.

Kerry and I began to make arrangements for the move. I called her every day to see how she was and we were both ecstatic about the baby. I was still writing deep into the night and would usually sleep in till about noon, but one morning I got a call around eight in the morning. As soon as I heard her speak I knew from the sound of her voice that something was wrong—that, coupled with the fact that it was only five a.m. in California. During the night she had lost the baby. I was crushed. I felt that feeling people talk about where your heart goes into the pit of your stomach, but I was worried about her. I had always been the strong one in the relationship. She would often ask me to tell her that everything would be okay, and when I did she'd believe me, but this time there was nothing I could do to make things right. I could only stay on the phone so we could share our sadness. When she hung up I turned and looked out the window and recalled how proud and happy I'd felt when I heard of my impending fatherhood. I lamented for an hour perhaps, then called her back to see how she was. I asked if she knew she had to get a D&C. She didn't, so she called her doctor to arrange it, but I was concerned for her.

From there it was difficult for both of us; she was in California and I was twenty-five hundred miles away. After a month or so the talk of me going out there had subsided and she threw out the idea of moving to Michigan instead, saying that we could live at The Point. She offered me all the leeway one could ask for; I could stay at the cottage and work on the next book and she would be no encumbrance and I could hit the town whenever I felt the urge. I told her it sounded cool and she was going to call her father to secure the cottage through the winter and into the spring. But as I thought about it through the night, something didn't feel right. Although it wasn't her intention I felt like I was going to be a kept man, and I was always an individualist first and foremost. I called her the next day and to her shock I said I couldn't do it. She took it as though I was rejecting her and within a week she requested that I no longer call her. I felt terrible—I at least wanted to maintain a friendship—but nonetheless I honored her wishes and didn't call her again until Christmas. When I did she sounded like a little girl, both in voice and in response. She would answer my questions with one-word answers and wait for me to ask another. There was no animosity or anger in her voice. Just depression. Again I worried about her, but there was nothing I could do; time would have to be the healer. Eventually time did its job and she moved past the experience through an eclectic group of friends that she had in Los Angeles. They had got her into self-realization groups and other sorts of new-age activities. I always looked at self-realization in a here-I-am sort of way, but I really believe that she believed in her beliefs. We stayed in touch for a couple more years, at which point she had moved and I had no way to get ahold of her. She has yet to call me. I again recall watching her drive away as I stood in the Starbucks parking lot, and I realize now what I only perceived at the time—that I was seeing her for the last time.

I continued to write. Parts of what happened on the road with Kerry were fictionalized and written into *The Potomac Circle*. The initial inspiration for the book had come from attending the 100 year jubilee of St. Francis School in Manistique and seeing people I hadn't seen in twenty-six years. That reunion prompted me to reflect upon my own past and the pasts of my classmates. I found it interesting to observe the metamorphosis we had gone through and it left a missing link between what we were and what we had become. I thought about all the choices we had had, how some of us made better choices than others, but in the end we would all be okay. The book came out in late 2000. I still feel that *The Potomac Circle* is my best story, perhaps because it's the one I relate to most. It was cool to have two books out, but I was still on an artistic roll. I first got the idea for the title and cover of *Fictional Numbers* with the titling of the third and final of the three short stories of which the book would be composed. As it was, all three shorts had a number in its title, and being works of fiction, the book titled itself. The cover was fun to create. Going with the numbers theme, I took pictures of friends holding different numbers and placed them eclectically on the front and back cover and throughout the book. Most of these people weren't only friends but supporters of my work, and I was glad to have the opportunity to do something for them. The book came out in the spring of 2001. The release of *Fictional Numbers* marked the third book to come out within a year. I was living such a unique life and so much of it was spontaneous. There were mornings (afternoons) where I'd wake up and think to myself, *I think I'll go to New York today,* and forty-five minutes later, after a shower and a quick job of packing, I'd be on the road. Once traveling I'd be just as spontaneous. I remember driving through Kansas City in the evening and seeing the lights of Kauffman Stadium. The game was already in the fifth inning, but I always liked that ballpark so I pulled in, got my ticket and watched the final four innings and rooted for the hometown Royals. I made these unplanned trips quite a few times over the three-year period where I wrote exclusively and found much of my material on the road.

I was on my way to Texas on one such occasion and had pulled over in Pacific, Missouri, which is just outside of St. Louis, standing outside my new Olds Alero having a cigarette. The window was down and I was listening to the radio as I stood and smoked when a weather advisory came on, saying that there was a major winter storm coming in from the west; the direction in which I was heading. I had heard of such storms closing down I-70 before and felt the urgency to get right back on the road, so I flicked my cigarette and resumed my westward trek. I hadn't gone twenty miles before the snow started to fly and the traffic slowed, and within the next half-hour we came to a standstill. I probably idled for five minutes or so before I realized that I only had a quarter tank of gas. I shut my engine off and stepped out of the car for another smoke. As I looked up the highway I saw a line of cars extending as far as I could see. The wind had picked up and was ripping through my coat. I wondered how long the ordeal would last. An hour went by, then two, then three. People were now out of their vehicles and communally walking from motorist to motorist, speculating on what the holdup was and for how long we'd be stranded. In the meantime the weather was getting worse. After four hours (about the time that I no longer had a smoke-free vehicle) the word came down that there was a major accident up ahead involving a semi and that traffic was backed up twenty-five miles. I had resorted to starting the car for five minutes every hour to try to warm up, but even with that limited amount of use I began to wonder if I'd make it to a gas station before running out of fuel. At around hour number six a couple of four wheel drives made their way through the ditch and a subsequent field and onto an access road. A couple of pickup trucks followed and I was considering the move heavily until another passenger car tried and got stuck in the middle of the ditch. After nine hours we began to move, but with all the wet snow that had fallen and the highway having been void of traffic for all that time it was like driving on a skating rink. I was cold and drained, and although I had driven a mere seventy miles I was ready for a hotel. Finding a hotel room when there's twenty-five miles of cars filled with like-minded people ahead of you isn't an easy task, and I would drive another fifty miles at fifteen miles per hour before I stopped for the night. By the next morning the roads were passable, even though in Oklahoma they simply threw sand on top of five inches of snow, making for a gritty slush on your windshield every time an adventurous semi driver passed. After a couple days in Oklahoma visiting my old dart-throwing buddy Mike Field, I made it to Texas.

Things were rolling in the direction I'd been hoping for, but I still lamented the loss of the baby. I was walking through Pennsylvania Park one Sunday afternoon when I recognized a couple sitting at a picnic table. I didn't know them well enough to feel inclined to talk to them, but as I observed their boy of about seven wheel around on his scooter, I couldn't help but think of what I had missed out on. The couple was about fifteen years younger than me and in the prime age of parenting. I went to the other end of the park and sat at the picnic table furthest from them and reflected upon the opportunities I had let pass. Although the loss of our child was an act of nature, there were other relationships that could have put me in that situation. There has always been a dichotomy in me and I've written it into my fiction novels through characters concerning the choices that must be made. Some of the choices of our generation had been war or pacifism, long-haired or conservative cut, free-spirited or domesticated. The dichotomy, of course, comes when these choices are split fifty-fifty in regards to passion. Inevitably you make a choice, whether consciously or not, and you go from there, but there are times when you look back at the other possibility and lament over what it could have brought you or what it could have made you. I had always felt that, if given the opportunity, I would have been a good father. Now, as I see time passing by and I realize that the opportunity probably won't be given to me, and after periods of lament, I think of how those perceived qualities could still be put to use.

About six months had passed between the time things ended with Kerry and when I met Julie. I felt a nonchalance when I first met her. She was attractive and intelligent and aware of the world around her, but I wasn't eager to get involved. I had regained my love of freedom and was satisfied with the occasional one-nighter. But the second time I saw her she gave me her number, and a few days later I called. We met at Sunset Park and did the obligatory gazing over the bay until the fall of night, then went back to my apartment. I remember her taking a look around and saying, "I thought you would have more books." (Since then I've kept all my books after reading them.) As she told me about herself I realized how attractive she was, and I was cloaked with intrigue when she told me she was a poet and a musician. I read her some prose and she read me some poetry and we both appreciated each other. It was supposed to be a short date, but she ended up spending the night. As the days and weeks passed I grew more fond of her. She would sometimes bring her guitar and play folk or Irish ballads, singing softly while I attentively listened. Even though Kerry was an actress, Julie stirred my creative side more than anyone I'd ever met. She was only twenty-three while I was forty-one, but the relationship was as natural as any I'd been in before or since. Our song was *Besame Mucho*. It happened that we each had vacations that were planned before we met; her going to Isle Royal and me meeting my friend Greg in Montreal and going to Quebec City from there. When I heard *Besame Mucho* three times while in French Quebec I took it as a sign that Julie and I were meant to be together. The sentiment was sustained for me as I returned. On vacation I recalled her saying that she thought about me all the time, and how sometimes she would say her name with my last name and that it sounded good. I felt a bit overwhelmed, but in the end I believe she overwhelmed herself. The back to back vacations, mine for seven days and then she took off for eleven, with only a couple days together in the middle, possibly gave her time to reflect upon our age difference and how fast things were moving. I don't know—I can only surmise. She left one day without explanation, right in the middle of the passion that was consuming us. I never got say goodbye. I felt the weight of unanswered questions for months and was left only with assumptions. Her lips had been as tantalizing as any I'd tasted, and to that I can add nothing. In her presence I was not a writer, but a mere speechless mongrel scratching at her door, damp and cold and hoping to be fed.

But sometimes positives come from negatives, and so it was with my experience with Julie. At a family picnic I had met her niece Beth, who was only a little younger than her. Then about a year later and after Julie had moved back to Pittsburgh, I recognized Beth waiting tables at one of the establishments I frequented. We made further acquaintance, and before too long Beth and I began to hang out. We would run into each other and go from there. Whatever she wanted to do I was up for and wherever I wanted to go she'd go with me. We had fun together and had good conversation—sometimes deep and sometimes whimsical—and I looked forward to being around her. As the years passed we remained close. She would come over and we would go through photos of my travels and I would listen to her adventures. I would tease her, referring to myself as Uncle Jacques, based on my relationship with her aunt, and in some ways I believe there was reality in that characterization.

I would see Julie one more time. Her nephew Randy was getting married, a wedding I had planned on attending anyway, and Beth had gotten word to me that Julie would be coming in from Pittsburgh for the festivities. I was out on the town the night before the wedding, standing by the door at The City Park, listening to a band from Chicago doing *Baba O'Riely*, and when she walked in I knew that nothing would be ordinary for the rest of the weekend. It had been close to five years since I'd seen her and I had no foresight to what her reaction would be. I looked her way as she was waiting to pay cover, not taking my eyes off her till she caught mine, and when she did I waved and smiled. She smiled, came and embraced me, the kind where you hold somebody tightly, release, and then hold each other again, and I knew things were going to be all right. We talked for about an hour, or perhaps shouted into each other's ear over the loudness of the band, but it was a good conversation. I didn't sleep well that night; I couldn't get my mind off of her. I hadn't realized how much I missed the inspiration she provided and I woke the next morning feeling as creative as I had in years. Randy was married the following afternoon on the veranda of The Perry Hotel, and after the ceremony Beth, Julie and her new boyfriend, and I went downstairs to the Noggin Room for a few drinks. Whether it was in good taste or not I showed Julie something she had written for me when we were together, written on the back of a religious card that a homeless man had given her in Galway, Ireland. It was from July of 2001 and it concluded by saying, "I can only acquiesce to your every whim and beckon call, like a daisy follows the sun." I'm not sure why, but I wanted her to see it. Perhaps it was because my life has been absent of such gestures since she had left. We went to the reception, which was twelve miles away, and it took me an extra ten minutes to find the house for Beth had transposed the address numbers, but I would have another four or five hours with Julie. I said many things I had wanted to say, some of them ego serving, but most importantly I got to tell her that after all the years that had passed she still, and always would, have a special place in my heart. It was a statement that she echoed, repeating the word *always*. The night would end with a stop at The City Park. I had dressed sharp, with a black suit coat with fine blue pinstripes, a blue shirt which I was told brought out the blue in my eyes, pants and tie that were gray and matched my hair. I have to say that I probably looked as good as I had in years, but when the blonde whom I had always thought to be attractive said that I looked hot and I should have no problem getting laid, and then when she proceeded to spill her drink on my suit, I had no problem. There would be no getting laid that night. For that weekend my thoughts belonged to Julie.

I was doing a book signing in my hometown when I was approached by Liliane Colburn, whom I had met years earlier when I was working in the produce department of a local supermarket. She had asked me a question and I picked up on her accent. I asked her if she was French—she was—and after a short conversation she agreed to help me expand upon the language of my heritage. Her son Mark was a navy SEAL, in fact, he a was a member of the elite skydiving team within the SEALs, The Leap Frogs. One day as I arrived at her house for my scheduled lesson, her neighbor came and passed on the message that Liliane wouldn't be able to keep her appointment and that in fact she'd be out of town for an indefinite period of time. Immediately I sensed that something had happened to Mark. My intuition was correct. Her son had been in a skydiving accident, as an inexperienced jumper failed to pull his chute on time, plunging through Mark's, breaking his neck and tearing a hole in his parachute in the process, leaving him ripping through the 3,000 feet of air that separated him from the ground below. Back to our encounter at the bookstore. She had a story to tell, as miraculously her son had survived, and she asked if I'd help her with this venture. I agreed. Over the next two years I listened to the tapes she made and wrote the story as I learned of the hardships she and her daughters experienced as they waited for their son and brother to emerge first from a coma and then from a vegetative state, and progress to the point where he gives motivational speeches at colleges. I learned a lot about brain injuries and personal fortitude, but mostly I learned the value of keeping hope when all seems lost. *The Green Room* came out in 2005.

We all have our friends, some of whom either have been or will become friends for life. From being an author I literally know hundreds of people, but of these there are probably less than ten who'd fit into the friends-for-life category. For as important as friendships are to me, it's acquaintances that I'd like to explore here; those you like and with whom you share some interests, but aren't close enough to do anything with on a one-on-one basis. One such person comes to mind. He was a sprightly individual of forty-three, an avid skier in the winter and cyclist in the summer and was seemingly in great health. I learned of his untimely and unexpected death while throwing darts with three other friends at The Mitchell Street Pub. One of the waitresses passed through and asked us if we'd heard about Joe, and when none of us had she told us the news. We stopped our game and stood at the round table where our drinks and lit cigarettes rested, and in our own way we told each other how shocking it was that such a vibrant personality could have left the world so early. I'd guess two minutes had passed when one of the guys said, "Jacques, you're up," and just like that we were back to our game, laughing and sharing stories and eyeing the girls that passed by as we threw. When I got home that night I reflected upon the situation and concluded that, as sad as it may be, we will get two minutes of remembrance when those who fit into this acquaintance category hear of our demise.

The most dramatic occurrence of my lifetime and our generation was the September 11th attacks on New York and Washington. It was the prime example of an event where one will always remember where they were and what they were doing when they heard the news. I had experienced that with the deaths of Elvis Presley and John Lennon and with the Challenger disaster, and folks a year or two older than me experienced it with the Kennedy assassination. On that fateful morning in September I was in Escanaba for my Uncle Elmer's funeral. There was a continental breakfast in the conference room of the hotel where I was staying, and like with the Challenger I noticed a conjugation in front of the TV. I moved closer to see what the fuss was and saw the two towers of the World Trade Center burning on the diagonal left side of the split-screen and the Pentagon smoldering on the diagonal right. I knew that we had been attacked and I was instantly captivated. I returned to my room and turned on the news, which wasn't hard to find because every station, even the sports channel, was broadcasting the event. Everything was happening fast and at that point we didn't know if the attacks were over or if subsequent ones were on the way. Sometimes it's strange what hits you the most. Despite the fact that the twin towers and Pentagon were ablaze, the seriousness of the day sunk into my bones when it was announced that all air travel was suspended throughout the country. The announcement gave validation to what had otherwise been surreal. Then came the crash of flight 93 in Shanksville, Pennsylvania, and we now know that that plane was heading for the Capital. I was going back and forth between all the stations trying to get the cutting edge report, but spending most of my time with ABC News and Peter Jennings. Not that this event needed to have definition of scale, but that definition came with seeing all the nightly news anchors in the morning. I was watching ABC when the towers collapsed. Jennings said that it appeared that parts of the building were breaking off, but he wasn't looking at his monitor for as he was saying it the first tower succumbed to the stress and crashed to the ground in front of all America. I had to go to the funeral mass, so I checked out of the hotel and went to pay my last respects to my dad's closest brother. Somewhere in the interim speculation broadened that the attack came from the Middle East, and as a result there was a run on gasoline as people feared shortages. I had planned to go back to Petoskey that evening, but by the time I was ready to leave every drop of gas in Escanaba had been sold. I checked back into the hotel I'd been in and resumed my vigil in front of the television. Soon, the man behind the attacks was unveiled; it was who we all thought it would be—Osama bin Laden. I eventually made it home, but stayed fixated on the coverage for several days. Then I got to the point where I just couldn't watch it anymore. Looking back now several images and accounts come to the forefront: the initial sight of the two towers and the Pentagon aflame, the grounding of domestic flights, fighter jets being deployed to patrol major U.S. cities, the towers collapsing, and President Bush with the megaphone amidst the rubble of the World Trade Center. I also recall the French and British being particularly sympathetic. Even though I can no longer remember what the French did, I do remember what they did in England. At the point of the ceremonious changing of the guard where they would normally play *God Save the Queen*, (or *King*, depending on the status of the monarchy) they broke tradition for the first time in the long history of this regal event and played *The Star Spangled Banner*.

The attacks on New York and Washington had put us all on edge and when anthrax began showing up in the mail we began to feel vulnerable. I wondered how it felt to live in a major city, one that had the figurative bulls eye painted on it. Yet, living in Northern Michigan, life still went on pretty much as it always had. But as a nation we were anxious for payback and it seemed long in coming, but in October American and British forces launched a bombing attack against the Taliban government in Afghanistan. With the assistance of the Northern Alliance we quickly crushed opposing Afghan forces and began sweeping the countryside in search of Al Qaeda fighters and Osama bin Laden. With the successes in Afghanistan, our focus began to shift toward Iraq. Saddam Hussein was becoming defiant again and after a series of U.N. resolutions President Bush positioned our forces for an attack. We all know what happened afterwards—a seemingly easy victory turned into a prolonged engagement that was followed by sectarian violence. My intent, as I mentioned earlier, isn't to turn this into a history book, but rather to recall this major series of events in our lives and reflect upon the historical significance of what I recall. I began by saying it was the most dramatic occurrence of my lifetime and I often wonder where it falls in the minds of the older Americans who remember Pearl Harbor.

Back to life in Northern Michigan. There is an annual summer music festival in the village of Bliss, which is roughly thirty miles north of Petoskey. I attended my first Blissfest in 2002. I'd heard people talking about it over the previous years but had this battle-of-the-bands picture in my head, and with that picture the festival didn't sound very interesting. As the years went by, though, I heard more people whose opinion I respected speak highly of it, along with the fact that John Sebastion and Richie Havens had previously headlined the event. I finally decided to see what it was all about. I drove down scenic M-119 through Harbor Springs and up to Cross Village, then took back roads for another three or four miles till I got to the grounds. It was nothing like I had pictured it to be; instead, it was wooded and slightly hilly with open fields for parking and camping, and another open field with three stages that were isolated from the campsites by about two-hundred yards of hardwood. From the back forty where I parked I went into the woods and found a flurry of activity. Campsites lined the trail I walked; many of them had banners or markers naming their site. Some sites had communal gatherings listening to backwoods musicians playing bluegrass with guitars, banjos, mandolins and bongos. There were workshops farther along the trail, and beyond them was The Song Tree, where more accomplished musicians played to a small crowd that sat on trunks of felled trees that served as benches. The trail split at that point, going to the main stage in one direction, while the other went toward the drum kiva, which was a stone fire pit entrenched in the hollowed center of a small hill. The event officially began on Friday afternoon (the second Friday in July) and ended late Sunday evening. The headline act that year was Janis Ian, not a huge name but still someone I remembered from the mid-seventies. In the field with the stages was a large crowd, thousands of people gathered from across the Midwest and Canada and conjugating in the middle of this otherwise obscure part of the country. It was a sixties throwback weekend, both in the delivery of the music and in the attire worn by the crowd. I knew many people there, including some of the musicians, and I hung with them at times, but I was still my individualist self above all else. I dug traversing the grounds and the trails that wound their way through the woods and taking in a little of everything. In the end, the food at the concessions was good, the music was good, camping was fun, but the experience as a whole was great and I would recommend that everyone take in the festival at least once.

It seems that in every artist's life there is a financial meltdown and mine came to a head in November of 2002. I had been living large and my savings account was getting small. I realized that I had to reevaluate my situation. I took a day job for the first time in three years and decided to sell my car and walk for one year. The day job would pay for my living expenses and being minus the expense of a car would allow me to restock a rainy-day fund. For the first time in my career as a writer I felt like a starving artist, but the strategy worked so well that I extended it for another year, but there were prices to be paid. I handled not having a vehicle most of the time; I was doing what I had to do to make myself solvent. My walk to work, though was a little under a mile and a half. In the winter the walk was brutal, but perhaps the most disconcerting occurrence was in the late spring. There was a field that I crossed through when it was dry, but at nesting time there was a sparrow who'd dive bomb me every morning. The worst part of it was that I knew it was coming, but not quite when. I'd see it fly diagonally from a tree on my left and take perch in a tree to my right. I'd turn back and watch for him, but he always outsmarted me and just when I thought I was in the clear it would blurt out two shrill chirps from about a foot away as it zoomed over my head. As much as I disliked that bird, there was another function in regards to not having a vehicle that I absolutely hated, and that was returning my bottles and cans. Whenever I did this I felt like a homeless person and I'd take the back street to the closest grocery store, which was seven blocks away. You could make the comparison to a twelve year-old boy whose mother asked him to hold her purse while she tried on a dress. I remember one time in particular. The road I mentioned had no sidewalk, so I had to walk the shoulder, and for some oddball reason there was a lot of oncoming traffic that day, which was pissing me off; I just wanted to get to the store, get my damn money for the bottles and cans and be done with it. As I walked I felt the occupants of each vehicle were evaluating me. After the last of a long string of vehicles had passed I'd had enough and said aloud, "Does every #$@!¢ car in this #$@!¢ town have to come down *this* #$@!¢ road, shaking my head and making a hands-out gesture as I did. It was then I realized what I must look like to anyone who happened to be looking out the window of their house—not only did I look like a homeless can collector, but now I was cursing aloud and making gestures. I realized the humor instantly and began to laugh, but then thought, *Yeah, this helps! Carrying cans and bitterly cursing one second and laughing the next.* But I couldn't hold it in, the irony was to rich. I let myself have my laugh. It felt good. After that day I was never troubled by taking my returnables back to the store. There were two other times that I really missed having my car. In October of '03 Greg was to be married in Estes Park, Colorado. He and his bride to be, Ann Marie, were moving from Florida to California and were traveling across country on their month long *Magical Mystery Tour*, as they had dubbed it, and would be wed before they reached their new home. Without a vehicle, having a day job, and having limited financial resources, I wasn't able to make it to my lifelong friend's wedding. Then in May of '04 my Uncle Pete Berger died. Once again I felt like a cad when I didn't make it to the funeral of the man whose roof I had stayed under for the nine-month school year that followed my mother's death. My two-year regrouping period ended as I was scanning the classifieds and found a deal on a car that I couldn't pass on. It was a Mercury Sable wagon, or *The While Whale* as J.R. Riley put it. The previous owner was ninety-five and could no longer drive, and although the car was thirteen years old it only had 36,000 miles on it. I took it to the Mitchell Street Pub that first night. After a couple hours of socializing, I found myself halfway home before I remembered that I had a car. (I had quit drinking some eight years earlier so the mistake of walking home was from habit, not inebriation.) I was parked in the back lot, which meant going back through the pub, and there was a good laugh when someone asked, "Back already?" and I had to reply, "No, I forgot I have a car."

I have never seen the country as divided as it was prior to the 2004 election. It wasn't just George W. Bush against John Kerry, it was conservatives against liberals, theocrats against secularists, neighbor against neighbor and friend against friend. Our states were categorized as red or blue, democrats were accused of being communists and republicans were being called Nazis. There were new battlegrounds in this war, namely talk radio and website blogs, and vitriol was being spewed from both mediums. The last time I remember such intensity in an election was in '72, but that election wasn't close; it was a landslide victory for Nixon. This time, however, the country was basically split in half, prodded by the polarizing effect that each candidate had. Kerry was being called the most liberal member of the senate and Bush was ultra conservative. The differences continued after the election. I had hoped that, no matter who won, that we as a nation could put everything behind us and accept the president for four years, but to this day passionate ridicule prevails. I had mentioned when I wrote about Reagan that I lean republican, but I think our country will be better when the Bush presidency ends in January of 2009, if only for the fact that maybe the political viciousness will soften and we can reunite as Americans.

I believe that our country would be better off if our representatives would abandon the alliance system of political parties and campaign strictly on their own beliefs, and then vote accordingly. Will this happen? Probably not, and more probable, not in our lifetime—it would be hard to break the established structure and it would be particularly hard to get adequate funding for the average citizen wanting to run for office. So we're left with our two-party system. I believe that, in the absence of any drastic changes, the best thing we can do is limit the term of the reigning party, regardless of which party we support. Whenever a party is in control too long it tends to push its agenda past the boundaries established for the good of the everyday American. When one party controls both legislative bodies and the presidency for too long it acts as though it has a mandate, and the danger is the possibility exists that it will try to take the country where the extreme fringes of the party want it to go, based on the premise that they keep getting elected. The enticement of the utopian thought of a nation without political parties can be proliferated by noting the benefit of a candidate not tied to party funding, hence not tied to its platform. For instance, a candidate may believe in points one, two, and four, but not three. Yet, if elected, the office holder becomes compelled to vote for three. This is comparable to attachments on bills that lead to pork-barrel spending. Likewise, I believe you can equate your position on the political spectrum to parenting. I sometimes wonder if I'm too conservative, and when I do it's because of something I agree with on the liberal landscape. On one such occasion I considered my ideology over a cigarette, wondering which philosophy was better for the world in which we live. I wondered how we should know when to cross over; when to focus our attention on the poor and when we should enforce global policies. It was then that I likened it to being a parent. You don't have a set playbook when it comes to raising your kids. Rather, you base it upon the situation; he breaks a window he's in trouble, he gets an A and he's praised. Perhaps we put too much emphasis on classifying ourselves as what we are politically.

The first time I spoke with Michelle Chenard was on January 31st, 1998. I remember the date because of the conversation. I had listened to her play at a couple locales and heard her mention that she had lived in The Upper Peninsula. I told her that I had grown up there, too, and when she asked how long it had been since I left I realized it had been ten years to the day. By the mid 2000s I was feeling an artistic kinship with Michelle as our careers were alike in many ways. I felt that we both had the talent to make the national scene; our time just hadn't come yet. Also, we had about the same popularity range geographically. We both liked each other's work and I looked to her for that first opinion that comes most honestly when it's artist to artist. Shortly after the release of *Falling From Delaware* she was co-hosting a local radio program, and she recommended me and joined the interview when the station came out with another program called *Bookends*. It wasn't until I gave her the first draft of this book, though, that she learned I had lived in Manistique, (in our initial encounter I had called Escanaba my hometown) and from that I learned that we had both attended Manistique schools from 1972 to 1974. I told her that my mother had written the high school fight song back in 1936, and she told me that her first boyfriend was my Uncle Pete's nephew, Rick. In talking with her later I learned we had both lived in the Orlando area as well. Shortly after these mutual realizations I was listening to her play at a local establishment. She spotted me and said, "This next song is for my friend Jacques," and then played *Sylvia's Mother*, and suddenly it was 1972 and I was back in Manistique.

One of the things I enjoy about being a writer is hitting the road with a carload of books. I particularly enjoy going to libraries as it takes me into the smaller towns that don't have bookstores and therefore I wouldn't otherwise visit. In doing this I've come to realize that every town has something to see, be it a quaint little park with a river running through it or historical markers denoting that community's touch with notoriety, or simply the small town look of its neighborhoods. I find myself being better received in these towns, too. In the larger cities I have to wait to speak with the contact person for whichever establishment I'm selling to, and oft times that contact person is busy and my visit seems like an inconvenience. In the small towns they chat colloquially and are glad I took the time to stop and see them. In the same way I enjoy these villages, it's a centering experience to take the rural roads that link these places to one another. It's Norman Rockwell's whitewashed fences versus long metal guardrails, rustic mom-and-pop stores versus rest areas, Mother Nature versus The Industrial Revolution. And when I do this I try to tune in the local AM radio station to further get a feel for the community. I can picture myself passing a farm house with an old red barn behind it and fields that go on as far as I can see, listening to an ad for so-and-so's body shop on Main Street America and hearing about upcoming community events. It reminds me of riding with Dad and Mom and listening to the sixties AM stations that had live local programming, in the days when our hometown station would play a variety of music so to suit everyone's taste. You could hear Sinatra followed by Dusty Springfield, and then Perry Como, who'd be followed by Martha and the Vandellas. Driving down these small state and county roads through mid to southern Michigan not only brought back memories, but for a moment brought the past into the present.

The summer of '06 was without a doubt a season of reunions. I had driven down to North Carolina to see Greg and his wife Ann Marie after not seeing them for the two years they lived in California, Julie had come to town for the wedding, I had met another old friend, David Ross, in the straits area on Memorial Day weekend after we'd been out of touch for four years, my old dart throwing buddy, Mike Field, returned to Indian River after seven years in Oklahoma, and I saw my cousin Paul after an eleven year hiatus when his daughter pitched in a softball tournament here in Petoskey. The way it was going I honestly thought I may even hear from Kerry. But there was a lesson for me with each encounter. I learned that relationships can withstand many years of remission and re-emerge without a beat missed. I only found it to be awkward for several minutes, then we'd go to talking about the past and laughing about the foolish things we had done or had encountered, and from there everything would be as natural as if no time of separation had existed. I also learned that although people's lives change they are still the same folks once you peel off any perception. Most importantly, though, it was reaffirmed to me how important certain people are and that with enough passage of time they fall into the friends-for-life category.

By the midway mark of the first decade of the new millennium many of us from the baby-boomer generation have past the halfway mark of our lives. We've been through good times and bad, the exciting and mundane, and my bet is that we're not about to be rendered passé quite yet. Surely there will be a shifting of gears, with the realization of age and the physical deterioration that comes with it. We'll change many of our physical activities into intellectual ones, or to ones of leisure. Afternoons playing football and basketball will change to golf or tennis. The question, "What's your sign?" shifts from astrological to The Seven Warning Signs. Those of us who have grandchildren will spend more time with them. We will contemplate the inescapable hand of death. We will die. And yet the planet will continue to circle the sun without us. Billions of people will never know we even existed, followed by billions and billions more as time passes through the continuum.

CHAPTER ELEVEN

As you may have noticed, I have divided this book into chapters that have roughly covered five-year increments. This final chapter, however, will be more analytical, observational, and theoretical. Here I will attempt to finish off previously developed thoughts and wrap up my take on the world in which we live. Perhaps you have noticed a symmetry between the life I have lived and yours. I love it when memories from my past are triggered, and in writing this I have unearthed long-forgotten moments. Hopefully I have stirred up such memories from your own pasts.

Those of you who have gone to Epcot Center at Walt Disney World know about *The World Showcase*, the circle of nations that rim a small man-made lake. There, you can walk into a simulation of Germany, visit the biergarten and eat sausage and spaetzle while listening to men in liederhosen play om-pah music, then walk down the path and be immersed in the culture of China, walk a little more and be in a courtyard filled with the shops and pubs of England. Thinking in a linear manner, it would be intriguing to apply the same concept to the decades of the twentieth century. Each American decade has a uniqueness and flavor and it'd be interesting to have an authentic representation of them: the frilly extravagance of The Roaring Twenties, the postwar pride and euphoria of the forties, the bobbie-socked innocence of the fifties, the cultural revolution of the sixties, the earthy naturalism of the seventies, and the gaudy materialism of the eighties. It would be a worthwhile flashback to be infused into the attire, architecture, and vernacular of each period with the music of the era filling the senses and completing the experience. You could be in a joint where cooks with greased-back hair and white tee-shirts fry your burger while you listen to Elvis singing *Don't Be Cruel* on the jukebox, then stroll some hundred yards down a path and visit a Bohemian coffee house where you could chat while listening to Dylan, and where the waitress would have a mod look and tell you to have a groovy day. I believe it's easy to forget the actualities of our past and it'd be good to be occasionally thrown back into those time periods. It would help us gain perspective of why we are who we are.

I don't believe in reincarnation. Having made that declaration, I sometimes feel that there's too much to experience in one lifetime and not enough time to recover from missteps and bad decisions. Earlier I wrote about dichotomies that ultimately come down to a choice, with the very essence of dichotomy dictating that what you left behind was still something important or interesting. Sometimes I wonder how we can be placed in a world that's such a tease. When I was a child I assumed that certain things would simply fall into place without effort. I figured that at a certain age I would be married, and a short while after that I would have two or three kids. I wondered what my home would look like, whether my children would be girls or boys, what kind of neighborhood it would be in, and if my kids would follow the same childhood routines as I had. My friend Dale's brother Patrick likes to say, referring to life, "This ain't no dress rehearsal," or as John Lennon quoted in a song, "Life is what happens to you while you're busy making other plans," but too many times I've found myself trapped in the snares of a fast-paced world. In regards to not living life to its fullest, I also believe that most people are conditioned to join the mainstream; drilled not to veer too far off their predetermined path. Some do aspire to grander things; feeling inspired or gifted, or they have that internal catalyst that makes them part from the rest and take Frost's road. But often times, these people have their own ghosts. They are seldom content with the present or with calling their current environs home. In the spring they dream of the excitement and leisure of summer, yet when it comes they crave the colors of autumn. When fall arrives they don't find fulfillment in the leaves so they long for exotic vacations that split winter and provide tolerability. Often enough when winter's doldrums are at their worst they miss their sabbatical and once again crave spring and the rebirth that comes with it. And so it goes year after year, a cycle of hope with revolutions matching the number of years in their lifetime. But I digress to the original point. I can understand how reincarnation almost begs to be believed in by some of the discontented. I can picture an ancient philosopher creating this concept based upon the shortcomings in his life, just as the Greeks and Romans created gods to suit their needs.

An indication that the world was evolving into a more complicated place came with the cloning of a sheep named Dolly, spotlighting the confluence of science and ethics. This confluence was front and center in the forties with the creation and eventual deployment of the atom bomb, but now there were implications of man taking on the role of God. We became aware that genetically engineered grain was on the market. Bills that would ban the cloning of humans were going through both chambers of congress. Meanwhile, more animals were being cloned overseas. Stem cell research became a highly controversial issue, with the debate pitting ethics against potential medical breakthroughs. As I watched from afar I couldn't believe how different the world was when juxtaposed with the one that existed when I was a child.

Our generation has seen many changes over our forty-two to sixty-two years of official baby-boomer existence. Society has gone from addressing some of our citizenry as Negroes to Coloreds to Blacks to African-Americans. We have gone from breakfasts of bacon and eggs to cereal to instant breakfast drinks to gourmet coffees. We began watching shows like *Gunsmoke* and *The Wild Wild West,* and from there went to *Petticoat Junction, M*A*S*H* and *Seinfeld.* We've gone from every network carrying *The Jerry Lewis Labor Day Telethon* for seventy-two straight hours on Labor Day Weekend to having over one hundred programming choices at our disposal with maybe only one or two carrying the telethon. We don't seem to mind that football games have nearly an hour added to them because of a bombardment of commercials, but we're becoming bored with baseball because there's too much time between pitches. As individuals we've gone from riding tricycles to bicycles to motorcycles to luxury foreign cars. Gone from being addressed as Sonny or Missy to Mr., Mrs. or Ms. We've matured and so has the world around us. I miss the simplicity of the past and not having all the controversy we have today. I miss having only four or five brands of laundry detergent to choose from, and perhaps ten viable cereal choices. I miss getting handwritten letters in the mail. I miss having three established anchormen on the nightly news. I miss the photographs that defined the times in a single shot, with pictures like the sailor kissing the girl in New York after W.W.II, or the marines hoisting the flagpole at Iwo Jima. Today all memorable events are on film and at what point does societies' mind freeze-frame the image into the one for posterity. I miss the time when we were less guarded and spoke freely with one another when we met, regardless if we knew them or not. I miss trusting or politicians, whether or not it was wise to blindly trust them in the past, it was one less thing we worried about. I miss understanding the technology of the times and not having to have it explained to me by someone twenty-five years my junior. I miss the aroma of walking through a hardwood forest, for years of smoking have compromised my sense of smell. I miss smudge pots, those kerosene burning contraptions used during road construction that looked like cannonballs. I miss watching professional sports in the days when the participants seemed like regular guys and not superhuman freaks with unbelievable skills. I think of the great linebackers of my youth—Willie Lanier, Dick Butkus, Ray Nitschke—and if you saw them on the street and didn't know who they were you might think they were tough looking guys, but it wouldn't be self-evident that they were athletes, and I think we related to them more because of it. They were men who looked like a fictional Mr. Phillips at the hardware store, Gus the butcher, or Nick the mechanic. Now I understand that there were times when the toughest linebackers were nearly knocked senseless by the likes of Jim Brown and I'm not suggesting that Mr. Phillips or Gus the butcher would have a chance at tackling him. The broader point is that we could hold pipe-dreams of becoming an NFL player because we saw people in our small towns that we could compare to pro football players, something we can't do anymore with the ripped behemoths on today's gridiron. In general, I miss what *was*.

I was raised a Catholic and remain so to this day, although I don't attend mass as regularly as I should. I have gone from a Christian by indoctrination to one who has been confirmed not by the sacrament of confirmation (which I believe is administered at too young an age) but by a life of contemplation and observation. I find faith by looking at the complexities of life. I find it in the senses we posses; the wonder of sight itself and how it can be transformed into an understandable image, or how a certain scent or sound can take us back thirty years and bring a fully-painted memory of what we were immersed in. I see it in the unlikely-to-be-random incredibility of the function of organs, the instinct of a newborn searching for its mother's breast, and how a large animal knows to avoid a smaller one that would be dangerous to it. Lastly, I feel the presence of God in emotions like love and compassion. It's hard to imagine the aforementioned being of happenstance; from a bolt of lightning charging a couple of particles. Now, I do believe that evolution occurred, but I believe there was a Superior hand guiding it along. Despite efforts by secularists to debunk the existence of God with this explanation or that, no one has explained where the original speck of dust came from—that is, how matter can create itself. They can come up with perhaps a feasible account for this or that happening, but they can't prove that it was the only way it could have happened. Plus, you have to consider the cumulative factor, that is, if you have a *possible* explanation for items 1, 2, 3, 4, and 5, what is the chance, remembering that we're only talking about possible explanations, that all five of the hypotheses are correct. So to summate: God gene, possible; Biblical timetables incorrect, probable but also subject to the comprehension of the audience of the times in which they were written; amino acids charged by lightning to initially form life which then evolved into every living form now known, I don't buy it but I have no qualm with anyone who does. I simply believe that many of life's wonders can be scientifically explained individually but not cumulatively.

I also believe that if one is to be religious, one mustn't be religious by default; *I won't steal or cheat in case there is a God.* As I previously opined, we are all indoctrinated into our religious beliefs, be it Christianity, Judaism, Islam, or Hinduism, and upon reaching an age of significance we decide for ourselves whether we believe what we were taught. When we come to that point of ultimate decision we should then be true to our beliefs, not flawless, of course, but steady in our resolve. Now some intellectuals consider Atheism to be a religion and I won't argue that point, except to clarify that my opinion about standing by affirmed beliefs pertains not to Atheists or agnostics—obviously an agnostic with set spiritual beliefs it would be oxymoronic. I write these beliefs because they are part of my life, just as my take on Vietnam was part of my life. I understand that there are differing opinions and with that I've tried to present my view and not lecture—and I think I've been fair—so I'll conclude by reiterating my belief in a Supreme Being and will do no coaxing on which religion best serves humanity.

Ever since I left Manistique there have been times when I look at my surroundings and ask myself *am I really here?* This obscure feeling of displacement mostly happened during the first few years that I lived in Escanaba, and understandably so, considering that it had been my first move and taking into account the changes in my life. However, I still find it happening on occasion after fourteen years in Petoskey. Likewise, there are times when I wake up, take my first step and my body feels worn and creaky—I again ask myself *is this really happening to me?* It still hasn't sunk in that I'm aging and I don't accept it well. Yet, I can still run up the stairs quite easily if I have the desire, so I must realize that there will come a time when I say *remember when you could run up the stairs?* The broader point in both examples is that change happens and there is little we can do to change change.

I concede that the best days of potential fatherhood have probably passed me. There are times when I'll stand on my front porch and smoke and see cars go by with nice families inside, then I look hard at myself and see an aging fellow—part hipster, part conventionalist—and I wonder what role I fill in the greater scheme of existence. At such times I question the point of anything and I feel the motivation draining, leaving me feeling like an old dog...you throw a ball and he looks at you as if to say, "Do you want me to get that? You threw it, *you* get it." Another thing that enters my mind is that new people I meet will never know what once was. I used to be a good athlete, for one. I could catch people's attention with how far I could throw a football or how fast I could hurl a baseball. On the basketball court I was quick. Now I have to sit back and listen to the younger guys tell gridiron and ballpark tales and refrain from saying what I once did, for words of conquests are rarely believed when they can't be validated. Even in writing this I do so only to highlight what we all either have or will yet go through. It's the previously mentioned period where one must make the transition from physical to mental, from athlete to intellectual. The only other option is to rest upon one past laurels and wait to die. It's interesting to reflect upon the development of how one comes to understand what life has in store. I wrote of the early morning of my life and how secure I felt. I wasn't responsible for even my own well being and I had no foresight of what would lie ahead. As a ten year old I looked at the future with wide eyes but limited understanding as I got a first glimpse of the freedoms that would soon come my way. At graduation I felt the world was mine. I could do whatever I pleased and go wherever I wanted, and technological advances brought an outlook that was exciting and progressive. It was somewhere in my mid-thirties when I first felt I had let some things get away; things that I fully expected would be part of my life. Now as I approach fifty my body is feeling the wear and tear from the aggressiveness of my younger days, and years of poor eating habits bring a new uncertainty of what awaits health wise. (The five fruits or vegetables a *month* for better health plan.) To conclude this thought, it seems like we get our information one step too late to make calculated decisions, leaving fate with a huge role in our ultimate outcomes.

It was a Sunday morning in the spring of the year when I realized that I'd been neglecting myself in many ways, partially by passing on travel events for reasons of thrift, and not paying attention to the physical part of aging, namely eating the aforementioned unhealthy diet, and smoking. I wanted to go to Harbor Springs that morning. At first I felt that I had too much to do. It was then that I had an epiphany. I looked at myself from a different angle, as if I was the father of myself, or more simply put, I was the person with authority over my requirements and desires. The question became how would the father I no longer had treat my wants and needs, and was I tending to those needs as he had when I young. I realized that if I had a son I wouldn't deny him as often as I'd been denying myself. I also would make my son eat his vegetables and not live off canned food and soda as I had been doing. There had been many times when I wanted to get out of town for a day or a weekend, but I'd been stuck in the mentality of my starving-artist days. Now I had the means and it was time to respect my needs, the same way that my dad had respected the needs of the little boy I had once been.

At certain times I'll hear a song from my past, or perhaps see an old movie, and crave the unattainable opportunity of going back, if even for one day, to that period of time. This is a concept that's so compelling to me that I wove it into my second book, *The Potomac Circle.* In it the main character, George Mills, has lost his wife and his job, and during an unwanted conversation in a bar in Idaho with someone whom he doesn't know, this question is posed: how much would he be willing to pay if he could go back for one random day to the best year of his life. He lets his mind wander into the notion as he recalls some of the wrong turns he has taken, and the idea stays with him as he leaves the bar and continues down the road. In the end, however, his love for his daughter makes him realize that the path he *did* take brought her into existence, and with that, he wouldn't change a thing. Whereas George contemplated returning to 1969, I believe that, if I had such a choice, it'd return to 1975. First, I would just drink in the memories; listening to Dave Tempe on WDBC playing *The Last Farewell* as I stood on the front porch on a warm summer evening, waking up the next morning to the smell of coffee, then going downstairs and finding Dad at the kitchen table listening to his morning news over eggs and toast, walking through the old neighborhood and going to the old hangouts, and standing in the longest line I'd ever seen to see *Jaws*. It's a tantalizing concept, turning the nostalgic back to contemporary, and if I had more than one day I'd take a hard look at some of the crossroads that awaited me back then; note the opportunities which I either hadn't recognized or assumed would be presented somewhere down the road. Essentially, I'd force myself to do the things that were hard but would benefit me later. I believe we all experience such longings at some time or another and it's intriguing to note how easily distant memories can be triggered. For me, just the memory of the smell of percolating coffee provokes the image of Dad at the breakfast table. I treasure such memories, and now I try to protect them. For example, I used to try to get hold of *all* my favorite songs from my youth, obscure stuff that I hadn't heard in thirty years. The problem was that after a few plays the flashback factor dissipated, the memories blurred, and the song simply became one that I liked to hear. (Keep in mind that I'm not talking about The Beatles or Dylan or the like, but really obscure seldom heard memory floggers like *Stay Awhile* by The Bells or *Master Jack* by Four Jacks and a Jill.) I have since learned to leave *some* of the old songs for when I occasionally hear them on the radio, and in doing so the poignancy of the memories remain preserved.

Life goes by fast and at times that fact is pointed out with blunt brutality. One such realization occurred when I was listening to an oldies station and heard *Call Me* by Blondie. My initial reaction was, "Come on, that's not an oldie." Then it hit me that the song had somehow gotten to be nearly a quarter century old. I made the transference to my renaissance of 1981, and back then a twenty-four year old song would've been from 1957. I reluctantly accepted that *Call Me* was a legitimate oldie, but then I maximized the concept. I know there are fifteen year-old kids that listen to oldies radio and I know that they play music that dates back to 1955, which would make the song fifty-one years old as of 2006. I went further into the thought and tried to imagine my fifteen year-old self listening to songs from 1924, which would be my equivalent to the previous scenario. Now, I did know those songs because my mom's music was from the early twenties to the late forties and she sang and played them often; songs like *Pack Up Your Troubles In Your Old Kit-Bag (And Smile, Smile, Smile), The Sunny Side of the Street, Ma He's Making Eyes At Me,* and *Side By Side.* They were sung by people like Bing Crosby, Pearl Bailey, Louis Armstrong, and Judy Garland. Looking back, they were great songs—happy songs—but I would never have listened to them voluntarily at age fifteen. Upon mentioning this thought to my friend Keith, he observed that perhaps this is because our kids' lives were more similar to ours than ours were to our parents'. It's an easily readable contrast; we and our children had grown up in relatively snug times—not hardened times like children of The Great Depression.

I'm often asked for advice in becoming a writer and my response is simple: don't become a writer, but if you must don't be too serious about it. There are downsides to everything and so it is with this craft, once the decision is made that it's what you want to do with the rest of your life. Throughout history writers have been characterized as having an edge or an aloofness, and having done this now for a considerable length of time I understand why. It starts with my head being full of ideas and I try to develop them, regardless of where I am or what I'm doing; consequently, my brain is always working. If I come upon a situation I explore its potential for development, regardless of how mundane it might be. For instance, we had stayed at a Howard Johnson's in Milwaukee the night before our army physical and in the morning we all ate in the hotel restaurant, arriving individually from our rooms. I remember sitting alone at a table. The waitress came up, I ordered something, and she told me I wasn't allowed to get it. I thought *how presumptuous of her!* Had that happened now it would be the exact type of thing I'd explore and develop for character fodder. I'd have it that the young man *was* a regular guest at the hotel and *not* with the military. I would create a reaction where he wonders why he can't get what he wants, have the girl fulfill her presumptuousness, then have the young man throw it back in her face. Is it a story? No, but it makes for a nice slice of sidebar. I edit everything, trying to find the most concise and least redundant way of stating myself. This, of course is not only good but necessary when writing, but unfortunately now through habit I find this process being used when my inner voice mulls day to day activities, like figuring out what I need from the grocery store. I might say, for instance, *I need apples, I need some cereal, I should get some garbage bags.* Even though this thought process needs no editing and its purpose will be fulfilled when I come home with these items, I nonetheless refine the thought to, *I need apples, some cereal, and garbage bags, too,* and then finally bring it to its book-ready form: *I need apples, cereal, and garbage bags.* Yet, even though this is involuntary it's probably necessary because if you think lazily you'll write and speak lazily. The editing extends out onto the street. Once while strolling downtown I was approached by a rather shabbily dressed young man and he asked, "Hey man, can you bum a smoke?" So I obliged him and asked for a cigarette. He was confused, of course, and I eventually did give him his smoke, but I was compelled to take him literally. I've become less tolerant of poor grammar, like when I overheard a lady at the grocery store ask for the new baby food with apples and chickens; the pluralization, of course, changed the actuality of chicken parts to the perception of three or four whole chickens inside the little jar. I bite my lip when I hear people I know misspeak, but cringe when I hear the national media do it. One of my pet peeves is the incorrect use of Islamic terrorists. They may report that a marketplace was bombed by Islamic terrorists. This is essentially saying that the marketplace was bombed by terrorists who happened to be Islamic. It's like saying a bank was robbed by a Roman Catholic or a Jew was charged with drunk and disorderly conduct. Am I nit-picking? Of course, but the correct way of reporting that story is to refer to the terrorists as Islamist. That implies their philosophy of theocracy, that the act was done in accord with their doctrine. The problem is that people dislike it when one gets too technical, thus I often have to make the decision whether to let something go and have it fester within me or point it out and subject myself to ridicule. But back to the advice-seeking young writers. If they convince me that they are serious I'll tell them a few things that work for me. One of these is that I never write if I don't feel it. I've read about famous authors who forced themselves to produce a certain number of pages a day, and that's fine if it worked for them, but I think writing is an art that needs to be created during periods of inspiration and to simply write for writing's sake then heavily tear through it in the editing process is a waste of time. Secondly, I encourage moderate description. The reader wants a picture painted, but also doesn't want to be bored. For as great as John Steinbeck was he'd frustrate me with page-long paragraphs of what the front of a house looked like. In his defense, he and earlier writers crafted stories in the days before visual arts, i.e. television and film. Some folks never traveled outside of their county, therefore the writer needed to paint pictures that needn't be painted with today's medium. Third, watch for impediments to your flow, be it from structure or content. Picture your words as a river; the more debris in the water the slower it moves, and too many bends will slow it down as well. In short, keep it simple and don't get too far off topic. The final tip I give is in regards to initial development, both of characters and setting. In the formative parts of my books I'll picture the scene and characters in my mind as if I'm watching a movie. I may envision some famous actor or actress as a model, then try to determine how they would carry themselves, what their mannerisms or idiosyncrasies might be, and perhaps isolate a syntax. Then after a chapter or two I find these characters have taken on a life of their own and I can predict how they would react in subsequent situations.

There is something in human nature that craves superlatives, and with that said I'm compelled to cast some opinions. Michael Jordan was the best athlete I've seen. Perhaps Mohammed Ali was the greatest heavyweight champ, but Mike Tyson was definitely the most dynamic fighter. No athlete (engaging in contact sports) was more graceful than O.J. Simpson, and in my opinion Ken Griffey Jr., while he was in Seattle, was the best baseball player, possessing the same combination of power and defense as Willie Mays. As a young boy I was able to see Mays play, but he was already an aging player when I became a fan of the game. Baseball was the sport of my youth, but football is the one I enjoy the most now. As a sports fan I have been fortunate; my teams, college and pro, have won thirteen championships. In the world of pop culture The Beatles were the best musical group and their existence created the biggest phenomenon of my lifetime—musical or otherwise. *The Russia House* is my favorite book. M*A*S*H was my favorite television show, with Hogan's Hero's being second. I like Pittsburgh more than any other city, followed by Burlington, Vermont. My tally of states visited holds at forty-seven, and of those California without a doubt had the most to offer. I'm contemplating a visit to China for the 2008 Olympics. If I go it would be nation eleven on my world tour.

For as much as I enjoyed the sixties and reflect upon them still, I believe the best time to have been young in this great land was during the post World War Two forties. There was an air of national pride stemming from our recent victories over Germany and Japan, and with much of Europe's industrial complex having been destroyed, more was being manufactured here than ever before.

Americans were thriving. People bought homes and began the exodus to the suburbs, furthering the need for infrastructure and creating even more jobs. People lived wholesome lives. They listened to the radio and read newspapers and weren't subjected to commercials with annoying salesmen or ads advocating the latest drug, followed by a list of ten or so embarrassing side effects. Baseball was the national pastime and fathers dressed in white shirts, ties, and top hats when they took their kids to see heroes like Ted Williams and Joe DiMaggio—with nicknames like The Splendid Splinter and The Yankee Clipper—who stayed with their teams throughout their careers and were loyal to the cities where they played. This wholesomeness can be exemplified in making a comparison between Ed Sullivan in the late sixties and Mick Jagger in the mid 2000s, placing them at roughly the same age but with quite different images; a microcosmic example of how society has changed. But we're not born into eras of our choosing. I look at the period shortly after my high school graduation and feel cheated in regards to music. Imagine if the music of the sixties and seventies were inverted but the culture remained as it was and you're at a peace rally listening to Abba or The Bee Gees. I understand that culture dictates the direction of music and for that reason the scenario I presented wouldn't happen, but nonetheless it frustrated me that the sixties were so vibrant while the late seventies were so meaningless.

Looking ahead, I'm not certain about what the future will hold and I'm not as excited about it as I'd been as a young man coming out of the seventies. Young people conform to change and have an understanding of new technology while the rest of us get left behind and must rely upon the ones we had once taught to keep us functional in the ever-changing world. We look back to simpler times and often disregard the benefits of technical advancements. One only has to look at the technology of the past ten years to understand the pros and cons. Cell phones save lives in emergency situations by providing a mobile conduit of communication, but research suggests they may cause brain tumors. Computers help us in innumerable ways but contribute to an inactive world that can make our youngsters lazy and obese. Advancements in medicine extend the length and quality of life, but many of the ailments come from poor diets mandated by a fast-paced society. The globe turns ten times faster than when I was young. We don't take the time to chat anymore, unless it's in a cyber chat room. The family unit isn't as cohesive as in the days when we gathered together each evening at the dinner table. The same thought can be extended into our communities. We used to have volunteers from the American Cancer Society go door to door, and if you donated they gave you a sticker that you proudly displayed at the front of your home. Today we get called by people states away and at hours we often find inconvenient. On Halloweens kids went throughout our town and collected treats without the need to have them x-rayed for foreign objects. In general, there isn't the neighbor-to-neighbor camaraderie that there was in the sixties. But I feel this way because I'm a product of my own times. Children born into this new world will assuredly feel the same when 2040 comes around and they long for the same comfort of a past that was simpler for them. As for me, I had mentioned that I'm beginning to feel the wear and tear of having been a rambunctious child and an athletic and adventurous teen. But also, I already find myself having occasional memory lapses. I'll sometimes forget names of people I have known for years or will have to search for words I have known since college. But I remember specific yet insignificant dates from many years ago, like the fact that I got a haircut in Buffalo, New York at three o'clock on June 4th of 1999. It's too bad that we can't delete outdated or useless information from our brains like we can with a computer, freeing room for what's prevalent. I don't believe I'll be one of those of whom people say, "He's so sharp for and eighty-five year old," or "I can't believe he's so active for someone who's ninety." But it would be presumptuous to assume I'll make it to eighty-five or ninety. In fact, if this passage was written by an all-knowing narrator he may refer to me by saying, *And although he doesn't know it, his lungs are already being invaded by cancer.*

There is no one place to feel safe as there had been in my child-hood—no backyard with lush green grass and parents flanking me. Now, every breath I take holds the potential to be my last, be it from a heart attack or a brick dropping out of the sky. On a brighter note, though, we have survived and are still doing so. Humanity has not succumbed to the doomsday forecasts of West Nile, SARS, or the swine, bird, or Hong Kong flu, nor have we experienced Armageddon. I believe Armageddon will eventually come, though. Too many countries are acquiring nuclear weapons, and more often than before emotion takes nations into war as opposed to strategy.

In every life there is a series of lasts, of which we are unaware of at the time. We experience a kiss, for instance, filled with love or passion or both, not knowing that a heart attack awaits, or shake hands with a best friend after a round of golf, oblivious to the car that will cross into his lane on the way home. This thought can be extended into less severe lasts, that is lasts that don't end in imminent death. For instance, at some point in a life there will come that final time one throws a baseball. Let's say Sam, like myself, could have been an avid baseball player as a kid, but there comes a day in his later years where he tosses a ball into the glove of a neighbor kid, then says, "That's enough for today." He lives for another fifteen or thirty years but never throws that red-seamed sphere again. The sad part is that when he threw the ball that day he didn't realize it would be the end to that part of his life. The same will happen to me soon and I only wish that I could have advanced knowledge so I could appreciate the finality of the situation and give it its due reverence: that I could momentarily hold the baseball in my hand and say, *okay, this is it!* The same can be said for the last time one has sex, or travels overseas, or out of state for that matter. Personally, when I think of lasts, I think of Kerry driving away as I stood and watched from the Starbucks parking lot, not aware that she was carrying my child. Our relationship had been so cool, and as I reflect upon it now, I think of the Green Day song and I hope she had the time of her life.

Despite the richness of memories we accrue as we reach our

older years, there is sadness that comes with the aging process. We lose friends and loved ones along the way and with each passing we feel more alone. We can't do many of the things we used to do, and with that we lose part of our spirit. I was recently driving through a neighborhood that borders a highway when I saw a gentleman who I'd guess to be in his upper seventies holding a young boy's hand. The child was tugging and wanted to go, unaware of the dangers of a highway, and I sensed it would only be a matter of months before the older fellow could no longer contain the child. I thought about what he must have been thinking: fear, first and foremost, that the boy would break loose and run into traffic, and sadness as he realized that, for the well being of the child, he would soon have to relinquish some of his grandfather privileges.

I believe I will always equate seventy year-olds with the W.W.II generation, regardless of how much time passes. Even as I write this, a person would have to be eighty at the youngest to have participated in the last great war to end all wars, but through the familiarity of past impression I look at anyone who has reached seventy and equate him as being part of that era, based upon the age the W.W.II veterans were when I began to appreciate that generation and all they stood for. Sadly, I realize that they're rapidly leaving us. I had grown up knowing many World War One vets and they were all in their eighties. Then they died, so my perception of them remains that of an eighty year-old. So it is with the W.W.II vets. I have to wonder if I'll feel that way when I look in the mirror and see *my* seventy-year-old reflection. I have not yet read Tom Brokaw's book *The Greatest Generation,* but based upon what I've heard I believe I share the same sentiment as him. I have such esteem for those who were born around the time of my parents. They were exemplary citizens and solid people. They raised their children well and provided for them amply. Those who survived the war built quaint suburban houses with fine-trimmed lawns and white picket fences. They worked hard from Monday to Friday and attended church on Sundays. They were friendly and accessible and genuine in nature. They liked baseball and fishing and taking their kids to the lake on hot summer afternoons. They always had stories to tell, never about the war, not to me at least, but there were lessons to be learned from each tale. Now they're leaving us at the rate of one thousand a day. When their exodus is complete I will miss them dearly. I will miss the supervision I always let them have over me. I'll miss their timeless advice and pureness of nature, and I'll feel my like dad is a step farther away. But as I say this I realize that we will become someone else's W.W.II generation. As times continue to progressively complicate themselves, we will be the ones from the era when things were simpler and easier to understand. Nature must instill this patriarchal instinct upon us, as I'm sure the previous generation went through the same period of loss and lamentation, and in the end my bet is that we'll be just as inspirational to those who follow us.

We from the *flower power* generation have come to an age where we begin to contemplate our ultimate and inescapable end, and with its approach we ponder our legacy, both as individuals and as part of a generation. This final self-evaluation can be brutal, gratifying, or even enlightening. Someone once posed the challenge to a roomful of people to give the first name of their great grandfather. Most of us couldn't, and thus we realized the short period of time we'll be remembered, so we must realize that in the midst of a civilization that has been around for roughly ten-thousand years and will continue on for an unknown period yet to come, we have a short time to make our mark or contribute in a lasting way. Can this be done? Sure. Today, for example, we have medical advances that extend our lives and ease our pains that were inconceivable one hundred years ago, and to go back to the challenge of naming our great grandfathers, I doubt that many of us could name the people who contributed to these advancements of civilization. Thus, it's not only by our names that we can be remembered but by our contributions. It's obvious that we don't all offer scientific potential, but it's been said that in one way or another, positively or negatively, we touch the lives of two-hundred fifty people during our own. Perhaps our actions or choices will mold a younger person, and perhaps he or she will influence someone of the generation that will follow them, and this will perpetuate and spread throughout the remainder of mankind's existence. Personally, I can see this manifestation in the small things that we do: a "Hello" to a social misfit, being a good parent, mentoring a child from a broken home, being one voice in a cause, or maybe being known as the person who is always friendly and smiling. Also, we think of ourselves as a generation. I consider the recently mentioned Greatest Generation, and those of us who came of age in sixties, as the two groups who most influenced our times. One was wholesome and heroic while the other sought to make the world a better place for all the earth's inhabitants. The latter were the children of the former and together they were parties to the *Generation Gap*. The latter held a view of the world that was diametrically opposed to the one their parents held. Another uniqueness to the baby-boomer generation was that a lot of them held their views into adulthood. Many people have liberal tendencies when they are young and then become more conservative as they age, but I believe the impact of being so influential during the sixties combined with the experience of bringing about social change kept many of them loyal to their ideology throughout their lives. Roughly two-hundred years have filtered classical music into what remains popular now, and I wonder where another two-hundred years of filtering will leave the artists of our time. Creativity and lyrics will be the measuring stick for who makes the cut and who doesn't. There will be no sentimental choices as none of us will exist when this musical evaluation is made. I don't foresee Elvis being part of this picture. His music was catchy and groundbreaking, but by then that broken ground will lack relevance. I believe that only three artists from our era will get significant play in the year 2206: The Beatles, Bob Dylan, and The Grateful Dead.

Our pondering continues as we approach an age where death's inexhaustible face looms. Inappropriate as it may be within the pages of this book about life, I must take a moment to mention The Great Equalizer. I'm sure there have been times when most of us have thought about death, be it from chest pains that turned out to be indigestion, reading a health guide and noticing you have the symptoms for a disease, or perhaps from a close call on the highway. It's funny how these events can bring sudden enlightenment; I have been most devout in my religion while in an emergency room. Close calls and paranoia aside, we contemplate how the end will come and what will come after. Some hope for a quick and painless death while others would prefer a more protracted end, giving them time for reflection and atonement. We consider those whom we leave behind and how they will be after our influence has morphed from direct to indirect. We hope that the lessons taught to our young will be remembered and the information we provided will be retained, but we have no choice other than to close our eyes, let go, and hope.

I near the conclusion of this synopsis of the times that took most of us from infancy to adulthood feeling fortunate to have been placed on this planet in this era of our destiny. I believe that any life can be as much of an adventure as one wants it to be, but I also believe that cultural factors such as music, social attitude, and worldly awareness can enrich us. And I believe that enough time has passed where the fermentation of our generation's story has ripened it into a sweet nectar. Where we will go from here no one knows, just as being here and evolving into who I am couldn't have been anticipated thirty years ago. I think of how fast those last thirty years have gone and realize that the next thirty, if I indeed have thirty years left, will go even faster. Someone may one day say that I died with plenty of life experiences, but with the desire to do so much more. Perhaps what is said upon our deaths is something we all should consider. As for me I hope that death will not come instantly, but that I will have time to reflect.

I wanted to make a trip back to Manistique before the book was done. It has been said that you can never go home again and I believe that to be true; regression does not intersect with the future and the future is where we're destined to head. But it does the soul good to ground itself on occasion by remembering who we were and recalling the zeitgeist. My hometown has been relegated to a once a year destination and with the infrequency of visits I notice the changes profoundly, changes where the aging of the town is a metaphor of myself. I drove down Arbutus Avenue to the house where I had lived as a boy, but I the edifice itself stirred few memories with the condition it was in. Much of the paint had peeled, leaving the wood worn and weathered. The grass hadn't been cut in some time and there was much clutter in the yard. Uncle Pete Gorsche's house was gone, too; it had been demolished some years ago. I thought of knocking on the door of my childhood home and asking the current residents if I could take a look inside. It would've been the first time in thirty-two years that my eyes met my never-to-be-forgotten memories. I could picture walking through the entrance and into the living room, void of piano, seeing different carpeting and furniture, and perhaps pictures on the wall that would betray both the era and the taste of when the dwelling had been my domain, and I knew there and then my memories would be better preserved by not entering. I parked in the alley and took a walk around the block. That's when I began see the little things that shifted my focus from what had changed to what remained the same as it was in 1965, or '68, or '72. The bump in the sidewalk in front of the MacGregor's was still there, still more prominent on the side toward the street and still available for a boy to catch air when speeding over it on his bike. I had to look hard, or better stated I did the opposite and let my vision blur, and when I did I saw the place where I grew from an infant to a child and to an older boy with goals and developing opinions.

About a month before I finished this book I received a call from Kerry. She had caught me at a loss as she spoke in accent, saying that it was Anna Maria from Italy. Now I meet a lot of people from all over the world and although initially I tried to fake it, I eventually came clean and admitted that I had no idea who she was. She said, "You used to pick me up at Harbor Point in your Monte Carlo." I smiled and sighed. "Kerry." She said she'd be up for ten days and wanted to coordinate some times when we could get together. I arranged it and when I hung up I smiled again when I flopped back on the bed. It had been six years since I'd seen her. Her life was a little different; she had a four year-old boy whom she was raising alone. I received security clearance for the ten day period and first went to see her on a Saturday afternoon. Her boy, Mac, liked me and watched as I showed him how to skip rocks. Then he wanted to see how far I could throw, so knowing that at my age I shouldn't throw all-out without warming up, I did anyway, to which he asked me to do it again, and again, then again. My arm was throbbing but I was impressing him and I liked that. We went for a walk to the very point of The Point, a place I remembered to be fairly secluded. Kerry and Mac wanted to go for a swim, but I was wearing jeans, as it had been cool that morning, but she talked me into peeling and in I went. On thing had changed since I'd last frequented Harbor Point, and that was the addition of a slow-moving Harbor Point Tour Boat, one of those that the peasants take to see when the rich and famous live, and Kerry laughed hysterically as it came into view. The tourists waved at us, not knowing my lack of attire as I stood shoulder deep in the cold Lake Michigan water. And with that Kerry and I were right back to where we had been six years ago. We got together three more times in Harbor Springs and made arrangements for her to come to Petoskey the on the day before she headed back to California. About an hour before she was to arrive I received a call saying that she'd rather leave the memories as they were instead of having an emotional departure. She had done it to me again. I hung up the phone and tossed it up in the air, not caring where it landed. Nothing had changed. Once again we'd had a great time together. We had connected on an artistic level, we had reminisced, we had stupid things happen that left us laughing, and Kerry couldn't say goodbye.

My heart breaks for all that has passed and for all time has stolen from me. My heart breaks for Kerry. My heart breaks for 1975. It breaks for the opportunities I missed. It breaks for who I could have become, without consideration of who I am. And that's when the desperation begins to cease and I realize what I have, what I offer, and the value of my memories. I think of the people I've met, the places I've visited, and the encounters I've had and how every part paints the whole. Then I understand that living well has made past memories worth missing. Meanwhile I will go on to visit more lands, meet more people, and garner more experiences that will hold high places in the pages of my life. And when I sense my end is near I'll bide my time and wait for the day where I once again see my dad, and my mom, and Ann Marie, and for the first time see the child I never met.